AN EXCITING NEW COOKBOOK

This cookbook has been prepared by arrangement with the Meredith Publishing Company. From the thousands of recipes they have published in *Better Homes and Gardens* and their many bestselling cookbooks, they have selected over 500 all-time favorites for this book. They have included both prize-winning recipes from loyal readers and new recipes created by BH&G's staff of food experts. All have been carefully tested in the BH&G test kitchens.

In this book you will find exciting new ways of preparing meats and vegetables. The big salad section contains recipes from the daintiest molded fruit salad to salads hearty enough to be meals in themselves.

There is an invaluable section containing dozens of ideas for quick, one-dish meals. Another section is devoted to that popular national pastime —outdoor cooking.

From simplest children's lunches to exotic recipes for your most important social occasions—this book answers your every need.

Most exciting of all (and for the first time in a paperback cookbook) over 270 recipes are beautifully illustrated with specially prepared photographs.

AMERICA'S FAVORITE RECIPES FROM BETTER HOMES AND GARDENS

BANTAM BOOKS, INC.
NEW YORK / TORONTO / LONDON

AMERICA'S FAVORITE RECIPES FROM BETTER HOMES AND GARDENS
A Bantam Book / published by arrangement with Meredith Press

Bantam Cookbook Shelf edition published November 1966

Library of Congress Catalog Card Number: 66-28830

*All rights reserved.
Copyright © 1966 by Meredith Publishing Company, Inc.
This book may not be reproduced in whole or in part, by mimeograph or any other means, without permission in writing.
For information address: Meredith Press,
1716 Locust Street, Des Moines, Iowa 50303.*

Published simultaneously in the United States and Canada

Bantam Books are published by Bantam Books, Inc., a subsidiary of Grosset & Dunlap, Inc. Its trade-mark, consisting of the words "Bantam Books" and the portrayal of a bantam, is registered in the United States Patent Office and in other countries. Marca Registrada. Bantam Books, Inc., 271 Madison Avenue, New York, N. Y. 10016.

PRINTED IN THE UNITED STATES OF AMERICA

Contents

1	1 · Meats, Poultry and Fish
63	2 · Vegetables
91	3 · Salads and Salad Dressings
125	4 · Desserts
195	5 · Breads, Sandwiches, Pancakes and Waffles
227	6 · Casseroles and One-dish Meals
273	7 · Outdoor Cooking
295	8 · Special Helps

Dear Reader:

Since 1923, *Better Homes and Gardens* has been reading, testing and publishing thousands of recipes shared with us by our readers. *America's Favorite Recipes* is a collection representing the best of these recipes. We call them America's favorites because they are indeed the tried and re-tried family favorites of hundreds of American homemakers. Some were initiated generations ago and became family food traditions. Others are the innovations of smart homemakers using present day convenience foods and streamlined preparation methods.

We're happy to present this collection of superb recipes within these covers; you're sure to find many recipes that will become your favorites.

THE EDITOR
Better Homes and Gardens

SECTION 1

Meats, Poultry and Fish

SECTION 1

Meats, Poultry and Fish

Stuffed Rolled Rib Roast

- ¼ cup chopped onion
- 1 clove garlic, minced
- 1 tablespoon brown sugar
- 1 teaspoon salt
  Dash pepper
- 1 teaspoon prepared mustard
- ¼ cup water
- 1 teaspoon Worcestershire sauce
- 1 cup soft bread crumbs (1½ slices)
- 3- to 4-pound rolled beef rib roast
- 1 3-ounce can sliced broiled mushrooms, drained (½ cup)
- 2 tablespoons chopped stuffed green olives
- ½ cup shredded sharp process American cheese

Combine onion, garlic, brown sugar, salt, pepper, mustard, water, Worcestershire, and bread crumbs. Unroll roast; spread with bread mixture and sprinkle with mushrooms, olives, and cheese. Reroll roast and tie securely; fasten ends with skewers. Place on rack in shallow baking pan. Roast at 325° to desired doneness, allowing 1½ to 2 hours for rare, 1¾ to 2¼ hours for medium, or 2 to 2½ hours for well-done. Makes 9 to 12 servings.

Savory Chuck Roast

- 3 to 4 pounds beef arm or blade pot roast
- 1 cup water
- 2 tablespoons soy sauce
- 1 tablespoon parsley flakes
- 1 teaspoon monosodium glutamate
- ½ teaspoon sage
- ½ teaspoon **fines herbes**
  Dash pepper
- ¼ cup cooking sherry

Trim excess fat from roast. Heat fat in Dutch oven; when you have about 2 tablespoons melted fat, remove trimmings. Brown meat on all sides in the hot fat. Mix water and seasonings; add. Cover; simmer 2¼ hours. Add sherry. Cover; cook ½ hour longer or till tender. Remove meat to hot platter. GRAVY: Skim off fat. Add water to meat juices to make 1½ cups. Blend ¼ cup flour and ½ cup cold water; gradually stir into meat juices. Cook and stir till gravy thickens; cook 5 minutes, stirring occasionally. Salt to taste. Makes 5 or 6 servings.

Pot Roast with Spaghetti

- 3 pounds beef arm or blade pot roast
- 1 8-ounce can (1 cup) tomato sauce
- 1 6-ounce can (⅔ cup) tomato paste
- ½ cup chopped onion
- 2 medium cloves garlic, minced
- 2 teaspoons oregano leaves, crushed
- 1 teaspoon thyme leaves, crushed
- ½ teaspoon basil leaves, crushed
- 1 teaspoon salt
- 7 ounces spaghetti, cooked and drained
- Shredded Parmesan cheese

Trim excess fat from roast. Heat fat in Dutch oven; when you have about 2 tablespoons melted fat, remove trimmings. Brown meat nicely on all sides in the hot fat. Combine tomato sauce, tomato paste, onion, and seasonings. Pour over meat. Simmer covered 2½ to 3 hours or till tender. Remove meat to hot platter. Simmer sauce uncovered till of desired consistency; skim off excess fat. Serve sauce with meat and hot cooked spaghetti. Pass Parmesan cheese. Makes 8 or 9 servings.

Pot Roast Norway

3 to 4 pounds beef arm or blade pot roast
1 8-ounce can (1 cup) seasoned tomato sauce
1 cup water
1 envelope onion-soup mix
2 teaspoons caraway seed
2 bay leaves

Trim off excess fat. Roll meat in flour; brown slowly on all sides in a little hot fat. Mix and add remaining ingredients. Cover; cook slowly 2½ hours or till tender. Remove to warm platter. GRAVY: Skim excess fat from liquid. For 1½ to 2 cups liquid, blend 3 tablespoons flour and ½ cup cold water. Gradually stir into liquid. Cook and stir till gravy thickens. Makes 6 to 8 servings.

Old English Fruited Pot Roast

Trim excess fat from 3- to 4-pound beef round or blade bone pot roast; heat fat in large skillet or Dutch oven till about 2 tablespoons melted fat has collected; remove trimmings. Brown meat slowly on all sides. Add ¼ cup Burgundy wine, ⅓ cup finely chopped carrot, ½ cup chopped onion, 1 clove garlic, minced, 1½ teaspoons salt, and ¼ teaspoon pepper. Cover; cook slowly 2½ to 3 hours or till tender. Meanwhile soak one 11-ounce package (1¾ cups) mixed dried fruits in 1½ cups hot water 1 hour. Drain; reserve liquid. Place fruits on meat last 45 minutes of cooking. Remove meat and fruit. Skim fat from pan juices; add reserved liquid to juices to make 1½ cups. Blend ½ cup cold water with 3 tablespoons flour; slowly stir into pan juices. Cook and stir till thick; pass with roast.

Barbecued Pot Roast

Instant meat tenderizer
3 to 4 pounds arm or blade pot roast
1 recipe Chef's Sauce

Use tenderizer on meat according to label directions; place in Dutch oven. Pour Chef's Sauce over. Cover; bake in slow oven (325°) 2½ to 3 hours or till tender. Make gravy from pan drippings. Six to 8 servings. CHEF'S SAUCE: Mix ½ cup bottled barbecue sauce, 1 to 2 tablespoons soy sauce, 1 tablespoon Worcestershire sauce, 1 clove garlic, minced, and dash *each* crushed thyme, basil, and oregano.

Mushroom Pot Roast

- 3 to 4 pounds beef pot roast
- 2 onions, sliced
- ½ cup water
- ¼ cup catsup
- ⅓ cup cooking sherry
- 1 clove garlic, minced
- ¼ teaspoon **each** dry mustard, marjoram, rosemary, thyme
- 1 bay leaf
- 1 6-ounce can (1⅓ cups) broiled sliced mushrooms

Trim off excess fat. Dredge meat in flour. Brown slowly on all sides in a little hot fat. Season generously with salt and pepper. Add onions. Mix and add remaining ingredients except mushrooms. Cover; cook slowly 2½ hours or till done. Add mushrooms (and liquid); heat. Remove meat to warm platter. Skim fat from stock. Blend 1 tablespoon flour and ¼ cup cold water; gradually stir into stock. Cook and stir till sauce thickens; salt to taste. Serve over meat. Makes 6 to 8 servings.

Fresh-brisket Feast

- 3 to 3½ pounds fresh boneless beef brisket
- 6 medium carrots, pared
- 2 onions, halved
- 2 stalks celery
- 1 tablespoon salt
- ¼ teaspoon pepper
- 10 whole cloves

Place brisket in Dutch oven; add vegetables and seasonings. Barely cover with water. Simmer (*do not boil*) covered, 3 to 4 hours. Transfer meat and vegetables to hot platter; keep hot. Cook diced potatoes in broth, if desired; or cook dumplings in broth. Thicken broth for gravy. Slice meat across grain. Pass Horseradish Sauce (p. 237). Serves 8 to 10.

Oven Beef Stew

- 2 tablespoons all-purpose flour
- 2 teaspoons salt
- Dash pepper
- 1½ pounds beef chuck, cut in 1-inch cubes
- 2 tablespoons fat
- 1 10¾-ounce can condensed tomato soup
- 1 cup water
- ½ cup chopped onion
- ½ teaspoon basil leaves, crushed
- 4 medium pared potatoes, cubed
- 4 medium carrots, cut in 1-inch pieces
- 1 medium onion, quartered
- ½ cup red Burgundy wine

Combine flour, salt, and pepper. Coat meat in seasoned flour; brown in hot fat in Dutch oven; add soup, water, chopped onion, and basil. Cover; bake in 375° oven 1 hour. Add vegetables and wine; cook 1 hour or till done. Serve over hot noodles. Makes 6 servings.

Polynesian Beef

Select a 3- to 4-pound beef pot roast. Trim off excess fat. Place meat in shallow dish; cover with 1 large onion, sliced. Mix 1 cup unsweetened pineapple juice, ¼ cup soy sauce, ½ teaspoon salt, and 1½ teaspoons ginger; pour over meat. Let stand 1 hour; turn once. Place meat and onion in large skillet or Dutch oven; pour marinade over. Cover; cook slowly 2½ hours or till tender. Cut 4 carrots lengthwise in *thin* slices; add to meat along with 1 cup bias-cut celery slices; sprinkle with salt. Simmer covered 10 to 12 minutes. Arrange ½ pound spinach and 1 cup sliced mushrooms on top; sprinkle with salt. Cook covered 5 to 7 minutes or till spinach is just done. Remove to warm platter. Skim fat from liquid. Blend 1 tablespoon cornstarch and 2 tablespoons cold water; slowly stir into liquid. Cook and stir till thick. Makes 6 to 8 servings.

Savory Stew, Bavarian Style

- 2 pounds beef chuck, cut in 1-inch cubes
- 2 tablespoons fat
- 3 cups water
- 2 medium onions, sliced
- 1 tablespoon salt
- ¼ teaspoon pepper
- 1 bay leaf
- 1½ teaspoons caraway seed
- ½ cup vinegar
- 2 tablespoons sugar
- 1 small head red cabbage
- ½ cup broken gingersnaps

Brown meat in hot fat; add water, onion, salt, pepper, bay leaf, and caraway. Cover; simmer 1 hour. Add vinegar and sugar. Cut cabbage in thin wedges; place atop meat. Cover; simmer 45 minutes or till tender. Remove cabbage to platter. Add gingersnaps to liquid; bring to boiling, stirring constantly. Makes 6 to 8 servings.

California Steak

- ¼ cup all-purpose flour
- 1 teaspoon salt
- ¼ teaspoon pepper
- 2 pounds round steak, about ¾ inch thick
- 2 tablespoons fat
- 1 medium onion, thinly sliced
- 1 10½-ounce can condensed beef broth
- ½ cup water
- ½ cup dairy sour cream
- 2 tablespoons all-purpose flour
- Poppy-seed Noodles

Combine ¼ cup flour, the salt, and pepper. Cut meat in 6 serving pieces and dredge in flour mixture; brown in hot fat. Add onion slices, beef broth, and water. Cover and *simmer* 1 hour or till tender. Remove steak and onions to serving platter. Blend sour cream and 2 tablespoons flour. Remove broth from heat and add sour-cream mixture; stir to blend. Cook, stirring constantly, *just* till gravy thickens. Serve with POPPY-SEED NOODLES: Cook 4 ounces (2 cups) medium noodles in boiling salted water till tender; drain. Add 2 tablespoons butter or margarine and 2 tablespoons poppy seed; toss. Makes 6 servings.

Herb-Stuffed Flank Steak

- ⅓ cup chopped onion
- 2 tablespoons butter or margarine
- 2 hard-cooked eggs, chopped
- 1 cup dairy sour cream
- 2 cups herb-seasoned croutons
- ½ cup hot water
- 1 beaten egg
- 1 1-pound flank steak
- Instant meat tenderizer
- 2 tablespoons hot fat

Cook onion in butter or margarine till tender. Stir in chopped eggs, ¼ cup of the sour cream, croutons, water, and beaten egg. Pound steak to thin rectangle. Use tenderizer according to package directions. Spread stuffing over meat; roll up from wide edge. Skewer securely. Brown in hot fat. Add ½ cup water. Cover; simmer till tender, about 1½ hours. Remove meat; add water to drippings to make ½ cup; stir in remaining sour cream. Heat just to boiling. Pass with meat. Makes 4 servings.

Southern Steak Bar-B-Q

¼ cup soft butter or margarine	¼ cup olive oil
2 tablespoons dry mustard	2 tablespoons Worcestershire sauce
2 teaspoons salt	
2 teaspoons sugar	2 tablespoons catsup
¾ teaspoon paprika	¾ teaspoon sugar
¼ teaspoon pepper	¾ teaspoon salt
2 pounds 1-inch-sirloin steak	

For seasoned butter, mix first 6 ingredients; spread *half* on one side of steak. In large skillet, brown meat buttered side down. As this browns, spread remaining butter over top; turn and brown. Remove to broiler pan. For sauce, mix remaining ingredients; add skillet drippings. Brush sauce on steak. Broil 5 inches from heat about 5 to 7 minutes on each side, brushing frequently with sauce. Makes 6 servings.

Steak Roll-ups

½ cup uncooked long-grain rice	2 tablespoons butter or margarine
¼ teaspoon **each** thyme and marjoram, crushed	2 pounds round steak, ½ inch thick
¼ cup sliced green onion	
¼ cup chopped green pepper	2 tablespoons fat
2 tablespoons chopped canned pimiento	½ envelope or can **dry** onion-soup mix (¼ cup)
1 3-ounce can broiled chopped mushrooms, drained (½ cup)	

Cook rice till tender; drain. Stir in next 7 ingredients. Cut steak in 6 pieces; pound each to 6 x 4 inches. Spread steaks with rice. Roll up; fasten with picks; brown in hot fat. Add soup and 1 cup water. Cover; simmer 1½ hours. Remove meat; add water to pan drippings to make 1 cup. Combine 2 tablespoons flour with ½ cup water; stir into liquid. Cook and stir till thickened. Makes 6 servings.

Beef Stroganoff

- 1 tablespoon all-purpose flour
- ½ teaspoon salt
- 1 pound beef sirloin, cut in ¼-inch-wide strips
- 2 tablespoons butter or margarine
- 1 cup thinly sliced mushrooms
- ½ cup chopped onion
- 1 clove garlic, minced
- 2 tablespoons butter or margarine
- 3 tablespoons all-purpose flour
- 1 tablespoon tomato paste
- 1¼ cups beef stock or 1 can condensed beef broth
- 1 cup dairy sour cream
- 2 tablespoons cooking sherry

Combine 1 tablespoon flour and the salt; dredge meat in mixture. Heat skillet, then add 2 tablespoons butter. When melted, add the sirloin strips and brown quickly, flipping meat to brown on all sides. Add mushroom slices, onion, and garlic; cook 3 or 4 minutes or till onion is barely tender. Remove the meat and mushrooms from skillet. Add 2 tablespoons butter to pan drippings; when melted, blend in 3 tablespoons flour. Add tomato paste. Slowly pour in cold meat stock—cook, stirring constantly, until mixture thickens. Return meat and mushrooms to skillet. Stir in sour cream and sherry; heat briefly. Serve with parsleyed rice, noodles, buckwheat groats, or pilaf. Makes 4 or 5 servings.

For serving or cook-at-the-table drama, use chafing dish or an electric skillet.

Quick Beef Stroganoff Cut 3 minute steaks in strips; brown in 2 tablespoons hot fat. Add 1 onion, sliced, and 1

clove garlic, crushed; cook 5 minutes. Combine 1 10½-ounce can condensed cream of mushroom soup, 1 cup dairy sour cream, one 3-ounce can mushrooms, 2 tablespoons catsup, 2 teaspoons Worcestershire sauce; add to meat; heat through and serve.

Swiss Steak in Foil

1 cup catsup	1 large onion, sliced
¼ cup all-purpose flour	2 tablespoons lemon juice, or 1 lemon, thinly sliced (optional)
2 pounds round steak, 1 inch thick	

Tear off 5-foot length of household-weight alumininum foil; fold double. Combine catsup and flour; spoon *half* of mixture in center of foil. Place steak atop; season with salt and pepper. Cover meat with onion slices and remaining catsup mixture. Sprinkle with lemon juice or top with lemon slices. Fold foil over and seal edges securely. Place in shallow baking pan. Bake in very hot oven (450°) for 1½ hours or till meat is tender. Remove foil; cut steak in pieces. Makes 5 or 6 servings.

Saucy Short Ribs

3 pounds beef short ribs	4 cups sliced onions
All-purpose flour	3 tablespoons all-purpose flour
Salt and pepper	1 teaspoon Worcestershire sauce
½ cup hot water	½ teaspoon kitchen bouquet

Trim excess fat from ribs; heat fat in Dutch oven. Roll ribs in flour. Brown in hot fat; spoon off fat. Season. Add water. Cover; simmer top-of-range or in slow oven (325°) until tender, about 2 hours. (Add more water if needed.) Lift meat to warm platter; keep hot; make ONION GRAVY: Skim fat from short-rib stock, reserving 3 tablespoons. Measure stock and add hot water to make 2 cups; set aside. Put reserved fat in skillet. Add sliced onions and cook till tender, but not brown. Remove from heat. Push onions to one side; blend flour into fat. Slowly stir in meat stock. Return to heat; cook and stir till gravy is bubbling all over. Add Worcestershire sauce and kitchen bouquet. Season to taste with salt and pepper. Cook slowly about 5 minutes more stirring now and then. Serve over short ribs. Makes 6 servings.

Beef Swiss Steak

Buy round or chuck steak cut 1 to 2 inches thick. Mix ½ cup all-purpose flour, 2 teaspoons salt, and ½ teaspoon pepper. Pound mixture into both sides of steak. Brown steak *slowly* on all sides in a little hot fat in Dutch oven or large skillet. Don't rush this browning step. Mix one 1-pound can (2 cups) tomatoes and 1 onion, chopped. Heat to boiling; pour over steak. Cover; cook in moderate oven (350°) 1½ to 2 hours or till meat is fork tender. Skim off excess fat. To carve, divide meat; turn one piece on edge and carve meat across grain; repeat.

Chicken-fried Round Steak

1½ pounds round steak, ½ inch thick
1 beaten egg
1 tablespoon milk
⅔ cup fine cracker crumbs
¼ cup salad oil
Salt and pepper

Pound steak thoroughly; cut in serving pieces. Blend egg and milk. Dip meat in egg mixture, then in crumbs. Slowly brown meat in hot oil, turning once; season. Cover; cook over low heat 30 to 45 minutes or till tender. Makes 4 to 6 servings.

Corned-beef Dinner

3 to 4 pounds corned-beef brisket
2 onions, sliced
2 cloves garlic, minced
6 whole cloves
2 bay leaves
6 small to medium potatoes, pared
6 small carrots, pared
6 cabbage wedges (1 medium head)

Barely cover corned beef with hot water. Add onions, seasonings. Cover; simmer about 1 hour *per pound* of meat, or till tender. Remove meat from liquid; add potatoes, carrots. Cover; bring to boiling, cook 10 minutes. Add cabbage; cook 20 minutes more. To glaze cooked meat, top with mustard, brown sugar, and ground cloves. Bake at 350° 15 to 20 minutes. Makes 6 servings.

Round Steak Sauerbraten

- 1½ pounds round steak, ½ inch thick
- 1 tablespoon fat
- 1 envelope brown gravy mix
- 2 cups water
- 1 tablespoon instant minced onion
- 2 tablespoons white wine vinegar
- 2 tablespoons brown sugar
- ½ teaspoon salt
- ¼ teaspoon pepper
- ½ teaspoon ginger
- 1 teaspoon Worcestershire sauce
- 1 bay leaf
- Hot buttered noodles

Cut meat in 1-inch squares. In a large skillet, brown meat on all sides in hot fat. Remove meat from skillet; add gravy mix and water. Bring to boiling, stirring constantly. Stir in remaining ingredients except noodles. Return meat to skillet; cover and simmer 1½ hours, stirring occasionally. Remove bay leaf. Serve meat over hot buttered noodles. Makes 5 to 6 servings.

Oriental Chi Chow

- 1 pound sirloin steak, 1-inch thick, cut in narrow strips
- ½ cup chopped green onions
- 1 meduim onion, cut in wedges
- 1 5-ounce can bamboo shoots, drained
- 1 5-ounce can water chestnuts, drained
- 1 3-ounce can broiled sliced mushrooms, drained (½ cup)
- 1 tablespoon sugar
- ½ cup condensed beef broth
- 2 teaspoons cornstarch
- ¼ cup soy sauce
- 1 1-pound can (2 cups) sliced peaches, drained

Brown meat, half at a time, in hot fat. Add next 7 ingredients. Cover; simmer 5 minutes. Blend cornstarch, 1 tablespoon cold water, and soy; add to meat. Cook and stir till thick. Add peaches; cover; heat through. Serve with GINGER RICE: Mix 2 cups hot rice with ½ teaspoon ginger. Makes 4 or 5 servings.

Minute-steak Scramble

- 4 cube steaks, cut in julienne strips
- ¼ teaspoon garlic salt
- ¼ teaspoon ginger
- ¼ cup salad oil
- 2 green peppers, cut in julienne strips
- 1 cup bias-cut celery slices
- 1 tablespoon cornstarch
- ¼ cup cold water
- 3 tablespoons soy sauce
- 2 tomatoes, peeled and cut in eighths

Season meat with garlic salt and ginger. Heat *half* the oil in skillet; add meat and brown quickly on all sides. Remove meat. Add remaining oil; heat. Add peppers and celery; cook just till slightly tender (about 3 minutes). Mix cornstarch, water, and soy sauce. Add to skillet; cook and stir till mixture thickens. Add meat and tomatoes; heat. Serve with hot rice. Pass soy sauce. Makes 4 servings.

Burger in the Round

- 1½ pounds ground beef
- ½ cup chopped onion
- 1½ teaspoons salt
- 1 teaspoon monosodium glutamate
- Dash pepper
- ¾ cup soft bread crumbs
- ¾ cup milk
- 1 slightly beaten egg
- 1 clove garlic, minced
- 1 cup coarsely chopped green pepper
- 1 tablespoon butter or margarine
- ¼ cup bottled barbecue sauce

Combine meat with next 7 ingredients; pat *half* the mixture into a shallow 8-inch round baking dish. Cook garlic and green pepper in butter till almost tender; spread over meat. Top green-pepper mixture with remaining meat mixture. Bake in moderate oven (350°) 35 minutes. Pour barbecue sauce over meat and garnish with green-pepper triangles; bake 10 minutes more. Cut in wedges. Makes 6 servings.

Beef-Mushroom Loaf

- 2 cups water
- 1 envelope or can **dry** mushroom-soup mix
- 2 pounds ground beef
- ½ cup cracker crumbs
- ¼ cup minced onion
- 2 tablespoons snipped parsley
- 1 slightly beaten egg
- 1½ teaspoons salt
- Dash pepper

Gradually stir water into soup mix; cook and stir till mixture boils; remove from heat. Combine remaining ingredients; mix well. Blend in *1 cup* of the soup. Shape mixture in loaf; place in shallow baking pan. Bake in 350° oven 1 hour. Remove loaf to platter. Mix remaining soup with pan drippings; add few drops kitchen bouquet; heat through. Makes 8 to 10 servings.

Meat Loaf—Italian Style

- 1 cup medium cracker crumbs (20 crackers)
- 1½ pounds ground beef
- 1 6-ounce can (⅔ cup) tomato paste
- 2 eggs
- 1 medium onion, finely chopped
- ¼ cup finely chopped green pepper
- ¾ teaspoon salt
- Dash pepper
- 1 12-ounce carton (1½ cups) small-curd cottage cheese
- 1 3-ounce can chopped, broiled mushrooms, drained (½ cup)
- 1 tablespoon snipped parsley
- ¼ teaspoon oregano

Set aside ½ cup of the cracker crumbs. Combine remaining crumbs with next 7 ingredients; mix well. Pat half the mixture in bottom of 8x8x2-inch baking pan. Combine reserved crumbs, cottage cheese, mushrooms, parsley, and oregano; spread evenly over meat in pan. Top with remaining meat mixture. Bake at 350° for 1 hour. Let stand 10 minutes before serving. Makes 8 servings.

Stuffed Burger Bundles

- 1 cup packaged herb-seasoned stuffing or 1¼ cups stuffing croutons
- ⅓ cup evaporated milk
- 1 pound ground beef
- 1 10½-ounce can condensed cream of mushroom soup
- 2 teaspoons Worcestershire sauce
- 1 tablespoon catsup

Prepare stuffing according to package directions. Combine evaporated milk and meat; divide in 5 patties. On waxed paper, pat each to 6-inch circle. Put ¼ cup stuffing in center of each; draw meat over stuffing; seal. Place in 1½-quart casserole. Combine remaining ingredients; pour over meat. Bake, uncovered, at 350° 35 to 40 minutes. Serves 5.

Parmesan Meat Loaf

1 pound ground beef
1 8-ounce carton (1 cup) large-curd cream-style cottage cheese
½ cup quick-cooking rolled oats
1 egg
¼ cup catsup
2 teaspoons prepared mustard
2 tablespoons chopped onion
1 teaspoon salt
Dash pepper
⅓ cup grated Parmesan cheese

Thoroughly mix all ingredients except Parmesan cheese. Lightly pack meat into 8x8x2-inch pan. Bake in moderate oven (350°) 20 minutes. Sprinkle top with cheese. Bake 10 minutes longer. Let stand 5 minutes; cut in squares. Makes 6 servings.

Little Cranberry Meat Loaves

1 pound ground beef
1 cup cooked rice
½ cup tomato juice
1 slightly beaten egg
¼ cup minced onion
1 tablespoon kitchen bouquet
1½ teaspoons salt
1 1-pound can (2 cups) whole cranberry sauce
⅓ cup brown sugar
1 tablespoon lemon juice

Combine meat with rice, tomato juice, egg, minced onion, kitchen bouquet, and salt; mix thoroughly. Shape meat mixture into 5 individual loaves; place in 13x9x2-inch baking pan. For topping, combine cranberry sauce, brown sugar, and lemon juice; spoon over loaves. Bake in moderate oven (350°) 40 minutes. Remove meat loaves to warm serving platter. Pour cranberry sauce from pan; pass with meat loaves. Makes 5 servings.

Hamburger-Biscuit Supper Pie

Brown 1 pound ground beef; spoon off excess fat. Stir in 1 tablespoon instant minced onion. Soak 1 tablespoon instant minced onion in ⅔ cup milk. Prepare 2 cups packaged biscuit mix according to package directions for rolled biscuits, using milk-onion mixture for liquid. Roll in two 8-inch circles, about ¼ inch thick. Press one circle into well-greased 8¼x1¾-inch round ovenware cake dish. To meat mixture add 1 cup shredded sharp process American cheese, ¼ cup mayonnaise, and 3 tablespoons snipped parsley; spread over biscuit. Top with second biscuit. Flute edge. Bake in moderate oven (375°) 15 to 20 minutes. Drizzle 1 tablespoon melted butter over top; sprinkle with 1 teaspoon instant minced onion. Bake 2 minutes or till onion is toasty. Cut in wedges. Pass VEGETABLE SAUCE: Mix 1 10¾-ounce can condensed cream of vegetable soup, ⅓ cup milk, and ¼ teaspoon monosodium glutamate. Heat and stir till hot.

Burger Skillet Stew

- 1 pound ground beef
- ⅓ cup fine dry bread crumbs
- ⅓ cup milk
- 1 slightly beaten egg
- 1 envelope spaghetti-sauce mix
- 1 tablespoon fat
- 1 can (1¼ cups) beef gravy
- ¼ cup water
- ½ cup chopped green pepper
- 4 medium carrots, cut in 1-inch pieces
- 1 medium onion, quartered

Combine ground beef, crumbs, milk, egg, and 3 *tablespoons* of the spaghetti-sauce mix. Shape in 12 balls; brown in hot fat. Blend remaining sauce mix with gravy and water. Add to meat balls with vegetables; simmer covered 50 to 60 minutes. Makes 4 to 6 servings.

Meat Balls in Gingersnap Sauce

- 1 pound ground beef
- 1 egg
- ¾ cup soft bread crumbs
- ¼ cup water
- ¼ cup finely chopped onion
- ½ teaspoon salt
- Dash pepper
- 1½ cups water
- 2 beef bouillon cubes
- ⅓ cup brown sugar
- ¼ cup dark raisins
- 2½ tablespoons lemon juice
- ½ cup coarse gingersnap crumbs

Combine meat with next 6 ingredients; shape in about twenty-five 1-inch balls. Bring 1½ cups water to boiling. Stir in bouillon cubes, sugar, raisins, lemon juice, and crumbs. Add meat balls; cook uncovered over *low* heat 10 minutes. Turn meat balls, spooning sauce over; cook 10 minutes longer, stirring occasionally. Makes 5 or 6 servings.

Gourmet Meat Balls

- 1 pound ground beef
- ¼ pound (½ cup) Braunschweiger
- ½ cup soft bread crumbs
- ¼ cup finely chopped onion
- 1 slightly beaten egg
- ½ cup milk
- 1 teaspoon salt
- Dash pepper
- 2 tablespoons fat
- ¼ cup dry mushroom-soup mix
- 1 cup cold water

Combine first 8 ingredients; mix well. Shape in eighteen 1½-inch balls; chill 1 hour. Brown meat balls, a few at a time, in hot fat, shaking frequently. Blend soup mix and water; add to meat. Cover; simmer 15 minutes. Serve with noodles. Serves 6.

Caraway Meat Loaf

- 1 tablespoon caraway seed
- 1 tablespoon instant minced onion
- 3 tablespoons red wine vinegar
- 1 pound ground beef
- ½ pound ground fresh pork
- 1½ cups soft bread crumbs
- ¾ cup milk
- 1 egg
- 1½ teaspoons salt
- Dash pepper

In large bowl, soak caraway seed and onion in vinegar 10 minutes. Add remaining ingredients; mix thoroughly. Shape in loaf in shallow baking dish. Bake in moderate oven (350°) 1½ hours. (If you wish to score loaf, press top with handle of wooden spoon or knife after baking ½ hour.) Makes 8 servings.

Pizza Loaf

1½ pounds ground beef
1 8-ounce can (1 cup) tomato sauce
¾ cup quick-cooking rolled oats
¼ cup chopped onion
1 egg
1 tablespoon Worcestershire sauce
1½ teaspoons salt
1½ teaspoons monosodium glutamate
¾ to 1 teaspoon oregano
¼ teaspoon pepper
1 6-ounce package sliced Mozzarella cheese

Combine all ingredients except cheese; mix thoroughly. Divide meat mixture in thirds. Pat ⅓ in bottom of 9½x5x3-inch loaf pan; cover with *half* the cheese. Repeat layers, ending with meat. Bake in moderate oven (350°) 1 hour. Makes 5 or 6 servings.

Tangy Frank Barbecue

2 tablespoons prepared mustard
2 8-ounce cans (2 cups) tomato sauce
½ cup dark corn syrup
⅓ cup vinegar
⅓ cup minced onion
2 tablespoons Worcestershire sauce
½ teaspoon celery seed
¼ to ½ teaspoon bottled hot pepper sauce
1 pound (8 to 10) frankfurters, scored diagonally

In skillet, blend mustard with small amount of tomato sauce; add remaining tomato sauce along with remaining ingredients, except franks. Cook over medium heat, stirring frequently, till mixture comes to boiling; reduce heat and simmer gently 30 minutes. Add franks; cook till franks are hot and plumped, 7 to 8 minutes. Serve in warm buns or over rice (if franks are to be served over rice, slice diagonally before adding to barbecue sauce). Makes 4 or 5 servings.

Pineapple Speared Franks

1 pound (8 to 10) frankfurters
Mustard
Catsup
8 to 10 canned pineapple spears
8 to 10 slices bacon

Slit frankfurters lengthwise; spread cut surfaces lightly with mustard, then catsup. Insert pineapple spears. Wrap slice of bacon around each frank; secure with toothpicks. Place cut side down on broiler rack; broil 6 inches from heat 7 to 8 minutes or till bacon is done on one side. Turn; broil 6 to 7 minutes. Remove toothpicks. Serve in warm buns, if desired. Makes 4 or 5 servings.

Franks Florentine

1 10-ounce package frozen chopped spinach, cooked and drained
1½ cups cooked rice
1 11-ounce can condensed Cheddar cheese soup
2 tablespoons minced onion
¼ cup milk
½ pound (4 to 5) frankfurters, halved crosswise

Spread spinach in bottom of 10x6x1½-inch baking dish. Combine rice, soup, onion, and milk; spoon over spinach. Score half franks with an X-shaped cut; arrange on casserole, pressing into rice. Bake in moderate oven (375°) 20 to 25 minutes or till heated through. Makes 4 servings.

Island Franks

Drain one 9-ounce can (1 cup) pineapple tidbits, reserving syrup. Slice ½ pound (4 or 5) frankfurters. In skillet, melt 2 tablespoons butter or margarine; add ½ cup sliced onion and 1 green pepper, cut in strips. Cover and cook over low heat 5 minutes. Dissolve 1 beef bouillon cube in ⅓ cup hot water. Mix 1 tablespoon cornstarch, 1 tablespoon brown sugar, dash salt, reserved pineapple syrup, 2 tablespoons vinegar, and 1 tablespoon soy sauce; add bouillon. Pour over vegetables. Cook and stir till mixture thickens. Add franks and pineapple. Heat thoroughly. Serve over hot rice. Makes 4 servings.

Wiener Wrap-ups

- 8 to 10 large cabbage leaves
- 1 pound (8 to 10) frankfurters
- Prepared mustard
- 1 cup canned cream-style corn
- 1 8-ounce can (1 cup) tomato sauce
- ¼ cup chopped onion
- ½ teaspoon dried basil **or** 2 teaspoons fresh basil
- ¼ teaspoon salt
- 4 ounces sharp process American cheese, shredded (1 cup)
- 1 1¾-ounce package corn chips, coarsely crushed (¾ cup)

Cook cabbage leaves in boiling salted water only till pliable, about 10 minutes; drain well. Brush one side of each frank with small amount of mustard; roll in a cabbage leaf. Arrange in an 11x7x1½-inch baking dish. Mix vegetables and seasonings; pour over franks. Cover; bake in moderate oven (350°) 35 minutes or till hot. Top with cheese and corn chips. Bake uncovered 5 minutes. Makes 4 or 5 servings.

Weiner-Bean Bake

- 1 10-ounce package frozen Limas
- 1 1-pound can (2 cups) pork and beans in tomato sauce
- 1 1-pound can (2 cups) kidney beans, drained
- ½ cup chili sauce
- ¼ cup molasses
- ½ to 1 teaspoon dry mustard
- ½ teaspoon Worcestershire sauce
- ½ envelope or can (¼ cup) **dry** onion-soup mix
- 1 pound (8 to 10) frankfurters, cut in 1-inch pieces

Cook Limas according to package directions; drain. Mix with pork and beans and kidney beans. Stir in remaining ingredients. Turn into 2-quart casserole or bean pot; bake covered in moderate oven (350°) 1 hour. Uncover; stir and continue baking 30 minutes. Makes 6 servings.

Frank-Noodle Supper Pie

- ½ pound (4 or 5) frankfurters, thinly sliced
- 1 cup medium noodles, cooked and drained
- ½ cup chopped onion
- 3 slightly beaten eggs
- 1 cup dairy sour cream
- ½ cup cream-style cottage cheese
- ½ teaspoon salt
- Dash pepper
- ½ cup packaged corn flake crumbs
- 1 tablespoon butter or margarine, melted

Reserve a few frankfurter slices for top; combine remainder with all ingredients except crumbs and butter; pour into a greased 9-inch pie plate. Mix crumbs and butter; sprinkle over top. Bake in moderate oven (375°) 25 minutes, topping with frank slices the last 5 minutes. Let stand 10 minutes; cut in wedges. Makes 6 servings.

Swiss Veal Foldovers

- 6 veal cutlets
- 6 square slices process Swiss cheese
- 6 square slices boiled ham
- 2 tablespoons all-purpose flour
- ¼ teaspoon paprika
- 2 tablespoons fat
- 1 10½-ounce can condensed cream of mushroom soup
- 1 cup light cream
- ¼ cup cooking sauterne

Pound each veal slice to a very thin rectangle (about 8x4 inches). Cut cheese and ham slices in half; stack alternately in center of each veal cutlet. Fold veal over to cover cheese and ham; roll carefully in mixture of flour and paprika. Brown in hot fat. Mix remaining ingredients; add to skillet. Cover; simmer, stirring occasionally, 30 minutes or till tender. Serve with hot rice. Makes 6 servings.

Veal Chops with Olive Sauce

- 4 veal chops, ½ inch thick
- Salt and pepper
- All-purpose flour
- 2 tablespoons fat
- 2 tablespoons all-purpose flour
- ½ teaspoon salt
- ½ teaspoon paprika
- 1 tablespoon chopped onion
- 2 teaspoons lemon juice
- 1 cup water
- ¼ cup sliced stuffed green olives

Sprinkle chops with salt and pepper; dip in flour. Slowly brown chops on both sides in hot fat; remove chops. Blend the 2 tablespoons flour into fat. Add salt, paprika, onion, and lemon juice. Add water. Cook and stir till mixture thickens. Return chops to skillet. Cover and simmer till tender, about 20 minutes. Add olives; cook uncovered 5 minutes. Makes 4 servings.

Baked Veal-and-Ham Birds

- 2 pounds veal round
- 8 slices boiled ham
- 8 slices (1 package) process Swiss cheese
- 1 slightly beaten egg
- 2 tablespoons milk or water
- ⅔ cup cornflake crumbs
- 1 10½-ounce can condensed cream of mushroom soup
- 2 tablespoons cooking sauterne
- ½ cup light cream

Have meatman cut veal in 8 slices, ¼ inch thick. Have him put them through tenderizing machine—*or*, at home, pound each slice to ⅛ inch. Top each veal slice with a ham slice. Cut each cheese slice in 4 strips and place in stacks on ham slices. *Loosely* roll up meat around cheese; secure with toothpicks. Brush rolls with mixture of the egg and milk; roll in crumbs to coat. Place seam side down in 13x9x1½-inch baking dish. Combine soup, sauterne, and cream; heat to bubbling; pour around rolls. Cover baking dish with foil; bake at 350° 50 minutes or till tender. Uncover and bake 10 minutes or till crumbs are crisp. Makes 8 servings.

Veal Scaloppine

- 3 pounds veal steak, ¼ to ⅓ inch thick
- ½ cup all-purpose flour
  Salt, pepper, and paprika
- 1 6-ounce can (1⅓ cups) broiled sliced mushrooms
- 1 bouillon cube
- 1 8-ounce can (1 cup) tomato sauce
- ¼ cup chopped green pepper
- 1 8-ounce package green noodles (tagliatelle verdi)

Pound meat thoroughly with meat pounder. Cut in serving pieces. Season flour with 1 teaspoon salt, dash pepper, and 2 teaspoons paprika. Coat meat in mixture. Brown in hot fat. Place in 13x9x2-inch baking dish. Drain mushrooms, reserving liquid. Add water to mushroom liquid to make 1 cup; heat to boiling. Dissolve bouillon cube in the hot liquid and pour over meat. Bake in moderate oven (350°) 30 minutes. Combine tomato sauce, green pepper, and mushrooms; pour over the meat and continue baking for 15 minutes more. Meanwhile, cook noodles until tender in boiling salted water; drain. Baste meat with the sauce just before serving. Sprinkle with Parmesan cheese. Serve with hot buttered noodles. Makes 8 or 9 servings.

Roast Stuffed Breast of Veal

Have meatman bone a 3-pound veal breast. Sprinkle inside surface of veal with salt. Top half the veal with Sausage-Apple Stuffing. Fold other half over stuffing and fasten together with metal skewers. Place on rack in shallow roasting pan; lay bacon slices on top to cover veal. Do not add water. Roast uncovered at 325° about 3 hours or till well done. Makes 6 servings.

Sausage-Apple Stuffing   Fry ½ pound bulk pork sausage till lightly browned; don't drain. Add 1 cup chopped tart apple, 1 cup soft medium bread crumbs, 1 cup medium cracker crumbs, 2 tablespoons chopped onion, ¾ cup hot water, ½ teaspoon salt, and dash pepper; mix.

Paprika Wiener Schnitzel

- 1½ pounds veal steak or cutlets, ½- to ¾-inch thick
- 1 medium onion, thinly sliced
- 1 clove garlic, minced
- ¼ cup all-purpose flour
- 1 cup dairy sour cream
- ⅓ cup condensed consomme
- 1 tablespoon paprika
- 3 drops bottled hot pepper sauce

Cut meat in serving pieces; pound till about double in area. Cook onion and garlic in hot fat till onion is tender but not brown; remove from skillet. Dip pounded veal steak in flour seasoned with 1 teaspoon salt and ¼ teaspoon pepper; brown on both sides in hot fat. Add cooked onion and garlic to meat; cover and cook slowly 15 minutes, or till meat is tender. Combine remaining ingredients and pour over meat. Cover tightly and simmer 10 to 15 minutes longer. Makes 4 servings.

Braised Rolled Veal Shoulder

Brown rolled veal shoulder on all sides in hot fat. Season with salt and pepper. Place on rack in roasting pan; add a little water; cover. Cook in slow oven (325°) until tender, about 45 minutes *per pound*. Vegetables may be added last 45 minutes.

Veal Chops

Select 4 to 6 veal chops, ¾ to 1 inch thick. Dip in flour;* brown in hot fat, season with salt and pepper. Add small amount of water, cover, cook slowly about 45 minutes or till done. Allow one chop per serving.

* *Or* dip chops into mixture of one slightly beaten egg and 1 tablespoon water, then into fine cracker or dry bread crumbs.

Holiday Pork Roast

Place 4- to 5-pound boned, rolled, and tied pork loin roast in shallow baking dish. Rub with mixture of 2 tablespoons dry mustard and 2 teaspoons thyme. Combine ½ cup sherry, ½ cup soy sauce, 2 cloves garlic, minced, and 1 teaspoon ginger; pour over meat. Let stand 3 to 4 hours at room temperature or overnight in refrigerator; turn occasionally. Remove meat from marinade; place on rack in shallow roasting pan; roast uncovered at 325° for 2½ to 3 hours till meat thermometer registers 185°. Melt one 10-ounce jar currant jelly; add 1 tablespoon soy sauce and 2 tablespoons sherry. Stir and simmer 2 minutes; pass with roast. Makes 10 to 12 servings.

Rice-stuffed Pork Shoulder

Select a 4- to 5-pound fresh boneless cushion shoulder. Enlarge pocket. Insert a few garlic cloves in fat side of meat. Sprinkle pocket of meat with salt; lightly stuff with Spanish-rice Stuffing*: Combine 3 cups hot cooked rice, one 8-ounce can (1 cup) tomato sauce, ½ cup chopped onion, ¼ cup chopped canned pimiento, 1 tablespoon brown sugar, 1 teaspoon chili powder, and 1 teaspoon salt. Close opening of pocket with skewers and tie with cord. Rub outside of roast with salt and ½ teaspoon rosemary. Place fat side up on rack in shallow pan (do not cover). Roast in slow oven (325°) 45 to 50 minutes *per pound* (about 4 hours) or till pork is well done. Allow ⅛ pound meat per serving.

* Bake extra stuffing in greased pan or casserole the last hour, basting occasionally with drippings.

Island Sweet-Sour Pork

1½ pounds boneless pork shoulder, cut in small cubes
1 tablespoon salad oil
1 teaspoon salt
Dash pepper
1 8¾-ounce can pineapple tidbits
½ cup barbecue sauce
1 tablespoon cornstarch
1 medium green pepper, cut in strips

Brown meat in hot oil in skillet. Season with salt and pepper. Drain pineapple, reserving syrup. Add water to syrup to make ¾ cup. Stir syrup and barbecue sauce into browned meat. Cover; simmer 40 to 45 minutes or till tender. Blend cornstarch with 2 tablespoons cold water; stir into meat. Cook and stir till thickened. Add pineapple and green pepper; heat through. Serve over rice. Six servings.

Cheese-stuffed Pork Chops

- 4 pork chops, 1 inch thick
- 1 3-ounce can (⅔ cup) broiled chopped mushrooms
- ¼ pound process Swiss cheese, diced (¾ cup)
- ¼ cup snipped parsley
- ½ teaspoon salt
- ½ cup fine dry bread crumbs
- ¼ teaspoon salt
- Dash pepper
- 1 beaten egg

Trim excess fat from chops. Cut a pocket in fat side of each chop (or have meatman do it). Drain mushrooms, reserving liquid. Combine mushrooms, cheese, parsley, and ½ teaspoon salt; stuff into pockets; toothpick and lace shut. Mix crumbs, ¼ teaspoon salt, and the pepper. Dip chops in egg, then in crumb mixture. Slowly brown chops in hot fat. Add reserved mushroom liquid; cover and simmer 1 hour or till chops are done. Remove chops. GRAVY: Blend 2 tablespoons flour and ¼ cup cold water to a smooth paste; gradually stir flour mixture into liquid in skillet. Cook and stir till gravy thickens. Makes 4 servings.

Gourmet Pork Chops

- 6 loin pork chops, about ½ inch thick
- 2 tablespoons all-purpose flour
- 1 teaspoon salt
- Dash pepper
- 1 10½-ounce can condensed cream of mushroom soup
- ¾ cup water
- ½ teaspoon ginger
- ¼ teaspoon rosemary, crushed
- 1 3½-ounce can French-fried onion rings
- ½ cup dairy sour cream

Trim excess fat from chops. Heat fat in skillet till about 2 tablespoons melted fat has collected; remove trimmings. Coat chops in mixture of flour, salt, and pepper. Brown in the hot fat. Place in 11x7x1½-inch baking dish. Combine soup, water, ginger, and rosemary; pour over chops. Sprinkle with half the onion rings. Cover; bake at 350° for 50 minutes, or till meat is tender. Uncover; sprinkle with remaining onion rings, and continue baking 10 minutes. Remove meat to platter. Blend sour cream into soup mixture; heat through. Pass with meat. Makes 6 servings. Serve with fluffy rice and fresh asparagus.

Fruit-top Pork Chops

    4 or 5 pork chops, about ½ inch thick
    1 tablespoon sugar
    1 teaspoon salt
    ¼ teaspoon curry powder
    1 cup orange juice
    ¼ cup water
    4 or 5 dried prunes
    8 or 10 dried apricot halves

Trim fat from chops. Heat fat in skillet; when you have about 2 tablespoons melted fat, remove trimmings. Slowly brown chops on both sides in hot fat. Combine sugar, salt, curry powder, orange juice, and water; pour over chops. Place dried fruits on top of chops. Cover; cook over low heat about 1 hour or till chops are done. (Add a little water to sauce, if necessary, to prevent chops from sticking.) Makes 4 or 5 servings.

Zesty Barbecue Pork Chops

    1 envelope tomato-soup mix
    ½ envelope or can (¼ cup) **dry** onion-soup mix
    ½ cup Italian salad dressing
    2 tablespoons vinegar
    2 cups water
    2 tablespoons brown sugar
    2 teaspoons Worcestershire sauce
    1 teaspoon prepared horseradish
    1 teaspoon prepared mustard
    6 pork chops

In saucepan, combine first 4 ingredients; gradually stir in water. Add remaining ingredients, except pork chops. Bring to boiling; simmer 10 minutes. Brown chops in hot fat; add 1 *cup of the* sauce. Simmer covered 1 hour, basting occasionally. Add sauce, as needed.

Apple-stuffed Pork Tenderloins

    2 1-pound whole pork tenderloins   1 cup apple juice
    1 recipe Apple Stuffing   4 slices bacon, halved

Cut each tenderloin lengthwise, *not quite through*; flatten out. Sprinkle generously with salt and pepper. Spread Apple Stuffing over one flattened loin; top with second one; skewer shut. Place in shallow baking pan. Pour apple juice over meat and lay bacon on top. Roast uncovered in 350° oven 1½ hours or till well-done. Remove skewers. Make gravy from pan drippings, adding kitchen bouquet for color, if desired. Six to 8 servings. APPLE STUFFING: Heat ⅓ cup apple juice with 1 tablespoon butter and 1 teaspoon sage. Stir in ¾ cup chopped unpared tart apple, ½ cup chopped onion, and ¾ cup packaged herb-seasoned stuffing.

Polynesian Pork Chops

    6 pork chops, ½ to ¾ inch   ½ cup thin bias-cut celery slices
      thick   2 teaspoons cornstarch
    3 oranges   ⅓ cup cold water
    ½ cup chopped onion   Hot cooked rice
    2 tablespoons soy sauce

Trim fat from chops. Heat fat in skillet; when you have about 2 tablespoons melted fat, remove trimmings. Brown chops in hot fat; season with salt and pepper. Pour off excess fat. Peel and section oranges, reserving any juice. Add water to juice to measure ½ cup; add to chops with onion and soy sauce. Cover; simmer 30 minutes. Add celery; simmer 5 minutes longer. Remove chops. Blend cornstarch and water; stir into sauce. Cook and stir till mixture thickens. Return chops to skillet; top each with orange sections. Cover; simmer just till hot. Serve with rice. Makes 6 servings.

Spareribs Cantonese

- 4 pounds spareribs, cut in serving pieces
- ½ cup soy sauce
- ¾ cup water
- 1 cup orange marmalade
- ½ teaspoon garlic powder
- Dash pepper
- 2 teaspoons grated fresh gingerroot **or** ½ teaspoon ground ginger

Place ribs, meaty side down, in shallow roasting pan. Roast in very hot oven (450°) for 30 minutes. Remove meat from oven; drain excess fat from ribs. Turn ribs meaty side up. Lower oven temperature to 350°; continue roasting ribs for 1 hour. Pour Orange Sauce over ribs; roast 30 minutes longer or till tender, basting ribs occasionally with the sauce. ORANGE SAUCE: Combine soy sauce, water, orange marmalade, garlic powder, pepper, and ginger; blend thoroughly. Makes 6 servings. Serve with fluffy rice and buttered Chinese pea pods.

Spareribs with Caraway Kraut

- 3 pounds spareribs, cut in serving pieces
- 2 teaspoons salt
- ¼ teaspoon pepper
- 1 1-pound 11-ounce can (3½ cups) sauerkraut
- 2 medium carrots, shredded
- 1 unpared tart apple, finely chopped
- 1½ cups tomato juice
- 2 tablespoons brown sugar
- 2 to 3 teaspoons caraway seed

Season ribs with salt and pepper; place in Dutch oven. Combine kraut (including liquid) with remaining ingredients and spoon over ribs. Bake, covered, in moderate oven (350°) 2½ to 3½ hours or till ribs are done, basting kraut with juices several times during the last hour. Use spoon to serve ribs and kraut so as to get all the good juices, too. Makes 4 to 6 servings.

Sausage Strata

- 6 slices bread
- 1 pound bulk pork sausage
- 1 teaspoon prepared mustard
- 4 ounces process Swiss cheese, shredded (1 cup)
- 3 slightly beaten eggs
- 1¼ cups milk
- ¾ cup light cream
- ½ teaspoon salt
- Dash pepper
- Dash nutmeg
- 1 teaspoon Worcestershire sauce

Trim crusts from bread; fit bread in bottom of 6 greased individual casseroles.* Brown sausage; *drain off all excess fat.* Stir in mustard. Spoon sausage evenly over bread; sprinkle with cheese. Combine remaining ingredients; pour over cheese. Bake in moderate oven (350°) 25 to 30 minutes or till set. Serve immediately.

*Or bake in a greased 10x6x1½-inch baking dish 30 to 35 minutes or till set.

Bacon Oriental

- 1 pound sliced bacon
- 1 medium onion, sliced
- 1 cup chopped celery
- 1 6-ounce can (1⅓ cups) broiled sliced mushrooms
- 2 tablespoons cornstarch
- ¼ cup cold water
- ½ teaspoon salt
- Dash pepper
- 1 tablespoon soy sauce
- 1 cup chopped green pepper
- 1 1-pound can bean sprouts, drained

Fry bacon till crisp; remove from pan and drain. Cook onion and celery in 1 tablespoon of the bacon fat till tender-crisp but not brown. Drain mushrooms, reserving liquid; add water to liquid to make 1½ cups. Dissolve cornstarch in ¼ cup water; combine with mushroom liquid, salt, pepper, and soy sauce. Add to onions and celery. Cook and stir till mixture thickens. Stir in mushrooms and remaining ingredients; heat through. Crumble bacon over top. Serve with rice. Makes 6 to 8 servings.

Yankee Bacon Bake

- ½ pound sliced bacon
- ½ cup cornmeal
- 2 cups milk
- ½ cup sifted all-purpose flour
- 1 tablespoon sugar
- 1 teaspoon baking powder
- ½ teaspoon salt
- 3 well-beaten egg yolks
- 3 stiffly beaten egg whites

Quarter bacon slices; fry till crisp; drain. Mix cornmeal with 1 cup of the milk; cook till consistency of mush; remove from heat. Sift together dry ingredients; blend into cornmeal mixture. Mix in remaining milk and egg yolks; fold in egg whites and bacon pieces. Bake in a greased 2-quart casserole in slow oven (325°) about 1 hour. Makes 6 servings.

Canadian Bacon-Bean Bake

- 1 1-pound can pork and beans in tomato sauce
- 1 tablespoon instant minced onion
- ¼ cup catsup
- 2 teaspoons prepared horseradish
- 2 teaspoons prepared mustard
- 1 teaspoon Worcestershire sauce
- 4 slices orange, about ¼ inch thick
- 8 slices Canadian-style bacon, about ¼ inch thick
- ⅓ cup brown sugar
- 2 tablespoons butter or margarine

Combine beans with minced onion, catsup, horseradish, mustard, and Worcestershire sauce. Pour into a 10x6x1½-inch baking dish. Bake in a moderate oven (350°) for 45 minutes. Arrange orange slices and bacon on top of bean mixture; sprinkle with brown sugar; dot with butter. Bake for an additional 30 minutes. Makes 4 servings.

Pineapple-Orange Glazed Ham

Pour ½ cup hot cider or hot water over ¼ cup raisins; let stand. Place 10- to 12-pound cook-before-eating ham, fat side up, on rack in shallow pan. Bake at 325° 3½ to 4 hours or to 160° internal temperature.* Half hour before ham is done, score fat in diamonds about ¼ inch deep. Spoon Pineapple-Orange Glaze over ham. Bake 30 minutes; baste with glaze 2 or 3 times. Remove ham to platter. Drain raisins; add to glaze remaining in pan; pass with ham. PINEAPPLE-ORANGE GLAZE: Combine 1 6-ounce can frozen pineapple-orange juice concentrate, ½ cup light corn syrup, ½ teaspoon cinnamon, and ¼ teaspoon cloves; bring to boiling.

*For fully-cooked ham, bake 2½ to 3 hours or to 130°.

Southern Luncheon Bake

- 6 ½-inch slices boned rolled ham (or canned ham slices)
- Whole cloves
- 6 canned pineapple rings
- 2 tablespoons butter or margarine, melted
- ½ teaspoon salt
- 2 cups mashed cooked or canned sweet potatoes
- 1 cup canned whole cranberry sauce
- 1 teaspoon grated orange peel
- ½ cup orange juice
- 2 tablespoons brown sugar

Arrange ham slices in shallow baking dish; stud sides with cloves. Place a pineapple ring on each ham slice. Beat butter and salt into potatoes and mound atop pineapple rings. In saucepan, combine cranberry sauce, orange peel, juice, and brown sugar; simmer about 5 minutes, stirring frequently; drizzle over potatoes. Bake in moderate oven (350°) 45 minutes, basting once or twice with sauce. Makes 6 servings.

Glazed Ham Slice with Cranberry-Raisin Sauce

- 1 1½-inch slice fully cooked ham (about 2 pounds)
- ½ cup light brown sugar
- 2 tablespoons cornstarch
- Dash ground cloves
- Dash salt
- ½ cup orange juice
- 1½ cups bottled cranberry-juice cocktail
- ½ cup raisins

Slash fat edge of ham at 2-inch intervals. Insert whole cloves in fat, if desired. Place ham in shallow baking dish. Bake in slow oven (325°) 30 minutes. Meanwhile make CRANBERRY-RAISIN SAUCE: Mix sugar, cornstarch, cloves, and salt. Add remaining ingredients. Cook and stir till mixture thickens and comes to boiling. Remove ham from oven. Spoon some of sauce over ham; bake 20 minutes or till glazed. Pass remaining sauce with the ham. Makes 6 servings.

Glazed Ham Balls

- 1 pound ground cooked ham
- ½ pound ground fresh pork
- ¾ cup soft bread crumbs
- 2 slightly beaten eggs
- ½ cup milk
- 2 tablespoons chopped onion
- 1 8¾-ounce can (1 cup) crushed pineapple
- ⅓ cup brown sugar
- 1 tablespoon vinegar
- 2 to 3 tablespoons prepared mustard

Thoroughly combine first 6 ingredients; shape in 1½-inch balls (about 18). Place in shallow baking pan. Mix remaining ingredients; spoon over ham balls. Bake in moderate oven (350°) 45 to 50 minutes, basting occasionally with glaze. Makes 6 to 8 servings.

Curried Ham Rolls

CURRY SAUCE: In saucepan, melt 3 tablespoons butter or margarine; blend in 2 tablespoons cornstarch, 1 teaspoon curry powder, 1 teaspoon monosodium glutamate, and ¼ teaspoon salt. Add 3 cups milk and ¾ cup golden raisins. Cook and stir till mixture thickens and comes to boiling.

RICE FILLING: Mix ½ *cup of the sauce* with 1½ cups cooked rice, 2 tablespoons finely chopped onion, 1 hard-cooked egg, chopped, 1 tablespoon minced parsley, ¼ teaspoon salt, and dash pepper. Spread filling over 12 slices boiled ham; roll up each. Place ham rolls, seam side down, in shallow baking dish. Cover with remaining sauce. Bake in moderate oven (350°) 35 to 40 minutes. Makes 6 servings.

Apricot-Glazed Ham Patties

1½ pounds ground cooked ham	1 teaspoon prepared mustard
½ cup soft bread crumbs	¼ teaspoon sage
½ cup milk	¼ teaspoon pepper
2 eggs	½ cup apricot **or** peach preserves
¼ cup chopped onion	2 teaspoons vinegar
¼ cup (1 ounce) crumbled blue cheese	1 teaspoon prepared mustard
1 tablespoon Worcestershire sauce	

Combine ham with next 9 ingredients. Shape in 6 patties. Place in 13x9x2-inch baking dish; bake at 350° for 30 minutes. Combine preserves, vinegar, and mustard; brush on ham patties. Bake 10 minutes more. Makes 6 servings.

Marmalade Ham-loaf Squares

- 1½ cups packaged herb-seasoned stuffing
- 2 cups milk
- 1½ pounds ground fresh pork
- 1½ pounds ground cooked ham
- ½ cup chopped onion
- ¼ teaspoon salt
- 1 cup orange marmalade
- 2 tablespoons vinegar
- 1 teaspoon dry mustard
- ¼ teaspoon cinnamon
- ¼ teaspoon cloves

Soak stuffing in milk 5 minutes; add meats, onion, and salt; mix well. Lightly pack into 9x9x2-inch baking dish. Bake in moderate oven (350°) 1¼ hours. Spoon off drippings. For MARMALADE GLAZE: Mix remaining ingredients; spread over loaf. Bake 10 minutes longer. Allow to stand a few minutes before cutting in squares. Top with orange cuts, if desired. Makes 9 to 12 servings.

Ham Logs with Raisin Sauce

- 1 pound ground cooked ham
- ½ pound ground fresh pork
- ¾ cup milk
- ½ cup quick-cooking rolled oats
- 1 egg
- 2 teaspoons prepared horseradish
- ½ teaspoon salt
- Dash freshly ground pepper
- 1 tablespoon cornstarch
- ¾ cup cold water
- 2 tablespoons lemon juice
- 2 tablespoons vinegar
- ½ cup brown sugar
- ¼ cup raisins

Combine first 8 ingredients; mix well. Shape in 6 logs, about 6½-inches long. Place in 11x7x1½-inch baking dish. Blend cornstarch and water; add remaining ingredients. Cook and stir till mixture bubbles; pour over ham logs. Bake in moderate oven (350°) 40 to 45 minutes, basting occasionally with the sauce. Makes 6 servings.

Ham Loaf—Red Mustard Sauce

- 1 10¾-ounce can condensed tomato soup
- 1 pound ground cooked ham
- 1 pound ground beef
- ½ cup chopped onion
- ⅓ cup milk
- ¾ cup medium cracker crumbs
- 1 slightly beaten egg

Reserve half the soup for sauce; combine remainder with other ingredients; mix well. Lightly pack into a 9½x5x3-inch loaf pan. Bake in moderate oven (350°) 1¼ hours. Spoon off excess fat. Let stand 5 minutes; then turn out on platter. Makes 8 to 10 servings. Serve with hot RED MUSTARD SAUCE: Mix reserved soup with 1 slightly beaten egg, 1 tablespoon sugar, 2 tablespoons prepared mustard, 1 tablespoon vinegar, and 1 tablespoon butter. Cook, stirring constantly, just till mixture thickens.

Roast Stuffed Lamb

- 4- to 5-pound lamb shoulder roast
- 1 cup chopped celery
- ¼ cup chopped onion
- 4 tablespoons butter or margarine, melted
- 6 cups soft bread crumbs (8 or 9 slices)
- ½ cup apricot nectar
- 2 beaten eggs
- 2 teaspoons poultry seasoning
- 1 teaspoon salt

Have meatman bone roast to form pocket. Cook celery and onion in butter or margarine till tender. Toss with remaining ingredients. Fill pocket with stuffing; skewer securely. Place roast on rack in shallow pan. Bake at 325° till meat thermometer registers 175° to 180° (about 3 to 3¾ hours). Remove strings and skewers before serving. Makes 8 servings.

Herbed Leg of Lamb

Select a 5- to 6-pound leg of lamb. Cut *deep* slits in meat at 2-inch intervals. Crush 4 cloves garlic; mix with 2 teaspoons *each* salt and crushed oregano, and ½ teaspoon pepper; press into slits. Place lamb, fat side up, on rack in open roasting pan. Mix 1 cup cooking claret, ¼ cup sliced green onions, and 2 tablespoons lemon juice. *Reserve* ½ cup of this mixture for gravy; brush part of remainder over meat. Brushing often with claret mixture, roast meat in 325° oven 30 to 35 minutes *per pound* or till meat thermometer reads 175° for medium. Lift roast to warm platter. GRAVY: Skim off fat. Add water to meat juices to make 1 cup. Measure 2 tablespoons fat back into pan; blend in 2 tablespoons flour. Stir in meat juices and reserved claret mixture. Cook and stir till bubbly; cook 1 minute. Season to taste. Makes 8 to 10 servings.

Barbecued Lamb Shanks

- 4 lamb shanks
- 1 medium onion, sliced
- ½ cup catsup
- ½ cup water
- 1 tablespoon brown sugar
- 1 tablespoon vinegar
- 1 tablespoon Worcestershire sauce
- 1 teaspoon salt
- 1 teaspoon dry mustard

Brown lamb shanks in small amount hot fat; spoon off excess fat. SAUCE: Mix remaining ingredients; pour over shanks. Cover; simmer 1½ to 2 hours or till meat is tender, turning occasionally. Makes 4 servings.

Savory Lamb Roll

- 1 clove garlic, minced
- 1 tablespoon all-purpose flour
- 2 teaspoons salt
- Dash pepper
- 1 tablespoon lemon juice
- 3- to 4-pound boned and rolled lamb shoulder

Combine garlic, flour, salt, pepper, and lemon juice; spread over roast. Place roast on large sheet of heavy foil; wrap securely. Place in shallow baking pan. Roast at 425° for 3 hours or till meat thermometer registers 175°; open foil last 30 minutes of baking. Remove meat to platter. Pour juices into 2-cup measure; add water to make 1¾ cups; transfer to saucepan. Stir in 3 tablespoons flour mixed with ½ cup cold water. Cook and stir till thickened. Add a dash of kitchen bouquet; season to taste. Makes 6 to 8 servings. Garnish with pears and mint jelly.

Orange-Thyme Lamb Chops

- 6 lamb shoulder chops, ¾ inch thick
- ¾ teaspoon thyme, crushed
- ½ teaspoon shredded orange peel
- ¼ cup orange juice
- Dash salt
- Dash pepper
- 1 3-ounce can broiled sliced mushrooms, drained (½ cup)

Trim excess fat from chops. Combine next 3 ingredients; pour over chops and marinate for 1 hour at room temperature or several hours in refrigerator. Drain, reserving marinade. Brown chops in small amount of fat; season with salt and pepper. Add reserved marinade and mushrooms. Cover; simmer 40 to 45 minutes or till tender. Uncover last few minutes of cooking. Serve with new potatoes, buttered carrots, and a crisp green salad.

Garden Lamb-chop Bake

- 4 lamb shoulder chops about ¾ inch thick
- 1 tablespoon fat
- 1 teaspoon salt
- Dash pepper
- ¼ cup extra-hot catsup
- 1 teaspoon basil
- 4 **thin** lemon slices
- 4 onion slices
- 4 green pepper rings
- 1 cup canned tomatoes, drained and broken up
- Coarsely shredded sharp process American cheese

Slash fat edges of chops and brown on both sides in hot fat. Season with salt and pepper. Place chops in shallow baking dish. Spread each with catsup; sprinkle with basil and top with a lemon slice, then onion and green pepper. Spoon tomatoes over and sprinkle with additional salt. Cover with foil and bake in moderate oven (350°) about 50 minutes or till done. Top with shredded cheese. Makes 4 servings.

Lamb Stew with Dumplings

- ¼ cup all-purpose flour
- 2 teaspoons salt
- 1 teaspoon paprika
- ¼ teaspoon pepper
- 2 pounds boneless lamb shoulder, cut in 1-inch cubes
- 2 tablespoons fat
- 2 cups water
- 1 8-ounce can (1 cup) tomato sauce
- 1 clove garlic, minced
- ½ teaspoon thyme leaves, crushed
- ½ teaspoon marjoram leaves, crushed
- 1 10-ounce package frozen baby Limas
- 6 medium carrots, cut in ½-inch pieces
- 6 small whole onions

Combine flour, salt, paprika, and pepper. Coat meat in seasoned flour; brown on all sides in hot fat. Add next 5 ingredients; cover and simmer 1 hour or till meat is almost tender. Add vegetables; cover and simmer 20 minutes or till done. Top with 10 to 12 small DUMPLINGS: To 1 cup packaged biscuit mix, add ⅓ cup milk. Mix well with a fork; spoon onto hot bubbling stew. Cook uncovered over low heat 5 minutes. Cover and cook 10 minutes. Makes 6 to 8 servings.

Spring Lamb Stew

- 2 pounds boneless lamb shoulder, cut in 1-inch cubes
- ¼ cup all-purpose flour
- 1 tablespoon fat
- 1 1-pound 13-ounce can (3½ cups) tomatoes
- 1½ teaspoons salt
- ¼ teaspoon pepper
- ¼ teaspoon thyme, crushed
- 1 10-ounce package frozen **or** 1 pound fresh cut green beans
- 2 medium onions, cut in ½-inch slices

Coat meat with flour; brown in hot fat in Dutch oven or heavy saucepan. Add tomatoes and seasonings. Cover; simmer 1½ hours or till meat is nearly tender; stir occasionally. Add beans and onions. Cover; simmer 20 to 25 minutes or till vegetables are tender. Makes 6 to 8 servings. Serve with a relish tray, toasted hard rolls, and whipped gelatin.

Ground Lamb with Lemon Sauce

- 1 pound ground lamb
- ½ cup chopped onion
- ⅓ cup packaged precooked rice
- ⅓ cup milk
- 1 beaten egg
- 1 teaspoon salt
- Dash pepper
- ½ cup snipped parsley
- 1 beef bouillon cube
- ¾ cup hot water
- 1 to 1½ tablespoons lemon juice
- 2 slightly beaten eggs

Combine lamb with next 6 ingredients. Form in 25 one-inch balls; roll in parsley. Dissolve bouillon cube in water; add meat balls. Cover and simmer (*don't boil*) 30 minutes, turning occasionally. Remove meat and make LEMON SAUCE: Beat lemon juice with eggs to blend. Stir small amount bouillon into egg mixture; return to hot bouillon; cook and stir till mixture thickens. Makes 5 or 6 servings.

Lamb Patties with Dill Sauce

- 1½ pounds ground lamb
- ½ cup quick-cooking rolled oats
- 1 slightly beaten egg
- ¼ cup finely chopped onion
- 1 teaspoon salt
- ¼ teaspoon thyme
- Dash pepper
- 6 slices bacon

Dill Sauce:
- 1 tablespoon finely chopped onion
- 1 tablespoon butter or margarine
- 2 teaspoons all-purpose flour
- 2 tablespoons grated Parmesan cheese
- ½ teaspoon dried dill weed
- ½ teaspoon paprika
- Dash salt
- 1 cup milk

Combine first 7 ingredients; shape in 6 patties. Wrap bacon slice around each patty; fasten with toothpick. Broil 5 inches from heat 10 minutes; turn and broil 5 minutes more. Serve with DILL SAUCE: Cook the 1 tablespoon onion in butter or margarine till tender. Blend in flour, Parmesan, and seasonings. Add milk all at once. Cook and stir till thickened. Six servings.

Shish Kabobs with Onion Marinade

- 1 envelope onion-soup mix
- 1 cup salad oil
- ½ cup red wine vinegar
- 1 tablespoon soy sauce
- 2 pounds boneless lamb, cut in 1-inch cubes
- Mushroom caps
- Quartered green peppers

Combine onion-soup mix, salad oil, vinegar, and soy sauce; add lamb cubes and stir to coat. Refrigerate overnight or let stand at room temperature 2 or 3 hours, turning meat occasionally. Fill skewers, alternating meat cubes with the vegetables. (For easier skewering, dip mushrooms and green pepper pieces first in boiling water for a minute.) Sprinkle with freshly ground pepper. Broil 5 inches from heat 8 to 10 minutes or till done, basting now and then with marinade. Serve on hot cooked rice, if you wish. Makes 6 to 8 servings.

Lamb Kabobs with Plum Sauce

- 1 1-pound can or jar purple plums
- ¼ cup lemon juice
- 1 tablespoon soy sauce
- 1 teaspoon Worcestershire sauce
- ½ clove garlic, crushed
- ½ teaspoon basil, crushed
- 1 pound boneless lamb, cut in 1-inch cubes
- ½ teaspoon salt
- Dash pepper

Drain plums, reserving ¼ cup syrup. Pit and sieve plums. Combine reserved syrup, sieved plums, and next 5 ingredients. Marinate lamb cubes in plum mixture several hours or overnight. Place meat on skewers; season with salt and pepper. Broil 4 inches from heat 10 to 12 minutes or till done, turning kabobs frequently and basting often with marinade. Simmer remaining marinade 5 minutes; serve with meat. Makes 4 servings.

Chicken Rosemary

- 1 teaspoon rosemary, finely crushed
- ⅓ cup sauterne
- 1 2½- to 3-pound ready-to-cook broiler-fryer chicken, cut up
- Salt and pepper
- 2 tablespoons fat
- 1 3-ounce can broiled sliced mushrooms, drained (½ cup)

Mix rosemary and sauterne; let stand several hours at room temperature. *Lightly* season chicken with salt and pepper; brown slowly in hot fat. Add sauterne mixture. Cover; simmer 45 minutes or till chicken is tender. Add mushrooms; heat through. Remove chicken to hot platter. Stir 2 tablespoons additional sauterne into pan drippings, if desired; serve sauce over chicken. Makes 4 servings.

Chicken Oahu

- 1 2½- to 3-pound ready-to-cook broiler-fryer chicken, cut up
- ¼ cup butter or margarine
- 1 1-pound 4½-ounce can (2½ cups) pineapple chunks
- 2 tablespoons brown sugar
- 1 teaspoon ginger
- ¼ teaspoon salt
- 1 8-ounce can (1 cup) tomato sauce
- ¾ cup chicken broth

Combine ¼ cup flour and ½ teaspoon salt; dredge chicken in mixture. Brown slowly in butter. Drain pineapple, reserving ½ *cup* syrup. Mix pineapple, reserved syrup, sugar, ginger, and salt; add to chicken. Stir in tomato sauce and broth. Simmer covered 20 minutes. Uncover; cook 25 minutes. Salt to taste. Serve with rice. Four servings.

Herbed Chicken en Casserole

- 3 large chicken breasts, cut in half
- Salt and pepper
- ¼ cup butter or margarine
- 1 10½-ounce can condensed cream of chicken soup
- ¾ cup cooking sauterne
- 1 5-ounce can (⅔ cup) water chestnuts, drained and sliced
- 1 3-ounce can broiled sliced mushrooms, drained (½ cup)
- 2 tablespoons chopped green pepper
- ¼ teaspoon crushed thyme

Lightly season chicken with salt and pepper; brown slowly in butter in skillet. Arrange browned chicken, skin side up, in 11x7x1½-inch baking dish. For the sauce, add soup to drippings in skillet; slowly add sauterne, stirring smooth. Add remaining ingredients; heat to boiling. Pour sauce over chicken. Cover with foil and bake in moderate oven (350°) 25 minutes. Uncover; continue baking 25 to 35 minutes or till chicken is tender. Serve with hot fluffy rice, if desired. Makes 6 servings.

Easy Chicken Divan

- 2 10-ounce packages frozen broccoli **or** 2 bunches fresh broccoli
- 2 cups sliced cooked chicken **or** 3 chicken breasts, cooked and boned
- 2 10½-ounce cans condensed cream of chicken soup
- 1 cup mayonnaise or salad dressing
- 1 teaspoon lemon juice
- ½ teaspoon curry powder
- ½ cup shredded sharp process American cheese
- ½ cup soft bread crumbs
- 1 tablespoon butter or margarine, melted

Cook broccoli in boiling salted water till tender; drain. Arrange broccoli in greased 11x7x1½-inch baking dish. Place chicken on top. Combine soup, mayonnaise, lemon juice, and curry powder; pour over chicken. Sprinkle with cheese. Combine bread crumbs and butter; sprinkle over all. Bake in moderate oven (350°) 25 to 30 minutes or till thoroughly heated. Trim with pimiento strips. Makes 6 to 8 servings.

Chicken Dinner Elegante

Thaw one 9-ounce package frozen artichoke hearts; arrange in 2½-quart casserole, along with 12 pared small new potatoes. Coat 3 halved chicken breasts with ¼ cup all-purpose flour; brown in ½ cup melted butter or margarine. Arrange atop vegetables in casserole. In same skillet, cook 2 tablespoons chopped green onion till tender. Stir in one 6-ounce can (1⅓ cups) broiled mushroom crowns (and liquid) and ¼ cup sherry; pour over chicken. Sprinkle with ½ teaspoon salt and dash pepper. Cover and bake in moderate oven (350°) 1½ hours. Remove chicken and vegetables to warm serving platter. Blend ½ cup dairy sour cream and 1 tablespoon all-purpose flour; add juices from casserole. Heat and stir, but *do not boil*; pass with chicken.*

* *Or* return chicken and vegetables to casserole; pour sauce over. Makes 6 servings.

Sesame-baked Chicken

- ⅔ cup fine cracker crumbs (15 crackers)
- ¼ cup toasted sesame seed*
- 1 2½- to 3-pound ready-to-cook broiler-fryer chicken, cut up
- ½ 6-ounce can (⅓ cup) evaporated milk
- ½ cup butter or margarine, melted

Combine cracker crumbs and toasted sesame seed. Dip chicken pieces in evaporated milk, then roll in cracker mixture. Pour melted butter into 11x7x1½-inch baking dish. Dip skin side of chicken pieces in butter; turn over and arrange, skin side up, in baking dish. Bake uncovered in a moderate oven (350°) for 1½ hours or till done. Remove to warm serving platter; garnish with parsley. Makes 3 or 4 servings.

* To toast sesame seed, place in a shallow, ungreased baking pan. Heat in a moderate oven (350°) for 10 minutes, stirring once or twice.

Skillet Cherry Chicken

- 1 12-ounce jar (1 cup) cherry preserves
- 2 tablespoons lemon juice
- 4 whole cloves
- ¼ teaspoon salt
- ¼ teaspoon allspice
- ¼ teaspoon mace
- ½ cup all-purpose flour
- 1 teaspoon salt
- 1 2½- to 3-pound ready-to-cook broiler-fryer chicken, cut up
- ¼ cup salad oil

Blend first 6 ingredients; set aside. Combine flour and salt in paper or plastic bag. Add 2 or 3 pieces of chicken at a time; shake to coat. Brown chicken in oil in skillet over medium heat, turning with tongs. Cover; cook 15 minutes. Drain off fat; add cherry sauce. Cover; simmer over very low heat, skin side up, 15 minutes. Turn; simmer 15 minutes more or till tender. Makes 4 servings.

Chicken and Ham

- 3 chicken breasts, boned and halved lengthwise
- 2 tablespoons butter or margarine
- ½ cup chopped onion
- 1 envelope or can **dry** chicken-noodle soup mix
- ⅔ cup long-grain rice
- ⅓ cup wild rice
- ½ teaspoon rosemary
- 2 cups water
- 1 envelope or can **dry** mushroom-soup mix
- ⅓ cup sauterne
- 1 3-ounce can broiled sliced mushrooms, drained (½ cup)
- 6 thin slices boiled ham

Brown chicken in butter; remove from skillet. Add onion to skillet; cook till tender. Add next 5 ingredients; bring to boiling. Pour into 9x9x2-inch baking dish; top with chicken. Bake, covered, in 350° oven 50 minutes. Prepare mushroom soup according to package directions; add wine and mushrooms. Lift chicken; slide ham under. Pour soup mixture over. Bake uncovered 15 minutes. Serves 6.

Chicken and Dressing Bake

- 1 7- or 8-ounce package herb-seasoned stuffing
- 1 10½-ounce can condensed cream of mushroom soup
- 2 cups chicken broth
- 2 well-beaten eggs
- 2½ cups diced cooked chicken
- ½ cup milk
- 2 tablespoons chopped canned pimiento

Toss stuffing with ½ *can of the soup*, the broth, and eggs. Spread in 11x7x1½-inch baking dish; top with chicken. Combine remaining soup with milk and pimiento; pour over all. Cover with foil; bake at 350° 45 minutes or till set. Makes 6 to 8 servings.

Turkey Croquettes

Melt 2 tablespoons butter; blend in 3 tablespoons flour. Gradually stir in ½ cup milk and ½ cup turkey or chicken broth. Cook and stir till mixture thickens; cool. Add 2 cups diced cooked turkey (or chicken), 1 tablespoon snipped parsley, and ¼ teaspoon rosemary, crushed; salt and pepper to taste. Cover; chill several hours. Trim crusts from 6 to 8 slices bread; tear slices into ½-inch pieces. Shape turkey mixture into eight 2½-inch balls (about ¼ cup each). Dip balls into 1 beaten egg, then roll in bread pieces, coating well. Place on greased jellyroll pan. (Chill till baking time, if desired.) Brush with melted butter. Bake in 350° oven 25 minutes or till hot and toasted. Makes 4 servings. Serve with CRANBERRY SAUCE: Heat 1 cup canned jellied cranberry sauce and ¼ cup cooking claret, beating till smooth.

Turkey Chow Mein

Cut 1 green pepper in thin strips; cook with 1 cup celery slices in 2 tablespoons butter or margarine for 2 minutes; add 1¾ cups turkey or chicken broth. Blend 2 tablespoons cornstarch with ¼ cup cold water and 2 tablespoons soy sauce; gradually stir into the broth. Add ½ envelope or ½ can *dry* onion-soup mix. Cook and stir till mixture thickens. Add 2 to 3 cups diced cooked turkey (or chicken), one 3-ounce can (⅔ cup) broiled sliced mushrooms, one 5-ounce can water chestnuts, drained and thinly sliced, and one 1-pound can bean sprouts, drained; heat. Serve with chow-mein noodles. Makes 6 servings.

Cheddar Turkey Casserole

- 1 cup packaged precooked rice
- 2 tablespoons instant minced onion
- ½ 10-ounce package frozen green peas, thawed and broken apart (about 1 cup)*
- 4 to 6 slices cooked turkey or 2 cups diced cooked turkey (or chicken)
- 1 11-ounce can condensed Cheddar cheese soup
- 1 cup milk
- 1 cup finely crushed rich round cheese crackers
- 3 tablespoons butter or margarine, melted

Prepare rice according to package directions, *adding the instant minced onion to the boiling water*. Fluff cooked rice with fork and spread in greased 10x6x1½-inch baking dish. Sprinkle with peas, then cover with turkey. Blend soup and milk; pour evenly over the turkey. Combine crumbs and butter; sprinkle over casserole. Bake in moderate oven (350°) 35 minutes or till heated through. Makes 4 to 6 servings.

*Or use 1 cup drained canned peas.

Turkey Crepes en Casserole

CREPES: Beat 1 egg just enough to blend; add 1 cup milk, 1 tablespoon melted butter or margarine, and 1 cup sifted all-purpose flour; beat smooth. Lightly grease a small skillet (about 6 inches in diameter); heat. Pour 2 tablespoons batter into skillet; lift pan and tilt from side to side till batter covers bottom. Return to heat; brown cake on *one side only*. Repeat with remaining pancakes (12 total). FILLING: Mix 1 cup finely diced cooked turkey or chicken, ½ cup canned or cooked spinach (well drained), ½ 10½-ounce can condensed cream of chicken soup, ¼ cup *each* medium cracker crumbs, grated Parmesan cheese, and chopped onion. Spoon a heaping tablespoon filling on *unbrowned* side of each pancake; roll up. Arrange, seam side down, in greased shallow baking dish. SAUCE: Combine remaining ½ *can* soup with 1 cup milk; pour over pancakes. Sprinkle with ⅓ cup toasted sliced almonds. Bake in 350° oven 30 minutes or till hot. Drizzle with melted butter. Makes 6 servings.

Squab

TO ROAST

Clean 4 squabs. Rub inside with salt, pepper. Brown giblets; add to favorite stuffing recipe; stuff squab; rub skin with butter. Place breast up on rack in shallow pan; roast uncovered in moderate oven (350°) till tender, 45 to 60 minutes. Makes 4 servings.

TO BROIL

Follow directions for Broiled Rock Cornish Game Hens. Broil 5 to 7 inches from heat for total of 20 to 30 minutes. Serve on buttered toast.

Roast Duckling with Cranberry Sauce

- 3½- to 4-pound ready-to-cook duckling
- 1 10½-ounce can condensed beef broth
- ¾ cup cranberry juice cocktail
- 2 tablespoons butter or margarine
- 2 tablespoons sugar
- 2 tablespoons vinegar
- 1 tablespoon cornstarch

Place duckling, breast up, on rack in shallow pan. Roast, uncovered, at 375° for 1½ hours, then at 425° for 15 minutes, or till tender. Meanwhile, place neck and giblets in saucepan. Add beef broth; simmer, covered, for 1 hour; strain. Serve giblets with duck. To strained broth, add cranberry juice cocktail; cook till reduced to 1 cup. In small pan, melt butter; blend in sugar; cook and stir till brown. Add vinegar and the cranberry-broth mixture. Remove duckling from roasting pan. Skim fat from meat juices; add juices to cranberry-broth mixture. Stir in cornstarch blended with about 1 tablespoon cranberry juice cocktail. Cook and stir till sauce boils; simmer 1 to 2 minutes. Pass with duckling.

Rock Cornish Game Hens

TO ROAST
- 4 1-pound ready-to-cook Rock Cornish game hens
- Salt and pepper
- ⅓ cup melted butter or margarine
- ¼ cup canned condensed consomme
- ¼ cup light corn syrup

Season hens inside and out with salt and pepper. Stuff each with ¼ cup stuffing, if desired. Place, breast side up, on rack in shallow roasting pan and brush well with butter. Roast uncovered in hot oven (400°) about 1 hour, or till tender. During last 15 minutes of baking time, baste several times with mixture of consomme and syrup. Makes 4 servings.

TO BROIL
Split birds in half lengthwise. Place skin side down in broiler pan (not rack); brush with melted butter. Season with salt and pepper. Broil 7 inches from heat about 30 minutes or till tender and drumstick moves up and down easily. Turn once; baste frequently. One bird makes 2 servings.

Sea-Food Pilaf

- ¾ cup uncooked long-grain rice
- 2 tablespoons butter or margarine
- 1 3-ounce can (⅔ cup) broiled sliced mushrooms
- 1 10½-ounce can condensed chicken with rice soup
- 1 6½- or 7½-ounce can crab meat, drained and flaked
- 1 4½- or 5-ounce can shrimp, drained
- ¼ cup dry sherry
- 1 tablespoon instant minced onion

In skillet, brown rice in butter, about 5 minutes. Add mushrooms (and liquid) and remaining ingredients. Turn into 1½-quart casserole. Bake covered in moderate oven (350°) 55 minutes. Fluff with fork. Bake uncovered 5 minutes longer. Makes 6 servings.

Shrimp on a Skewer

- ⅓ cup salad oil
- ⅓ cup lemon juice
- 3 or 4 cloves garlic, minced
- 1½ teaspoons salt
- ½ teaspoon paprika
- ¼ teaspoon pepper
- 1 pound (about 30) raw cleaned shrimp (2 pounds in shell)
- 2 medium green peppers, cut in wedges
- 2 medium onions, cut in wedges
- 12 red cherry tomatoes

Combine first 6 ingredients; pour over shrimp and refrigerate at least 2 hours. Drain, reserving marinade. On 6 greased 12-inch skewers, alternate shrimp, green pepper, and onion. Brush with marinade. Broil 3 inches from heat about 13 minutes, turning once and brushing often with marinade. During last 2 or 3 minutes, place tomatoes on skewers.

Haddock-Shrimp Bake

- 2 pounds fresh or frozen haddock or sole fillets
- 1 10-ounce can frozen condensed cream of shrimp soup, thawed
- ¼ cup butter or margarine, melted
- ½ teaspoon grated onion
- ½ teaspoon Worcestershire sauce
- ¼ teaspoon garlic salt
- 1¼ cups crushed rich round crackers (30 crackers)

Slightly thaw frozen fillets. Place fillets in greased 13x9x2-inch baking dish; spread with soup. Bake in 375° oven 20 minutes. Combine butter and seasonings; mix with cracker crumbs; sprinkle over fish. Bake 10 minutes longer. Makes 6 to 8 servings.

Deviled Oysters on the Half Shell

- 14 oysters in shell
- 2 tablespoons finely chopped shallots
- 1 tablespoon butter or margarine
- 2 tablespoons all-purpose flour
- ½ teaspoon salt
- ⅛ teaspoon nutmeg
- Dash cayenne
- 1 tablespoon Worcestershire sauce
- ½ teaspoon chopped parsley
- ½ teaspoon prepared mustard
- 1 3-ounce can chopped mushrooms, drained
- 1 slightly beaten egg yolk
- ½ cup cracker crumbs
- 1 tablespoon butter or margarine, melted

Open oysters and reserve ⅓ cup of the liquor. With a knife, remove oysters from shells; wash thoroughly and chop. Wash shells. Cook shallots in 1 tablespoon butter till just tender; blend in flour and let brown. Stir in reserved oyster liquor, salt, nutmeg, cayenne, Worcestershire, parsley, mustard, and mushrooms; add oysters. Cook about 3 minutes, stirring constantly. Remove from heat and add egg yolk. Spoon mixture into deep halves of oyster shells. Combine cracker crumbs and melted butter; sprinkle over oyster mixture. Bake in a moderate oven (350°) for about 10 minutes. Serve immediately. Makes 2 to 3 servings.

Clam Puff

- 2 7- or 7½-ounce cans minced clams
- 1 cup fine cracker crumbs (24 crackers)
- 2 tablespoons instant minced onion
- 4 well-beaten eggs
- 2 tablespoons snipped parsley
- ½ teaspoon salt
- Dash bottled hot pepper sauce

Drain clams, reserving liquor; add milk to liquor to make 1 cup. Combine liquid with cracker crumbs and onion. Let stand 15 minutes. Fold in clams, eggs, parsley, salt, and hot pepper sauce. Pour into 1½-quart souffle dish. Bake in slow oven (325°) 60 to 65 minutes or till done. Six servings.

Broiled Scallops

1 pound scallops
Salt to taste
Pepper to taste
Dash paprika
Butter

Place 1 pound scallops in shallow pan or pie plate. Sprinkle with salt, pepper, and paprika, then dot with butter. Broil 3 inches from heat for 6 to 9 minutes or until scallops are very delicately browned, spooning pan drippings over scallops several times. To serve, garnish with lemon wedges and sprigs of parsley; pass Tartare Sauce. Makes 2 to 3 servings.

Tartare Sauce

1 cup mayonnaise
2 tablespoons minced parsley
1 tablespoon minced onion
1 tablespoon chopped stuffed green olives
2 tablespoons well drained green pickle relish

Combine all ingredients in a mixing bowl. Mix well. Refrigerate sauce 3 hours before serving. Serve with Broiled Scallops.

Baked Lobster Savannah

2 2-pound lobsters
½ cup sliced fresh mushrooms
¼ cup diced green peppers
3 tablespoons butter
2 tablespoons all-purpose flour
1 cup milk
¼ cup sherry
1 teaspoon paprika
2 tablespoons chopped canned pimiento
Grated cheese
Fresh bread crumbs

Plunge lobsters in boiling salted water; cover and boil 25 minutes. Remove and let cool. Cut off claws and legs so only body remains. Hold lobster with its top side up; using kitchen shears, cut an oval opening in top of shell, from base of head to tail. Remove all meat from body and claws; cube. Cook mushrooms and green pepper in butter till tender. Blend in flour; add milk; cook and stir till mixture thickens and boils. Add sherry, paprika, and salt to taste; cook 5 minutes. Add lobster and pimiento. Pile filling in lobster shells; top with cheese and crumbs. Bake at 375° 15 minutes. Serves 2.

Crab Meat with Chinese Cabbage

- 2 tablespoons salad oil
- 4 medium green onions, sliced (¼ cup)
- 1 tablespoon sherry
- ½ teaspoon salt
- ½ teaspoon sugar
- ¼ teaspoon ginger
- 1 head Chinese cabbage, cut in 1-inch pieces (6 cups)
- 1 cup chicken broth
- 1½ tablespoons cornstarch
- 1 6½- or 7½-ounce can crab meat, flaked

Heat oil in skillet, add next 5 ingredients and dash of pepper; stir 1 minute. Add cabbage and broth; cover; simmer 5 minutes or till tender-crisp. Blend cornstarch with 2 tablespoons cold water; add to cabbage. Cook and stir till thickened. Add crab; heat through. Serve over heated Chinese noodles. Four servings.

Fiesta Salmon Bake

DEVILED EGGS: Halve 4 hard-cooked eggs lengthwise; remove yolks and mash; mix with 2 tablespoons mayonnaise, ¼ teaspoon *each* salt and dry mustard, and dash bottled hot pepper sauce. Refill whites. SALMON LAYER: Drain one 1-pound can (2 cups) salmon or two 6½- or 7-ounce cans tuna. Break in chunks and line bottom of 10x6x1½-inch baking dish; sprinkle with 1 teaspoon lemon juice. Top with half the CHEESE SAUCE: Melt ¼ cup butter or margarine; blend in ¼ cup all-purpose flour and ½ teaspoon salt. Stir in 2 cups milk; cook and stir till mixture thickens. Stir in ¾ cup shredded process American cheese. Arrange Deviled Eggs and pitted ripe olives atop. *Cover* with remaining sauce. Sprinkle with 1 cup crushed potato chips. Bake in moderate oven (375°) 25 minutes or till hot. Makes 5 or 6 servings.

Trout Almondine

- 6 8-ounce trout, cleaned
- Salt and pepper to taste
- 2 slightly beaten eggs
- ½ cup light cream
- ½ cup all-purpose flour
- ¼ cup salad oil
- ¼ cup butter or margarine
- ½ cup slivered blanched almonds
- ½ cup butter or margarine, melted
- 2 tablespoons lemon juice

Bone whole trout; season with salt and pepper. Combine slightly-beaten eggs and cream. Dip trout in flour, then in egg and cream mixture. Heat salad oil and ¼ cup butter together. Fry trout in combined oil and butter until golden brown on both sides, about 5 minutes for each side. Add almonds to ½ cup melted butter and cook until browned. Removed from heat; stir in 2 tablespoons lemon juice. Place trout on a warm platter; pour almond sauce over and serve immediately. Makes 6 servings.

Truite Farcie

- 6 mushrooms, thinly sliced
- 2 leeks, cut in julienne strips
- 1 medium carrot, cut in julienne strips
- 1 medium celery branch, cut in julienne strips
- 1 truffle, thinly sliced
- ¼ cup butter or margarine
- ¼ cup port
- 2 tablespoons cognac
- 2 tablespoons dry vermouth
- 6 trout, boned
- Salt and pepper to taste
- 1 cup dry white wine
- 1 cup Court Bouillon
- 4 egg yolks
- ½ cup whipping cream
- Salt and pepper to taste

Cook vegetables in ¼ cup butter for 2 to 3 minutes. Add port, cognac, and dry vermouth. Cook about 2 minutes longer or till liquid is reduced to a glaze. Season inside of trout with salt and pepper. Stuff with vegetable mixture. Poach fish in enough white wine to cover, about 1 cup, for 5 minutes or until fish flakes. Remove fish to hot platter; keep warm. To make sauce, combine Court Bouillon with egg yolks and cream. Beat over *hot, not boiling* water till thickened. Season with salt and pepper; pour over stuffed trout. Sprinkle with paprika and garnish with lemon wedges. Makes 6 servings.

Two-Way Oriental Tuna

- ¼ cup mayonnaise or salad dressing
- 1 tablespoon minced onion
- 1 teaspoon lemon juice
- 1 teaspoon soy sauce
- ½ teaspoon curry powder
- 1 6½- or 7-ounce can tuna, flaked
- 1 5-ounce can (½ cup) water chestnuts, drained and sliced
- 6 to 8 thin slices French bread

Combine mayonnaise, onion, lemon juice, soy sauce, and curry powder; blend. Add tuna and water chestnuts; toss gently. Spread on French-bread slices.* Broil 2 to 3 inches from heat 3 to 4 minutes or till hot. Makes 6 to 8 sandwiches.

*Or chill tuna mixture. Serve as salad in crisp lettuce cups. Makes 3 to 4 servings.

Herbed Fish

- 1 pound frozen fish fillets, partially thawed
- ⅓ cup chopped onion
- 1 small clove garlic, minced
- 2 tablespoons butter or margarine
- ½ teaspoon tarragon, crushed
- ¼ teaspoon thyme, crushed
- ¼ teaspoon salt
- Dash pepper
- ¼ cup corn flake crumbs

Place fillets in greased 10x6x1½-inch baking dish. Cook onion and garlic in butter till tender. Stir in seasonings; cook 1 minute. Spread over fish. Top with crumbs. Bake in 500° oven 12 minutes or till fish flakes easily with a fork. Makes 4 servings.

Tuna Florentine

- 3 tablespoons butter or margarine
- 1 onion, sliced
- 1 1-pound can (2 cups) tomatoes
- 1 8-ounce can (1 cup) tomato sauce
- 1 teaspoon salt
- 1 6½- or 7-ounce can tuna
- 4 ounces (2 cups) medium noodles, cooked
- 1 10-ounce package frozen chopped spinach, cooked and drained
- ¼ cup shredded Parmesan cheese

Melt butter; add onion and cook till tender. Add next 3 ingredients. Simmer uncovered about 20 minutes. Break tuna in chunks; add with noodles. Turn into 2-quart casserole. Spoon spinach around edge and sprinkle with cheese. Bake in moderate oven (375°) about 25 minutes. Makes 6 servings.

Salmon or Tuna Ring

- 1 1-pound can (2 cups) red salmon or two 6½- or 7-ounce cans tuna, drained and flaked
- 1 cup fine dry bread crumbs
- ½ cup chopped celery
- ¼ cup chopped green pepper
- 2 tablespoons minced onion
- 1 tablespoon lemon juice
- 1 cup evaporated milk
- 1 beaten egg
- 1 recipe Olive-Almond Sauce

Combine the salmon, crumbs, vegetables, and lemon juice. Combine milk and egg; add to salmon mixture, mixing gently. Turn into well-greased 5-cup ring mold. Bake in moderate oven (350°) about 30 to 35 minutes. Invert on warm platter and serve with OLIVE-ALMOND SAUCE: Combine ¼ cup mayonnaise, 1 tablespoon all-purpose flour, and ¼ teaspoon salt; blend till smooth. Measure ⅔ cup evaporated milk, and add water to make 1¼ cups; slowly add to mayonnaise mixture. Cook and stir till thick. Add ¼ cup sliced stuffed green olives and ¼ cup chopped salted almonds. Makes 6 servings.

SECTION 2

Vegetables

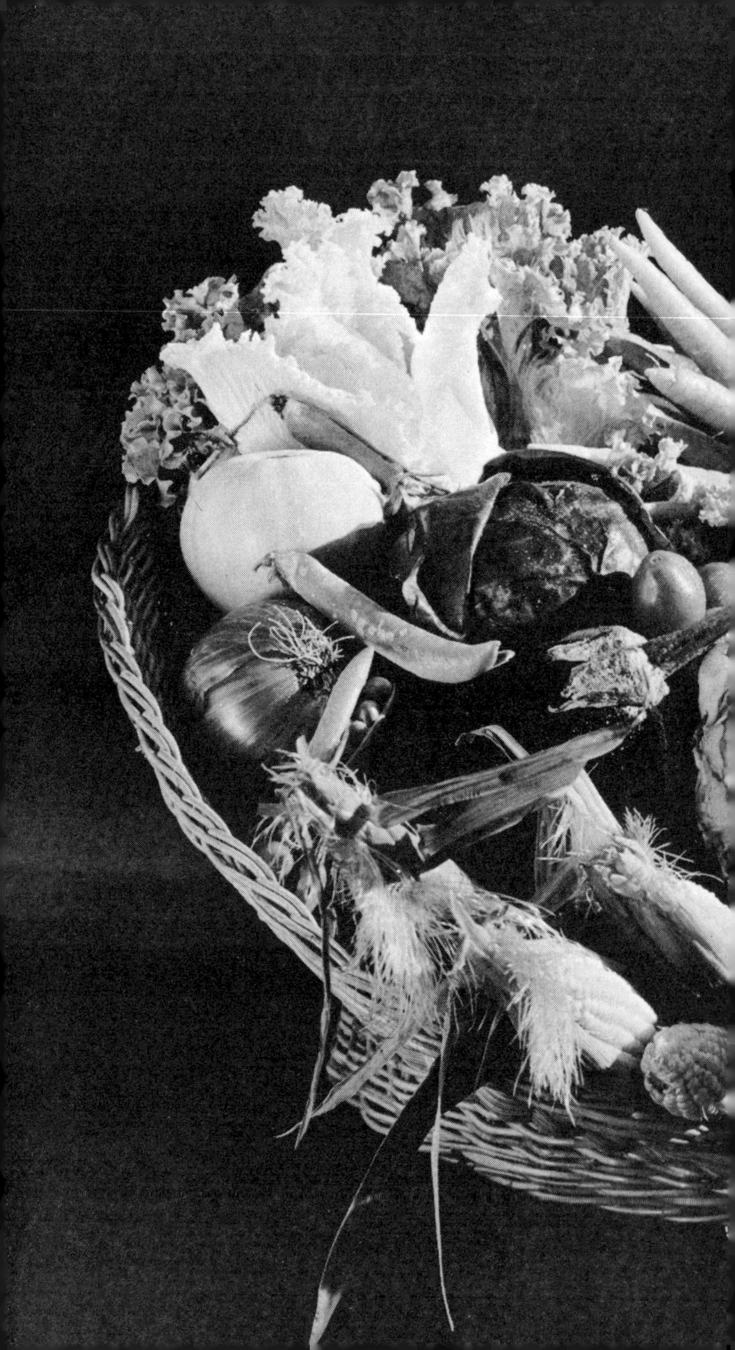

SECTION 2
Vegetables

How to Cook an Artichoke (French Type)

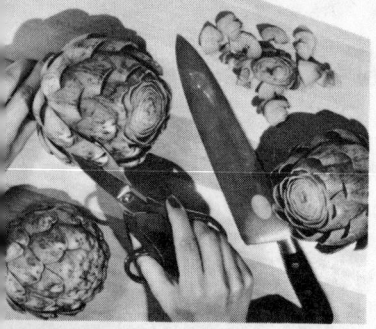

TO CLEAN
Give artichokes a shower of cold running water. With sharp knife, cut off about 1 inch from top. Chop off stem even with base or leave about 1 inch. Pull off loose leaves around bottom. Snip sharp leaf tips off artichokes. Brush cut edges with lemon juice.

TO COOK
Place artichokes upright in large pan with boiling salted water to cover. (One-fourth cup olive oil and 3 or 4 cloves garlic may be added. Or a few lemon slices.) Cover; simmer 25 to 30 minutes or till you can easily pierce stalk or pull out a leaf readily. Drain. Cut off any stem.

Artichoke Velvet

- 2 9-ounce packages frozen artichoke hearts
- 1 pint fresh mushrooms, sliced
- 2 tablespoons butter or margarine
- 1 1 1/16-ounce package chicken gravy mix
- Dash thyme
- Dash marjoram
- 4 ounces Swiss cheese, diced (1 cup)
- 1 tablespoon dry white wine

Cook artichokes according to package directions; drain. Cook mushrooms in butter till tender. Combine artichokes and mushrooms in 1-quart casserole. Prepare chicken gravy mix using package directions. Remove from heat; add herbs and cheese; stir till cheese melts. Add wine; pour over vegetables. Bake covered at 350° for 30 minutes. Serves 6 to 8.

Asparagus Delicious

2 pounds fresh (or 2 10-ounce packages frozen) asparagus spears	Dash white pepper
1 tablespoon butter or margarine	1 cup milk
1 tablespoon all-purpose flour	½ cup shredded sharp process American cheese
⅛ teaspoon salt	¼ cup slivered blanched almonds, toasted

Cook asparagus and drain. Place in warm serving dish and keep hot. Melt butter in a small saucepan over low heat. Combine flour, salt, and white pepper; blend into melted butter. Add the milk all at once. Cook quickly, stirring constantly, until mixture thickens and boils. Cook and stir 2 minutes longer.. Add the shredded cheese and stir until melted. Pour cheese sauce over hot asparagus at once; top with toasted almonds. Serve hot. Serves 4.

Green Beans Bearnaise

1 pound fresh green beans, French-cut or 1 9-ounce package frozen or 1 1-pound can (2 cups) French-style green beans	½ cup finely diced fully cooked ham
	1 small clove garlic, minced
	½ teaspoon salt
	Dash pepper
1 tablespoon butter or margarine	1 medium tomato, cut in wedges

Cook fresh or frozen green beans in small amount of boiling water till just tender; drain. Or heat canned beans and drain. Melt butter in saucepan; add ham and garlic; cook till garlic is softened. Stir in beans, salt, and pepper. Top with tomato; cover, heat through. Makes 4 servings.

Potluck Bean Bake

1 1-pound can (2 cups) beans in barbecue sauce	1 1-pound can (2 cups) cut green beans, drained
1 8-ounce can (1 cup) Limas with ham	1 teaspoon instant minced onion

Combine ingredients in 1½-quart casserole. Stir to mix. Bake in moderate oven (350°) for about 1½ hours. Let stand 10 minutes before serving. Makes 8 servings.

Hearty Baked Beans

- 1½ cups dry navy beans
- 1½ cups dry baby Limas
- 6 cups cold water
- 1 large onion, chopped (1 cup)
- 1 teaspoon salt
- 2 bay leaves
- ½ teaspoon thyme
- ¼ teaspoon pepper
- 1½ to 2 pounds boneless smoked pork shoulder
- 1 1-pound can (2 cups) tomatoes
- 2 cups sliced celery
- ⅓ cup dark corn syrup

Rinse beans; cover with cold water in large kettle. Bring to boiling; simmer 2 minutes. Remove from heat; cover; let stand 1 hour. Stir in next 5 ingredients. Add meat; cover and simmer 1 hour. Remove meat; let stand till cool enough to slice. Dice, discarding fat. Combine beans, meat, and remaining ingredients; pour into 2½-quart bean pot or casserole. Bake, covered, in 350° oven 2 hours. Uncover; bake 2 hours, stirring several times. Remove bay leaves. 8 to 10 servings.

Savory Green Beans

- 2 1-pound cans (4 cups) green beans, drained
- 1 teaspoon summer savory
- 2 tablespoons finely chopped canned pimiento
- ⅓ cup butter or margarine
- ½ teaspoon salt
- Dash pepper

Combine beans with remaining ingredients. Heat slowly; stir often. Makes 6 servings.

Zippy Beet Relish

6 cups finely chopped cabbage
6 cups cooked beets, shredded or 3 1-pound cans shoestring beets, drained
3 cups sugar
2 cups vinegar
1 cup water
3 to 4 tablespoons prepared horseradish
1½ teaspoons salt

Combine cabbage and beets; pack in hot sterilized jars. In saucepan, combine sugar, vinegar, water, horseradish, and salt; heat to boiling and pour over vegetables in jars. Seal; let stand several days to a week before serving. Serve chilled. Makes about 10½ cups relish.

Company Beets with Pineapple

2 tablespoons brown sugar
1 tablespoon cornstarch
¼ teaspoon salt
1 8¾-ounce can (1 cup) pineapple tidbits
1 tablespoon butter or margarine
1 tablespoon lemon juice
1 1-pound can (2 cups) sliced beets, drained

Combine brown sugar, cornstarch, and salt in saucepan. Stir in pineapple (with syrup). Cook, stirring constantly, till mixture thickens and bubbles. Add butter, lemon juice, and beets. Heat through, about 5 minutes. Makes 4 servings.

Broccoli Italienne

- 2 10-ounce packages frozen broccoli spears **or** 2 pounds fresh broccoli
- ½ teaspoon oregano, crushed
- ½ cup mayonnaise or salad dressing
- ¼ cup shredded sharp process American cheese
- 1 tablespoon milk

Cook broccoli till tender in boiling salted water to which oregano has been added; drain. In top of double boiler, mix mayonnaise, cheese, and milk; heat over hot, not boiling water, stirring till cheese melts and mixture is hot. Serve with broccoli. Makes 6 servings.

Broccoli Parmesan

- 2 10-ounce packages frozen broccoli spears **or** 2 pounds fresh broccoli
- 2 tablespoons butter or margarine
- ¼ cup chopped onion
- 1 10½-ounce can condensed cream of chicken soup
- ⅔ cup milk
- ⅓ cup grated Parmesan cheese

Cook broccoli in boiling *unsalted* water till tender; drain well. Melt butter in saucepan; add onion and cook till tender but not brown. Blend in soup, milk, and cheese. Heat thoroughly. Serve sauce over hot broccoli. Makes 6 to 8 servings.

Broccoli Casserole

- 2 tablespoons butter, melted
- 2 tablespoons all-purpose flour
- 1 3-ounce package cream cheese, softened
- ¼ cup crumbled blue cheese (1 ounce)
- 1 cup milk
- 2 10-ounce packages frozen chopped broccoli, cooked and drained
- ⅓ cup rich round crackers, crushed (about 10)

In a large saucepan blend butter, flour, and cheeses. Add milk; cook and stir till mixture boils. Stir in cooked broccoli.

Place in a 1-quart casserole; top with cracker crumbs. Bake at 350° for 30 minutes. Serves 8 to 10.

Brussels Sprouts Souffle

- ¼ cup butter or margarine
- ¼ cup all-purpose flour
- ½ teaspoon salt
- 1 cup milk
- 4 egg yolks
- 4 ounces Cheddar cheese, shredded (1 cup)
- 1 10-ounce package frozen Brussels sprouts, cooked, drained, and finely chopped (about 2 cups)
- 4 egg whites

Melt butter and blend in the flour and salt. Add milk all at once and cook quickly till mixture thickens, stirring constantly. Beat egg yolks till thick and lemon-colored. Blend some of the hot mixture into egg yolks; return to hot mixture and stir rapidly. Stir in cheese and finely chopped sprouts. Remove pan from heat. Beat egg whites until stiff but not dry; fold into hot mixture. Turn into an *ungreased* 2-quart souffle dish. Bake in a moderate oven (350°) for 40 minutes or till knife inserted comes out clean. Makes 4 to 6 servings.

Brussels Sprouts Polonaise

- 2 pounds Brussels sprouts (about 8 cups)
- ¼ cup butter or margarine
- ¼ cup fine dry bread crumbs
- 1 hard-cooked egg yolk, sieved
- 2 tablespoons snipped parsley

Cut very large Brussels sprouts in half; cook sprouts, covered, in boiling salted water for 12 to 15 minutes or till just tender; drain. Heat butter in small saucepan or skillet till it begins to brown; add crumbs, egg yolk, and parsley. Spoon mixture over sprouts; toss lightly. Serves 6 to 8.

Blue Cheesed Sprouts

- 2 pints fresh Brussels sprouts **or** 2 10-ounce packages frozen Brussels sprouts
- 2 tablespoons (½ ounce) blue cheese, crumbled
- ¼ cup butter or margarine

Wash and trim fresh sprouts; cook covered in boiling salted water for about 15 minutes or till tender. Or cook frozen Brussels sprouts according to package directions. Drain thoroughly. Melt butter and blend in blue cheese. Toss with hot drained sprouts. Serves 6.

Zippy Glazed Carrots

- 2 tablespoons butter or margarine
- ¼ cup brown sugar
- 2 tablespoons prepared mustard
- ¼ teaspoon salt
- 3 cups sliced carrots, cooked and drained
- 1 tablespoon snipped parsley

Melt butter in skillet. Stir in brown sugar, mustard, and salt. Add cooked carrots; heat, stirring constantly, till carrots are nicely glazed, about 5 minutes. Sprinkle with parsley. Makes 4 servings.

Sunshine Carrots

- 5 medium carrots
- 1 tablespoon sugar
- 1 teaspoon cornstarch
- ¼ teaspoon salt
- ¼ teaspoon ginger
- ¼ cup orange juice
- 2 tablespoons butter or margarine

Slice carrots crosswise on the bias—about 1 inch thick. Cook, covered, in boiling salted water till just tender, about 20 minutes; drain. Meanwhile, combine sugar, cornstarch, salt, and ginger in small saucepan. Add orange juice; cook, stirring constantly, till mixture thickens and bubbles. Boil 1 minute. Stir in butter. Pour over hot carrots, tossing to coat evenly. Makes 4 servings.

Cheese-frosted Cauliflower

- 1 medium head cauliflower
  Salt
- ½ cup mayonnaise or salad dressing
- 2 teaspoons prepared mustard
- ¾ cup shredded sharp process American cheese

Leaving the cauliflower whole, remove leaves and woody base; wash. Cook cauliflower 12 to 15 minutes in boiling salted water to cover; drain well. Place cauliflower in shallow baking

Cauliflower Scallop

- 1 10½-ounce can condensed cream of celery soup
- 2 beaten eggs
- ½ cup shredded sharp Cheddar cheese
- ½ cup soft bread crumbs
- ¼ cup snipped parsley
- ¼ cup chopped canned pimiento
- 1 tablespoon instant minced onion
- ½ teaspoon salt
- Dash pepper
- 2 9-ounce packages frozen cauliflower, thawed

Mix together all ingredients. Place in 10x6x1½-inch baking dish. Bake at 375° for 45 minutes or till firm. Serves 6 to 8.

Western Corn-on-the-Cob

- 4 or 5 ears sweet corn
- ½ cup soft butter or margarine
- 1 tablespoon prepared mustard
- 1 teaspoon prepared horseradish
- 1 teaspoon salt
- Dash freshly ground pepper
- Snipped parsley

Husk corn and strip off the silk;* spread each ear with a little Horseradish Butter. Wrap each loosely in foil and bake in very hot oven (450°) 20 to 25 minutes. HORSERADISH BUTTER: Combine butter, mustard, horseradish, salt, and pepper; cream till light and fluffy. Sprinkle extra butter with parsley and pass with corn.

* *Or* roast in foil or in the husks, Indian style, over hot coals on grill.

Corn Curry

3 tablespoons butter
1½ to 2 cups cut fresh or
  frozen corn*
2 tablespoons chopped green
  pepper
2 tablespoons chopped onion
¼ to ½ teaspoon curry powder
½ cup dairy sour cream
Salt and pepper

Melt butter in skillet. Add vegetables and curry. Cover; cook over low heat till vegetables are just tender, 8 to 10 minutes. Stir in sour cream; season to taste. Heat, stirring constantly. Four servings.

*Or use drained canned whole-kernel corn or leftover corn cut off the cob; add with sour cream.

Scalloped Corn and Oysters

¼ cup finely chopped celery
1 10-ounce can frozen
  condensed oyster stew,
  thawed
1 1-pound can (2 cups)
  cream-style corn
1½ cups medium cracker
  crumbs

1 cup milk
1 slightly beaten egg
¼ teaspoon salt
  Dash freshly ground pepper
2 tablespoons butter or
  margarine, melted
½ cup medium cracker crumbs

Combine first 8 ingredients. Pour into greased 1½-quart casserole. Mix butter with ½ cup cracker crumbs; sprinkle over top. Bake in moderate oven (350°) 1 hour or till knife inserted halfway to center comes out clean. Makes 6 servings.

Scalloped Eggplant

- 1 large eggplant, diced (4 cups)
- ⅓ cup milk
- 1 10½-ounce can condensed cream of mushroom soup
- 1 slightly beaten egg
- ½ cup chopped onion
- ¾ cup packaged herb-seasoned stuffing
- 1 recipe Cheese Topper

Cook diced eggplant in boiling salted water till tender, 6 to 7 minutes; drain. Meanwhile, gradually stir milk into soup; blend in egg. Add drained eggplant, onion, and stuffing; toss lightly to mix. Turn into greased 10x6x1½-inch baking dish. For CHEESE TOPPER: Finely crush ½ cup packaged herb-seasoned stuffing; toss with 2 tablespoons melted butter or margarine; sprinkle over casserole. Top with 4 ounces sharp process American cheese, shredded (1 cup). Bake casserole in moderate oven (350°) 20 minutes or till hot. Makes 6 to 8 servings.

Roman Eggplant

- 1 medium eggplant, pared and cut in ½-inch slices
- ½ cup butter or margarine, melted
- ¾ cup fine dry bread crumbs
- ¼ teaspoon salt
- 1 8- or 10¾-ounce can (about 1 cup) spaghetti sauce with mushrooms
- 1 tablespoon crushed oregano leaves
- 4 ounces sharp process American cheese or Mozzarella cheese, shredded (1 cup)

Dip eggplant in butter, then in mixture of bread crumbs and salt. Place on greased baking sheet. Spoon sauce atop each slice; sprinkle with oregano and cheese. Bake in hot oven (450°) 10 to 12 minutes or till done. Makes 4 or 5 servings.

Mushrooms and Chicken Livers

- 1 8-ounce package frozen chicken livers, thawed
- 2 tablespoons butter or margarine
- 1 6-ounce can broiled sliced mushrooms, drained (1 cup), **or** 1 pint fresh, sliced
- ¼ cup chopped green onion
- ½ cup dairy sour cream
- 1½ teaspoons soy sauce
- 1½ teaspoons chili sauce
- Dash pepper

Cut chicken livers in large pieces; cover and cook in butter in skillet till almost tender, about 10 minutes. Add mushrooms and green onions; cook just till onions and livers are tender. Combine remaining ingredients; add to livers. Heat and stir just till sauce is hot. Serve over toast points. Makes 4 servings.

Cheese-stuffed Mushrooms

- 2 6-ounce cans (2⅔ cups) broiled mushroom crowns*
- 1 tablespoon finely chopped onion
- 1 teaspoon salad oil
- ¼ cup finely chopped salami
- ¼ cup smoke-flavored cheese spread
- 1 tablespoon catsup
- Fine soft bread crumbs

Drain mushrooms. Hollow out crowns and chop enough pieces to make 3 tablespoons; cook pieces with onion in oil. Stir in next 3 ingredients. Stuff into mushroom crowns; sprinkle with crumbs. Heat on baking sheet in 425° oven 6 to 8 minutes or till hot.

*Or use 2 pints fresh mushrooms. Wash; trim off tips of stems. Remove stems and chop enough pieces to make ⅓ cup. Continue as above.

Mushrooms Mornay

- 2 6-ounce cans broiled mushroom crowns, drained (2 cups)*
- 1 6½- or 7½-ounce can (about 1 cup) crab meat, flaked
- 2 teaspoons lemon juice
- 3 tablespoons butter or margarine
- 3 tablespoons all-purpose flour
- 1½ cups milk
- 2 slightly beaten egg yolks
- 6 ounces sharp process American cheese, shredded (1½ cups)
- 2 tablespoons sherry

Arrange mushrooms, hollow side up, in 8-inch round baking dish. Cover with crab meat; sprinkle with lemon juice. Melt butter in saucepan; blend in flour. Add milk all at once; cook and stir till mixture thickens and bubbles. Add small amount of hot mixture to egg yolks; return to sauce and cook 1 minute. Remove from heat; stir in 1¼ *cups of the cheese* and the sherry. Pour sauce over crab; sprinkle with ¼ cup cheese. Bake in moderate oven (350°) 20 minutes or till very hot. Serve over rice or toast points. Makes 6 servings.

*Or use 2 pints fresh mushrooms. Wash. Remove stems; arrange crowns and stems in baking dish.

Creole Onions

- 8 medium onions, sliced ½-inch thick
- 2 slices bacon, diced
- 1 tablespoon minced green pepper
- 1 small clove garlic, minced
- 1 8-ounce can (1 cup) tomato sauce
- ½ cup chopped fully cooked ham
- ¼ teaspoon salt
- Dash pepper
- ½ cup grated sharp process American cheese

Cook onion rings in boiling salted water for 10 to 12 minutes, or till tender. Drain *well*. Place in a 1½-quart casserole. Fry bacon till crisp; add green pepper and garlic, and cook till tender. Stir in next 4 ingredients. Pour mixture over onions; bake uncovered at 350° for 20 to 25 minutes. Sprinkle with cheese and return to oven to melt cheese. Serves 8.

Gourmet Onions

- 3 tablespoons butter or margarine
- ½ teaspoon monosodium glutamate
- ½ teaspoon sugar
- ¼ teaspoon salt
- ¼ teaspoon pepper
- ¼ cup sherry
- 10 to 12 small onions, peeled, cooked, and drained
- ¼ cup shredded Parmesan cheese

Melt butter in saucepan; stir in monosodium glutamate, sugar, salt, pepper, and sherry. Add onions and heat quickly (about 5 minutes), stirring now and then. Turn into serving dish and sprinkle with cheese. Serves 6.

Quick Creole Peas

- 1 10-ounce package frozen peas
- ¼ cup chopped onion
- ¼ cup chopped green pepper
- 2 tablespoons butter or margarine
- 1 8-ounce can (1 cup) tomatoes
- ½ teaspoon salt
- Dash pepper
- 1 tablespoon cornstarch

Cook peas according to package directions; drain. Cook onion and green pepper in butter till tender but not brown. Reserve 2 tablespoons tomato liquid. Cut tomatoes in pieces and add to cooked onion. Stir in salt, pepper, and the drained peas. Heat mixture to boiling. Combine cornstarch with the reserved tomato liquid and stir into peas. Cook and stir till mixture thickens and boils. Makes 3 or 4 servings.

Luxe Peas and Celery

- 2 tablespoons butter or margarine
- ½ cup bias-cut celery slices
- 1 3-ounce can broiled sliced mushrooms, drained (½ cup)
- 2 tablespoons chopped canned pimiento
- 2 tablespoons finely chopped onion
- ½ teaspoon salt
- ¼ teaspoon savory
  Dash freshly ground pepper
- 1 1-pound can (2 cups) peas, drained or 1 10-ounce package frozen peas, cooked and drained

Melt butter in skillet. Add celery, mushrooms, pimiento, onion, salt, savory, and pepper. Cook uncovered, stirring frequently, till celery is crisp-done, about 5 to 7 minutes. Add peas; heat just till hot. Makes 4 servings.

Garden Pepper Boats

- 3 medium green peppers
- ¼ cup chopped onion
- 2 tablespoons butter or margarine
- 1 cup canned whole kernel corn or fresh cut corn
- 1 medium tomato, chopped (¾ cup)
- ½ cup cooked baby Limas
- 1 tablespoon butter or margarine, melted
- ½ cup soft bread crumbs

Remove tops and seeds from peppers. Cut in half lengthwise. Cook peppers in boiling salted water 5 minutes; drain. Cook onion in 2 tablespoons melted butter till tender but not brown. Add corn, tomato, and Limas; mix well. Season pepper shells with salt and pepper to taste. Fill peppers with vegetable mixture. Combine 1 tablespoon melted butter and bread crumbs; sprinkle atop peppers. Place in 10x6x1½-inch baking dish. Bake in moderate oven (350°) for 30 minutes. Serves 6.

Green Peppers and Tomatoes

- ½ cup thinly sliced onion
- 2 cloves garlic, minced
- 1 tablespoon olive oil
- 2 cups stewed tomatoes or 1 1-pound can tomatoes
- 2 teaspoons sugar
- 1 teaspoon salt
- Dash pepper
- ½ teaspoon basil
- 4 to 5 large green peppers, cut in strips ¾-inch wide (4 cups)
- 3 tablespoons olive oil

Cook onion and garlic in 1 tablespoon hot oil until tender; add tomatoes and seasonings. Simmer uncovered till sauce is slightly thick, about 20 minutes. Cook pepper in 3 tablespoons oil, turning frequently, till tender but still *crisp*. Lift to serving dish; season; top with tomato sauce. Serves 6.

Mashed Potatoes
Step-by-step

Pare potatoes. Cook in boiling salted water till tender. Drain, then shake over low heat to dry. Remove pan from heat. Mash potatoes with potato masher, or with electric mixer, using lowest speed.

Adding hot milk as needed, beat well with wooden spoon or electric mixer till light and fluffy (gradually increase speed of mixer). Add salt, pepper, lump of butter; beat in. Pile into bowl, top with butter.

Cottage Mashed Potatoes

Instant mashed or whipped potatoes (enough for 4 servings)
1½ tablespoons instant minced onion
1 8-ounce carton (1 cup) large-curd cream-style cottage cheese

Decreasing the water by ½ cup, prepare instant potatoes according to package directions, *but adding the instant onion to the boiling water before adding the potatoes.* With a fork, fold in cheese. Turn into a 1-quart casserole. Dot with butter; sprinkle with paprika. Bake in moderate oven (350°) 30 minutes or till lightly browned. Makes 4 or 5 servings.

Parmesan Double-potato Bake

Packaged dry hash brown potatoes (enough for 4 servings)
1 10¼-ounce can frozen condensed cream of potato soup
1 soup-can milk
1 tablespoon instant minced onion
1 tablespoon chopped parsley
Dash pepper
⅓ cup shredded Parmesan cheese

Prepare potatoes according to basic recipe on package. Combine remaining ingredients except cheese. Heat till soup thaws; add to drained potatoes, mixing gently. Turn into 10x6x1½-inch baking dish. Sprinkle with cheese. Bake in moderate oven (350°) 35 minutes or till lightly browned. Top with parsley. Makes 6 servings.

Potatoes in Lemon Sauce

2 pounds small potatoes
¼ cup butter or margarine
1 tablespoon lemon juice
1 tablespoon snipped green onion tops
Dash pepper
Dash nutmeg
1 teaspoon grated lemon peel

Pare potatoes; cook in boiling salted water, covered, till done, about 30 minutes. Drain and set aside. In small saucepan, heat butter with next 4 ingredients. Pour over potatoes, coating each potato well. Sprinkle with grated lemon peel. Makes 6 servings.

Blue Cheese and Bacon Potatoes

>   3 medium baking potatoes
> ½ cup milk
>   3 tablespoons butter or margarine
> ½ teaspoon salt
>
> Dash pepper
>   3 tablespoons blue cheese dressing
>   3 slices bacon, crisp-cooked and drained

Scrub potatoes with brush. Rub with fat and puncture skin with a fork. Bake in a hot oven (425°) for 1 hour. Cut slice from top of potatoes. Scoop out insides; mash. Add milk, butter, salt, and pepper; beat till fluffy. Pile lightly into shells. Garnish each potato with a tablespoon blue cheese dressing and crumble a strip of bacon over each. Return to oven 5 minutes to heat. Serve at once. Makes 3 servings.

California Sweet-potato Bake

>   4 medium sweet potatoes
> ½ cup brown sugar
>   1 tablespoon cornstarch
> ¼ teaspoon salt
>   1 cup orange juice
> ¼ cup raisins
> ¼ cup butter or margarine
>   3 tablespoons cooking sherry
>   2 tablespoons chopped California walnuts
> ½ teaspoon shredded orange peel

Cook potatoes in boiling salted water till tender; drain; peel, and halve lengthwise.* Arrange in shallow baking dish or pan. Sprinkle lightly with salt. Mix brown sugar, cornstarch, and the ¼ teaspoon salt. Blend in orange juice; add raisins. Stir while bringing quickly to boiling. Add remaining ingredients; pour over potatoes. Bake uncovered in moderate oven (350°) 20 minutes or till potatoes are well glazed. Makes 4 servings.

* Or use a 1-pound 2-ounce can (3 cups) sweet potatoes.

Spiced Apricot Sweets

1 1-pound 1-ounce can apricot halves
Whole cloves
1½ pounds sweet potatoes, cooked, peeled, and quartered
1 tablespoon sugar
1 tablespoon butter or margarine

Drain syrup from apricots into a 2-quart saucepan; add 3 whole cloves. Boil till reduced to ⅓ cup, about 8 to 10 minutes. Place *half* the sweet potatoes on bottom of 1½-quart casserole; top with *half* the apricots. Repeat layers. Stick a clove into each apricot half in the top layer. Pour reduced syrup over all; sprinkle with sugar and dot with butter. Bake in a moderate oven (350°) for 30 minutes. Makes 6 servings.

Rutabaga and Apple Bake

3 cups pared rutabaga slices
1 medium apple, thinly sliced
6 tablespoons brown sugar
2 tablespoons butter or margarine

Cook rutabaga slices in boiling salted water till just tender; drain. Place *half* the rutabag slices in a greased 1-quart casserole along with *half* the apple slices. Sprinkle with *half* the brown sugar; dot with *half* the butter; sprinkle with salt. Repeat layers using remaining ingredients. Bake covered in moderate oven (350°) for 30 minutes. Makes 4 to 6 servings.

Sauerkraut Provencale

- ⅓ cup chopped onion
- 2 tablespoons butter, melted
- ⅓ cup canned condensed beef broth
- 1 1-pound can (2 cups) sauerkraut, drained
- 2 tablespoons chopped canned pimiento
- ½ cup dairy sour cream
- Poppy seed

Cook onion in butter till tender but not brown. Add broth, sauerkraut, and pimiento; mix lightly. Simmer covered for 10 minutes. Serve topped with sour cream and sprinkled with poppy seed. Makes 4 servings.

Spinach Delight

- 2 10-ounce packages frozen chopped spinach, cooked and drained
- 4 slices bacon, crisp-cooked and crumbled
- 1 5-ounce can (⅔ cup) water chestnuts, drained and sliced
- 1 10-ounce package frozen Welsh rarebit, thawed (about 1 cup)
- 1 cup canned French-fried onions

Place cooked spinach in 10x6x1½-inch baking dish. Top with bacon and water chestnuts. Spread Welsh rarebit evenly over top. Garnish with French-fried onions. Bake in moderate oven (350°) for 20 to 25 minutes or till heated through. Serves 6 to 8.

Dilly Squash

- 1 pound yellow summer squash
- 2 tablespoons butter or margarine
- 1 tablespoon fresh snipped parsley
- ¼ teaspoon dill weed
- ¼ teaspoon salt
- Dash onion powder

Slice squash crosswise ¼-inch thick. Melt butter in skillet. Add squash, parsley, dill weed, salt, and onion powder. Cover and cook over low heat for 8 to 10 minutes or till tender, stirring occasionally. Serve piping hot. Makes 4 to 6 servings.

Glazed Squash with Onions

- 3 medium acorn squash
- 2 cups drained cooked or canned small onions
- ½ cup broken California walnuts
- ⅓ cup butter or margarine, melted
- ⅓ cup light molasses
- ¼ teaspoon salt
- ¼ teaspoon cinnamon

Cut squash in half lengthwise; remove seeds. Bake cut side down in shallow pan or baking dish in moderate oven (350°) 35 to 40 minutes or till almost tender. Turn squash halves cut side up and sprinkle with salt. Fill with onions and walnuts. Combine remaining ingredients; spoon over squash and filling. Continue baking 15 to 20 minutes or till squash is tender, brushing occasionally with sauce to glaze. Makes 6 servings.

Savory Succotash

- 1 1-pound can (2 cups) French-style green beans, drained
- 1 1-pound can (2 cups) whole kernel corn, drained
- ½ cup mayonnaise or salad dressing
- ½ cup shredded sharp process American cheese
- ½ cup chopped green pepper
- ½ cup chopped celery
- 2 tablespoons chopped onion
- 1 cup soft bread crumbs
- 2 tablespoons butter or margarine, melted

Combine first 7 ingredients; place in a 10x6x1½-inch baking dish. Combine crumbs and butter; sprinkle over top. Bake in a moderate oven (350°) 30 minutes or till crumbs are toasted. Makes 6 to 8 servings.

Spicy Whole Tomatoes

- ¼ cup butter or margarine
- ½ cup chopped onion
- 2 tablespoons brown sugar
- 6 whole cloves
- 2 bay leaves, crumbled
- 2 inches stick cinnamon, broken in pieces
- 1½ teaspoons salt
- Dash cracked pepper
- 6 medium tomatoes, peeled and cored

Melt butter in skillet; add onion, brown sugar, cloves, bay leaves, cinnamon, salt, and pepper; cook till onion is tender. Add tomatoes, cored side down; spoon butter mixture over. Cover; simmer 5 minutes. Carefully turn tomatoes. Simmer uncovered 5 to 10 minutes longer or till tomatoes are tender, basting often. Serve whole tomatoes in sauce dishes with sauce spooned over. Makes 6 servings.

Tomatoes with Dill Sauce

- ½ cup dairy sour cream
- ¼ cup mayonnaise or salad dressing
- 2 tablespoons finely chopped onion
- 1 teaspoon snipped fresh dill weed **or** ¼ teaspoon dried dill weed
- ¼ teaspoon salt
- 4 large firm-ripe tomatoes

Combine sour cream, mayonnaise, onion, dill, and salt, mixing well. Chill. Spoon over hot broiled tomatoes: Core tomatoes and cut in half crosswise. Season cut surfaces with salt and pepper; dot with butter or margarine. Broil, cut side up, 3 inches from heat about 5 minutes or till hot through (don't turn). Makes 8 servings.

Oriental Tomato Skillet

- 2 tablespoons butter or margarine
- ½ cup chopped onion
- 2 medium unpared zucchini squash, cut in quarters
- 3 medium tomatoes, cut in wedges
- 1 3-ounce can broiled sliced mushrooms, drained (½ cup)
- ¼ teaspoon salt
- ¼ teaspoon curry powder
- ¼ teaspoon ginger
- Dash freshly ground pepper

Melt butter in skillet; add onion and zucchini. Cover; cook over medium heat 5 minutes. Stir in remaining ingredients. Cover and cook 5 minutes longer or till vegetables are tender but slightly crisp. Makes 4 to 6 servings.

Lemon Turnips

- 2 cups turnip sticks
- 1 tablespoon butter or margarine
- 2 teaspoons snipped parsley
- 1 teaspoon finely chopped onion
- 1 teaspoon lemon juice

Cook turnip sticks in boiling salted water till just tender, about 20 minutes; drain. Add remaining ingredients. Toss to coat. Serves 4.

California Vegetable Bowl

- ¼ cup butter or margarine
- 4 cups sliced unpared zucchini squash (about 1 pound)
- 1½ cups cut fresh or frozen corn*
- ½ cup chopped onion
- ⅓ cup chopped green pepper
- ½ teaspoon salt
- 1 tablespoon fresh snipped dill **or** 1 teaspoon dried

Melt butter in skillet; add zucchini, corn, onion, and green pepper. Sprinkle with salt. Cover and cook, stirring occasionally, 10 to 12 minutes, or till vegetables are done to your liking. Sprinkle with dill. Makes 4 to 6 servings.

Or use drained canned whole-kernel corn.

Vegetable Chow Mein

- ¼ cup butter or margarine
- 3 cups coarsely shredded cabbage
- 1 cup bias-cut celery slices
- 1 cup thinly sliced carrot rounds
- 1 green pepper, cut in strips
- ½ cup chopped onion
- 1 teaspoon salt
- Dash pepper
- 1 6-ounce can (⅔ cup) evaporated milk

Melt butter in a large skillet; add vegetables, salt, and pepper. Cover and cook over medium heat just till vegetables are slightly tender, about 5 minutes. Add milk; heat thoroughly, stirring gently once or twice. Makes 6 servings.

Vegetable Medley Relish

- 1 10-ounce package frozen mixed vegetables
- 2 medium tomatoes, chopped (1½ cups)
- 1 large onion, chopped (1 cup)
- 1 medium cucumber, chopped (1 cup)
- 1 cup sugar
- 1 cup vinegar
- 1 teaspoon salt
- 1 teaspoon celery seed
- 1 teaspoon turmeric
- ½ teaspoon mustard seed

In a saucepan, combine vegetables, sugar, vinegar, and spices; heat to boiling and simmer, uncovered, for 30 minutes. Serve chilled. Makes about 4½ cups relish.

Vegetable Trio with Zippy Sauce

- 1 cup mayonnaise or salad dressing
- 2 hard-cooked eggs, chopped
- 3 tablespoons lemon juice
- 2 tablespoons minced onion
- 1 teaspoon Worcestershire sauce
- 1 teaspoon prepared mustard
- ¼ teaspoon garlic salt
- Dash bottled hot pepper sauce
- 1 10-ounce package frozen French-style green beans
- 1 10-ounce package frozen peas
- 1 10-ounce package frozen baby Limas

Combine ingredients, except vegetables; heat and stir over *low heat* just till hot through. Cook vegetables according to package directions; drain and mix. Pour hot sauce over vegetables. Makes 8 to 10 servings.

Green Rice Bake

- 2 slightly beaten eggs
- 2 cups milk
- ¾ cup packaged precooked rice
- ⅓ cup finely chopped onion
- 1 10-ounce package frozen chopped spinach, cooked and drained
- 4 ounces sharp process American cheese, shredded (1 cup)
- ½ teaspoon garlic salt

Combine eggs and milk. Add remaining ingredients. Pour into 10x6x1½-inch baking dish. Bake in slow oven (325°) 35 to 40 minutes or till firm. Makes 4 to 6 servings.

SECTION 3

Salads and Salad Dressings

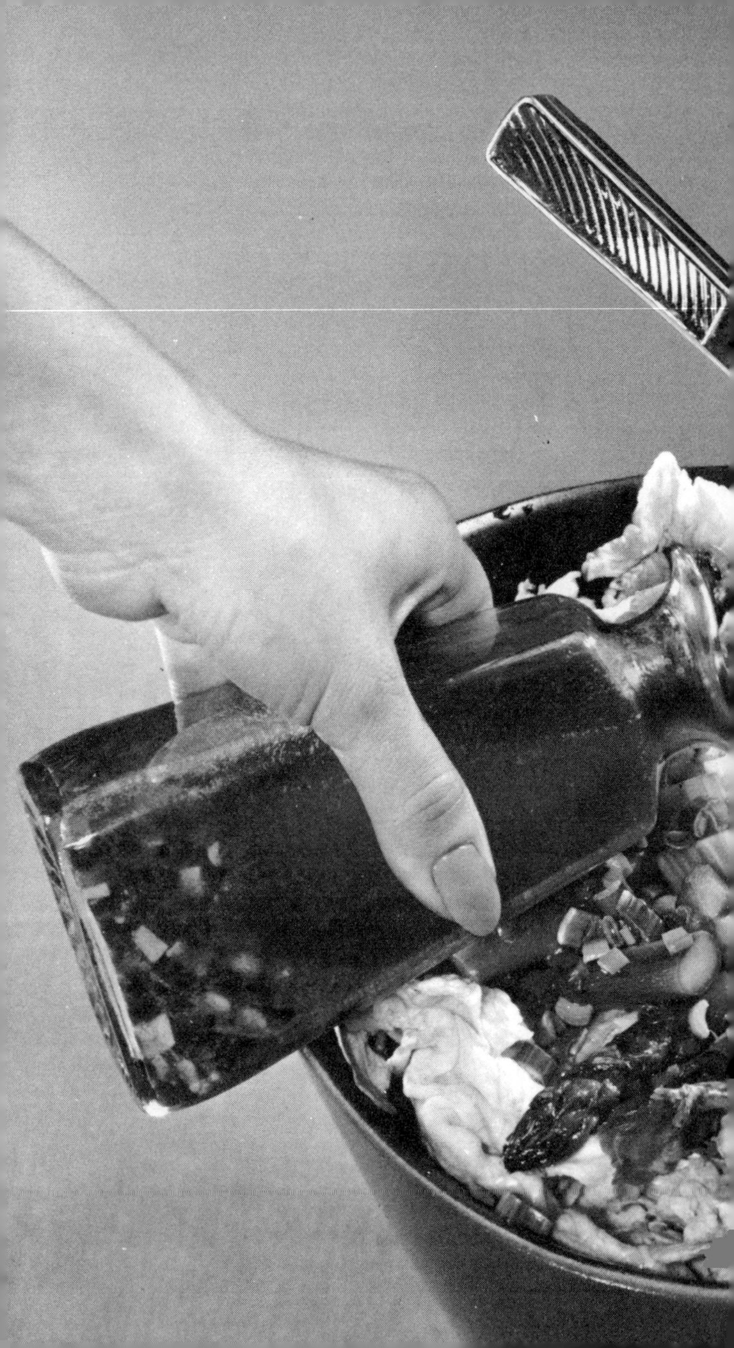

SECTION 3
Salads and Salad Dressings

Asparagus Toss with Harlequin Dressing

- 1 pound fresh asparagus, cut in 2-inch pieces (2 cups)
- 1 small head lettuce, torn in bite-size pieces (4 cups)
- 1 cup sliced celery
- ¼ cup sliced green onions and tops
- ½ cup salad oil
- 2 tablespoons white wine vinegar
- 2 tablespoons lemon juice
- ¼ cup finely chopped cooked beets
- 1 hard-cooked egg, finely chopped
- 1 tablespoon snipped parsley
- 1 teaspoon paprika
- 1 teaspoon sugar
- 1 teaspoon salt
- ½ teaspoon dry mustard
- 4 drops bottled hot pepper sauce

Cook asparagus till just tender; drain. Chill. Combine with lettuce, celery, and onion. For dressing,* combine remaining ingredients in jar; cover and shake well. Pour over salad; toss lightly. Makes 6 to 8 servings.

* *Or* use one envelope French salad-dressing mix and omit last 5 ingredients listed above.

Artichoke-Pimiento Bowl

- ½ cup olive or salad oil
- ⅓ cup vinegar
- 2 tablespoons water
- 4 thin slices onion
- 1 tablespoon sugar
- 1 clove garlic, crushed
- ¼ teaspoon celery seed
- ½ teaspoon salt
- Dash pepper
- 1 9-ounce package frozen artichoke hearts
- 1 4-ounce can or jar chopped pimientos
- 1 2-ounce can anchovy fillets, diced
- 2 cups torn head lettuce
- 2 cups torn romaine lettuce
- 2 cups torn small spinach leaves

In saucepan, combine first 9 ingredients for dressing; bring to boiling. Add artichoke hearts. Cook till tender, about 3 to 5 minutes. Cool; stir in pimiento and anchovies. Chill in dressing till serving time. Drain off dressing, and reserve. Add artichoke mixture to salad greens; toss with enough reserved dressing to coat. Makes 8 to 10 servings.

Green Bean Salad Mediterranean

- 1 9-ounce package frozen French-style green beans, thawed
- 1 medium onion, thinly sliced and separated in rings
- 1 3-ounce can broiled sliced mushrooms, drained (½ cup)
- ⅓ cup Italian dressing
- ¼ teaspoon salt
- Dash freshly ground pepper
- 2 medium tomatoes, cut in wedges

Pour boiling water over beans; let stand about 5 minutes; drain thoroughly. Place in salad bowl with onion rings and mushrooms. Combine salad dressing, salt, and pepper. Add to salad and toss. Marinate in refrigerator at least 2 hours, tossing occasionally. Just before serving, arrange the tomato wedges on salad. Makes 4 to 6 servings.

Mexican Bean Salad

- 1 1-pound can (2 cups) cut green beans
- 1 1-pound can (2 cups) dark red kidney beans
- 1 1-pound can (2 cups) chick peas or garbanzo beans
- 1 cup garlic French dressing
- Crisp salad greens

Drain beans and peas. Toss with dressing. Chill several hours or overnight, stirring a few times. Just before serving, stir again; drain off excess dressing. Spoon salad onto lettuce-lined plates. Sprinkle with sweet pickle relish, if desired. Makes 10 servings.

Mustard Beans

    1 cup sugar
    ½ cup cider vinegar
    3 tablespoons prepared mustard
    ½ teaspoon instant minced onion
    ¼ teaspoon salt
    1 1-pound can yellow wax beans, drained or 1 9-ounce package frozen yellow wax beans, thawed

Combine all ingredients except beans; bring to boiling point, stirring till sugar is dissolved. Add beans; simmer uncovered 5 minutes; cool. Cover; refrigerate overnight. Serve as relish or salad ingredient.

Borsch Salad Molds

    1 3-ounce package lemon-flavored gelatin
    ¾ cup boiling water
    ¼ teaspoon salt
    1 cup dairy sour cream
    2 4½-ounce jars (1 cup) strained beets
    1 tablespoon lemon juice
    1 teaspoon grated onion

Dissolve gelatin in boiling water; add remaining ingredients; beat smooth with electric or rotary beater. Pour into 6 individual molds; chill till firm, about 6 hours. Unmold on red onion slices. Serve with chilled marinated cooked or canned peas.

Orange-glazed Beets

    ¼ cup honey
    ½ to 1 teaspoon shredded orange peel
    ¼ cup orange juice
    ¼ cup lemon juice
    ½ teaspoon salt
    1 1-pound can (2 cups) julienne-style beets, well-drained

In a small mixing bowl, combine honey, orange peel and juice, lemon juice, and salt. Add drained beets; mix gently. Refrigerate several hours or overnight, turning occasionally. Drain and serve as a relish.

Campfire Coleslaw

    8 cups finely shredded crisp cabbage
    1 cup thin-sliced raw cauliflower
    ¼ cup chopped onion
    ¼ cup sliced radishes
    ¼ cup chopped green pepper
    Zippy Garlic Dressing

Combine chilled vegetables. Toss with ZIPPY GARLIC DRESSING: Combine 1 cup dairy sour cream, ½ envelope cheese-garlic salad-dressing mix, ¼ cup milk, 1 tablespoon salad oil, 1 tablespoon lemon juice, and ½ teaspoon salt; stir well. Trim salad with green pepper rings. Makes 6 to 8 servings.

Blue Cheese Slaw

- 6 cups shredded cabbage
- 2 tablespoons chopped canned pimiento
- 2 tablespoons chopped green onion tops
- ½ cup dairy sour cream
- 2 tablespoons mayonnaise or salad dressing
- 1 tablespoon lemon juice
- ½ teaspoon sugar
- Dash salt
- 1 4-ounce package blue cheese, crumbled (1 cup)

Combine cabbage, pimiento, and onion tops; chill thoroughly. Mix together remaining ingredients; chill. Pour over cabbage and toss lightly. If desired, garnish with slices of hard-cooked egg and Bologna ruffles. Makes 4 to 6 servings.

Perfection Salad

In a mixing bowl, thoroughly combine 2 envelopes (2 tablespoons) unflavored gelatin, ½ cup sugar, and 1 teaspoon salt. Add 1½ cups boiling water and stir to dissolve gelatin. Then add 1½ cups cold water, ½ cup vinegar, and 2 tablespoons lemon juice. Chill till mixture is partially set. Add 2 cups finely shredded cabbage, 1 cup chopped celery, ¼ cup chopped green pepper, ¼ cup diced canned pimiento, and ⅓ cup stuffed green olives, sliced. Pour into 8½x4½x2½-inch loaf pan. Chill till firm. Garnish with carrot curls and ripe olives.

Original Caesar Salad

3 medium heads romaine
lettuce, chilled, dry, and crisp
About ⅓ cup Garlic Olive Oil
2 to 3 tablespoons wine vinegar
1 lemon, halved
1 or 2 1-minute coddled eggs

Dash Worcestershire sauce
Salt and freshly ground
pepper
⅓ cup grated Parmesan cheese
About 1 cup Caesar Croutons

Break romaine leaves in 2- or 3-inch widths. At *last minute* before serving, place romaine in chilled salad bowl. Drizzle with Garlic Olive Oil, then vinegar. Squeeze lemon over, using fork to help free juice. Break in eggs. Season with Worcestershire and salt. Grind pepper over all. Sprinkle with Parmesan cheese. Roll-toss 6 or 7 times, or till dressing is well combined and every leaf is coated. Add Croutons; toss once or twice. Serve *at once* on chilled dinner plates. Garnish with rolled anchovies, if desired. Makes 6 servings as main course. GARLIC OLIVE OIL: Prepare one to several days early. Slice 6 cloves of garlic lengthwise in quarters; let stand in 1 cup olive oil (or use salad oil or half of each). CAESAR CROUTONS: Cut each slice of bread in 5 strips one way, then across 5 times to make squares. Spread out on baking sheet; pour a little Garlic Olive Oil over. Heat at 225° for 2 hours or till very dry. Sprinkle with grated Parmesan cheese. Store in covered jar in refrigerator.

Cauliflower-Cheese Toss

¼ cup olive oil
¼ cup salad oil
¼ cup white wine vinegar
1 teaspoon salt **and** dash pepper
1 medium onion, thinly sliced
and separated in rings
½ small head cauliflower, sliced
(about 3 cups)

½ cup sliced radishes
Romaine leaves
1 medium head lettuce,
torn in bite-size pieces
(about 8 cups)
2 ounces blue cheese, crumbled
(½ cup)

Combine olive oil, salad oil, vinegar, salt, and pepper. Add sliced vegetables to mixture. Marinate for at least 30 minutes. Line salad bowl with romaine leaves; add the torn lettuce; sprinkle crumbled cheese over lettuce. Just before serving, add marinade mixture and toss gently with lettuce and blue cheese. Makes 6 servings.

Carrot Relish Cups

- 1 3-ounce package orange-flavored gelatin
- ¼ cup sugar
- 1½ cups boiling water
- 1 8-ounce package cream cheese, softened
- ½ cup orange juice
- ½ teaspoon shredded lemon peel
- 2 tablespoons lemon juice
- 1 cup shredded carrots
- 1 cup chopped unpared apple

Dissolve gelatin and sugar in boiling water. Add cream cheese and beat smooth with electric or rotary beater. Stir in orange juice, lemon peel, and lemon juice. Chill till partially set. Add carrots and apple. Spoon into 6 to 8 individual molds. Chill till firm. Unmold. Garnish with carrot curls and orange sections.

Pickled Carrots

- 6 medium carrots (about 1 pound), scraped and cut in 3-inch lengths
- ¾ cup sugar
- ¾ cup vinegar
- ¾ cup water
- 1 tablespoon mustard seed
- 2½ inches stick cinnamon, broken
- 3 whole cloves

Precook carrots 5 minutes. Drain; cut in thin sticks. Combine next 4 ingredients. Tie cinnamon and cloves in cloth bag; add to sugar-water mixture. Simmer 10 minutes; pour over carrots. Cool; refrigerate 8 hours or overnight. Drain well before serving.

Confetti Relish Mold

- 2 beef bouillon cubes
- 1 3-ounce package lemon-flavored gelatin
- 1 cup boiling water
- 2 tablespoons tarragon vinegar
- ½ teaspoon salt
- 1 cup dairy sour cream
- ½ cup chopped unpared cucumber
- ¼ cup finely chopped green pepper
- ¼ cup sliced radishes
- 2 tablespoons sliced green onions

Dissolve bouillon cubes and gelatin in boiling water; add vinegar and salt. Chill till partially set. Add sour cream; beat smooth. Add vegetables; pour into a 3-cup mold. Chill till firm. Makes 6 servings.

Spring Salad Souffle

- 1 3-ounce package lime-flavored gelatin
- ½ cup water
- 1 10½-ounce can condensed cream of asparagus soup
- ½ cup mayonnaise or salad dressing
- 1 tablespoon vinegar
- 1 teaspoon grated onion
- Dash pepper
- ½ cup shredded unpared cucumber
- ¼ cup diced celery
- 1 tablespoon snipped parsley

In saucepan, mix gelatin and water. Gradually blend in soup; heat and stir till gelatin dissolves. Add next 4 ingredients. Beat smooth with rotary or electric beater. Chill till partially set. Turn into large chilled bowl; beat till thick and fluffy. Fold in vegetables. Spoon into 5-cup ring mold or 6 to 8 individual molds; chill firm.

Cheese Marinated Onions

- 3 ounces blue cheese, crumbled (about ¾ cup)
- ½ cup salad oil
- 2 tablespoons lemon juice
- 1 teaspoon salt
- ½ teaspoon sugar
- Dash pepper
- Dash paprika
- 4 medium onions, thinly sliced (about 4 cups onion rings)

Mix all ingredients except onions. Pour over onion rings and chill thoroughly. Serve as a meat relish or add to a green salad.

Zippy Mushrooms

- ⅔ cup tarragon vinegar
- ½ cup salad oil
- 1 medium clove garlic, minced
- 1 tablespoon sugar
- 1½ teaspoons salt
- Dash freshly ground pepper
- 2 tablespoons water
- Dash bottled hot pepper sauce
- 1 medium onion, sliced and separated in rings
- 2 6-ounce cans broiled mushroom crowns, drained, **or** 2 pints fresh mushrooms, washed and trimmed

Combine first 8 ingredients. Add onions and mushrooms. Cover and refrigerate mixture for at least 8 hours, stirring several times. Drain and serve as a relish.

Candied Dill Pickles

- 1 1-quart jar whole dill pickles
- ½ cup tarragon vinegar
- 2¾ cups sugar
- 2 tablespoons mixed pickling spices

Drain pickles; cut in ¼-inch slices. (Use a crinkle cutter for a fancy look.) Combine pickle slices, vinegar, and sugar. Tie spices in small piece of cheesecloth; add. Let mixture stand at room temperature, stirring occasionally, till sugar dissolves (about 4 hours). Return half the pickles to their jar; add spice bag. Add remaining pickles, then fill jar with the syrup. Cover and refrigerate at least 4 days before serving. Remove spice bag in 1 week, if desired. Makes 1 quart.

Potato Salad Special

- 3 cups diced cooked potatoes
- 1½ cups sliced raw cauliflower
- 1 cup diced celery
- 2 hard-cooked eggs, chopped
- ¼ cup chopped onion
- 6 slices crisp-cooked bacon, crumbled
- 1 cup mayonnaise or salad dressing
- 1 tablespoon bacon fat
- 2 teaspoons caraway seed (optional)

Combine potatoes, cauliflower, celery, eggs, onion, and bacon. Mix mayonnaise, bacon fat, and caraway seed. Pour over salad; toss lightly; salt to taste. Chill. Makes 5 or 6 servings.

Pepped-up Potato Salad

- 1½ teaspoons mustard seed
- 1 teaspoon celery seed
- 3 tablespoons vinegar
- 1½ teaspoons salt
- ½ cup finely chopped green onions and tops
- 5 cups diced cooked potatoes
- ¾ cup mayonnaise or salad dressing
- 2 hard-cooked eggs, chopped

Soak mustard seed and celery seed in vinegar (several hours or overnight, if possible). Combine seed mixture with salt and green onions. Add potatoes and mix lightly. Add mayonnaise and chopped eggs; toss to mix. Chill thoroughly. Trim with hard-cooked egg wedges and green onions. Makes 6 servings.

Deviled Potato Salad

- 8 hard-cooked eggs
- 3 tablespoons vinegar
- 3 tablespoons prepared mustard
- 1 cup mayonnaise or salad dressing
- ½ cup dairy sour cream
- ½ teaspoon celery salt
- 1 teaspoon salt
- 6 medium potatoes, cooked and cubed (4 to 4½ cups)
- 2 tablespoons chopped onion

Cut eggs in half; remove yolks; mash and blend with vinegar and mustard. Add mayonnaise, sour cream, celery salt, and salt; mix well. Chop egg whites; combine with potatoes and onion. Fold in egg yolk mixture; chill. Garnish with tomato wedges and cucumber slices. Makes 6 to 8 servings.

Dublin Potato Salad

- 1 teaspoon **each** celery seed and mustard seed
- 2 tablespoons vinegar
- 3 cups warm diced cooked potatoes
- 2 teaspoons sugar
- ½ teaspoon salt
- 1 12-ounce can corned beef, chilled and diced
- 2 cups finely shredded crisp cabbage
- ¼ cup finely chopped dill pickle
- ¼ cup chopped green onions
- ¾ cup mayonnaise or salad dressing
- 2 tablespoons milk
- 1 tablespoon vinegar
- ½ teaspoon salt

Soak celery and mustard seeds in 2 tablespoons vinegar; drizzle over *warm* potatoes. Sprinkle with sugar and ½ teaspoon salt. Chill. Add meat, cabbage, pickle, and onions. Mix remaining ingredients; pour over potato mixture; toss lightly. Makes 7 or 8 servings.

Hot Potato Salad

- ½ pound bacon
- ⅓ cup vinegar **plus** water to make ½ cup
- 1 slightly beaten egg
- 1 teaspoon sugar
- 1 teaspoon salt
- ¼ teaspoon pepper
- 5 cups diced cooked potatoes
- ½ cup chopped onion

Cook bacon crisp; crumble. Combine ⅓ cup bacon drippings with next 5 ingredients. Heat and stir till thickened. Add potatoes, onion, and bacon; toss, heat through. Serves 6.

Fiesta Corn in Tomato Cups

- 1 12-ounce can (1½ cups) whole kernel corn, well drained
- ¼ cup **each** chopped green pepper, chopped canned pimiento, sliced green onions, and sliced ripe olives
- ½ cup diced celery
- Dash freshly ground pepper
- 1 recipe Chili Dressing
- 6 to 8 large ripe tomatoes

Combine all ingredients except dressing and tomatoes; pour Chili Dressing over vegetables and mix well. Chill thoroughly. At serving time, drain corn mixture well. Turn tomatoes stem end down; cut each *not quite through* in wedges; spread apart. Spoon corn mixture into center. Makes 6 to 8 servings. CHILI DRESSING: In jar, mix ⅓ cup catsup, ¼ cup salad oil, ¼ cup tarragon vinegar, 1 tablespoon sugar, ¾ teaspoon chili powder, ½ teaspoon salt, 2 dashes bottled hot pepper sauce, and 1 small clove garlic, minced; cover and shake.

Tomato Relish Salad

- 3 medium tomatoes, sliced
- 1 cup thinly sliced unpared cucumber
- 1 medium onion, thinly sliced
- ½ cup thinly sliced carrot rounds
- ½ cup thinly sliced celery
- ½ cup tarragon vinegar
- ⅓ cup water
- ¼ cup sugar
- 1 teaspoon paprika
- 1 teaspoon basil leaves, crushed
- ½ teaspoon salt
- ¼ teaspoon freshly ground pepper

Arrange the tomato slices, cucumber, onion, carrot rounds, and celery in rows in 10x6x1½-inch baking dish. Combine vinegar, water, sugar, paprika, basil, salt, and pepper; pour over vegetables. Cover and chill at least 4 hours or overnight, turning vegetables occasionally. Makes 6 to 8 servings.

Sarah's Salad

- 2 cups torn head lettuce
- 2 cups torn curly endive
- 2 cups torn romaine lettuce
- 6 tablespoons mayonnaise or salad dressing
- 1 medium red or white onion, thinly sliced
- 1½ cups drained cooked peas
- 1 cup julienne strips natural Swiss cheese
- 6 slices bacon, crisp-cooked and crumbled

Place a *third* of the salad greens into a bowl; dot with several tablespoons of the mayonnaise. Top with a *third* of the onion slices; sprinkle with sugar (about 1 teaspoon). Dash with salt (about ¼ teaspoon) and freshly ground pepper. Add a *third* of the peas and cheese. Repeat layers, seasoning each. *Do not toss.* Cover; chill 2 hours. Just before serving, top with bacon and toss. Makes 6 servings.

Shoestring Toss

- 1 cup julienne carrot strips, cooked and drained
- 1 cup drained cooked or canned French-style green beans
- 1 cup celery strips
- ½ cup French dressing
- ½ medium head lettuce
- 1 small head romaine
- 1 head Bibb lettuce
- 2 hard-cooked eggs, sliced

Combine carrots, beans, and celery; pour French dressing over. Chill at least 3 hours. Drain off excess dressing; reserve. Line large salad bowl with part of greens; break in remaining greens in bite-size pieces. Arrange marinated vegetables and the egg slices over greens. Dash with salt and freshly ground pepper. Toss lightly, adding enough reserved dressing to coat leaves. Makes 6 servings.

Italian Salad Bowl

- ½ medium head lettuce, torn into bite-size pieces
- ½ medium head romaine, torn into bite-size pieces
- 2 cups thinly sliced raw zucchini
- ½ cup sliced radishes
- ½ cup sliced fresh mushrooms (optional)
- 3 green onions, sliced
- Salt and pepper
- Italian dressing
- 2 ounces blue cheese, crumbled (½ cup)

In large bowl, combine lettuce, romaine, zucchini, radishes, mushrooms, and sliced green onions. Season to taste. Toss lightly with dressing; sprinkle crumbled blue cheese over top. Makes 6 servings.

Tangy Spinach Toss

- ¼ cup butter or margarine
- 2 tablespoons sliced green onion
- 2 tablespoons all-purpose flour
- ¼ teaspoon salt
- 1 cup water
- 2 tablespoons lemon juice
- 1 tablespoon prepared horseradish
- ½ teaspoon Worcestershire sauce
- 2 hard-cooked eggs
- 1 pound fresh spinach, torn in bite-size pieces

Cook onion in butter about 1 minute; blend in flour and salt. Add water, lemon juice, horseradish, and Worcestershire; cook and stir till mixture boils. Dice *one* egg; add to dressing. Pour dressing over spinach in salad bowl; toss lightly. Slice remaining egg for garnish; sprinkle with paprika; serve at once. Makes 6 to 8 servings.

Taos Salad

- 2 cups chopped lettuce
- 1 1-pound can (2 cups) dark red kidney beans, drained
- 2 medium tomatoes, chopped and drained
- 1 tablespoon chopped, canned green chiles
- 1 medium avocado, mashed
- ½ cup dairy sour cream
- 2 tablespoons Italian dressing
- 1 teaspoon chili powder
- 1 teaspoon instant minced onion
- ¼ teaspoon salt
- Dash pepper
- ½ cup shredded sharp natural Cheddar cheese
- ½ cup crushed corn chips

Combine lettuce, kidney beans, tomato, and chiles in salad bowl; chill thoroughly. Blend avocado and sour cream. Add next 5 ingredients; mix well; chill. Season salad with salt and pepper. Toss with avocado dressing. Top with cheese and corn chips. Garnish with ripe olives, if desired. Makes 4 to 6 servings.

Guacamole Salad Bowl

- ½ medium head lettuce
- 2 tomatoes, cut in wedges
- ½ cup sliced pitted ripe olives
- ¼ cup chopped green onions
- 1 cup corn chips
- 1 6½- or 7-ounce can tuna, drained
- 1 recipe Avocado Dressing
- ½ cup shredded natural Cheddar cheese

Break lettuce into bowl. Add tomatoes, olives, onions, corn chips, and tuna. Toss lightly with Avocado Dressing. Top with cheese and additional ripe olives. Makes 4 servings.
AVOCADO DRESSING: Combine ½ cup mashed ripe avocado, 1 tablespoon lemon juice, ½ cup dairy sour cream, ⅛ cup salad oil, 1 clove garlic, crushed, ½ teaspoon sugar, ½ teaspoon chili powder, ¼ teaspoon *each* salt and bottled hot pepper sauce; beat with electric beater or blender.

Hot Tuna-Macaroni Toss

- ½ 7-ounce package (1 cup) elbow macaroni
- ¼ cup Italian salad dressing
- 1 teaspoon celery seed
- ¾ teaspoon dry mustard
- ½ teaspoon salt
- Dash pepper
- 1 6½- or 7-ounce can (1 cup) tuna, flaked
- ½ cup diced celery
- ½ cup diced green pepper
- 3 tablespoons mayonnaise or salad dressing

Cook macaroni in boiling salted water till tender; drain. In skillet, mix Italian dressing and seasonings; heat just to boiling. Add macaroni, tuna, celery, and green pepper. Toss lightly and heat just through. Stir in the salad dressing. Top with green-pepper rings; serve at once. Serves 6.

Western Tuna Toss

- 1 6½- or 7-ounce can tuna
- ¼ cup wine vinegar
- ½ teaspoon crushed basil leaves
- Dash coarsely ground pepper
- Dash salt
- 1 small head lettuce
- 2 medium tomatoes, cut in wedges
- 1 small onion, thinly sliced

Place tuna (undrained) into salad bowl. With fork, break tuna into bite-size chunks. (If needed, add 2 tablespoons salad oil or olive oil to dress lettuce.) Add vinegar and seasonings. Break lettuce in bite-size pieces into bowl. Add tomatoes and onion; toss lightly. Makes 4 servings.

Blue-cheese Waldorf Salad

- 2 cups diced unpared tart apples
- 1 cup diced celery
- ½ cup broken California walnuts
- ¼ cup crumbled blue cheese
- ¼ cup dairy sour cream
- ¼ cup mayonnaise or salad dressing
- Dash salt

Combine apples, celery, and walnuts. Mix remaining ingredients; add to salad and toss. Chill. Serve on crisp greens. Makes 6 servings.

Pear-Waldorf with Swiss Cheese

- 1 cup diced, pared fresh pears
- 3 tart medium apples, pared and diced (about 3 cups)
- 2 tablespoons lemon juice,
- ¾ cup diced Swiss cheese
- ½ cup celery slices
- ½ cup broken California walnuts
- ⅔ cup mayonnaise or salad dressing
- Salad greens

Sprinkle pear and apple cubes with lemon juice. Add cheese, celery, and nuts. Toss lightly with mayonnaise. Chill. Serve on salad greens.* Trim with pear wedges or apple rings, if desired. Makes 6 servings.

* *Or* heap salad mixture on greens in center of large plate and trim with PEAR CROWN: Arrange 6 or 8 pared fresh, or canned, pear halves, pointed ends up, around salad, to form crown. Top each pear half with a maraschino cherry (with stem on).

Apple-Melon Toss with Cheese

- 2 cups diced unpared apple
- 1 cup celery slices
- 1½ cups cantaloupe or honeydew balls
- ½ cup dairy sour cream
- ⅓ cup mayonnaise or salad dressing
- 2 ounces blue cheese, crumbled (⅓ to ½ cup)

Mix apple cubes, celery slices, and melon balls. Blend sour cream and mayonnaise; stir in blue cheese. Add to apple mixture and toss lightly. Chill. Serve in lettuce cups. Makes 4 or 5 servings.

Avocado Fruit Toss

- 1 small head lettuce
- ½ head curly endive
- 2 medium, ripe avocados
- 1 cup orange sections
- 1 cup grapefruit sections
- French dressing
- Pomegranate seeds, if desired

Tear lettuce and endive into bite-size pieces. Halve and seed avocados. Peel; slice into bowl. Add orange and grapefruit sections. Toss with enough clear French dressing to coat. Sprinkle with pomegranate seeds. Makes 8 or 9 servings.

Avocado Fruit Squares

- 1 large ripe avocado
- 2 tablespoons lemon juice
- 1 3-ounce package cream cheese, softened
- 2 tablespoons sugar
- ¼ cup mayonnaise or salad dressing
- ¼ teaspoon salt
- 1 cup well-drained diced canned peaches
- ¼ cup well-drained chopped maraschino cherries
- ½ cup whipping cream, whipped

Halve and seed avocado. Peel; dice into bowl. Sprinkle with *1 tablespoon* of the lemon juice. Blend cheese, remaining lemon juice, the sugar, mayonnaise, and salt. Add fruits; fold in whipped cream. Pour into refrigerator tray; freeze firm, 6 hours or overnight. Before serving, let stand at room temperature about 15 minutes; cut in squares. (For circles, freeze in a 1-quart round ice-cream or freezer carton or in No. 2½ cans; slice.) Trim with kabobs of cherries and avocado balls, if desired. Makes 5 or 6 servings.

Frosted Apricot Squares

Drain one 1-pound 14-ounce can (3½ cups) unpeeled apricot halves, reserving syrup. Cut apricots in quarters. Add water to syrup to make 1¾ cups; add ¼ teaspoon salt, 6 inches stick cinnamon, and ½ teaspoon whole cloves; simmer covered 10 minutes. Remove from heat and let stand 10 minutes to steep; strain. Dissolve two 3-ounce packages orange-flavored gelatin in *hot* mixture. Drain one 8¾-ounce can (1 cup) crushed pineapple, reserving syrup; add water to syrup to make 2 cups; add to gelatin mixture along with 3 tablespoons lemon juice. Chill till partially set. Stir in apricots and 1 cup halved seedless green grapes. Pour into 11x7x1½-inch baking pan. Chill till firm. Soften one 3-ounce package cream cheese; mix with pineapple; spread over gelatin. Sprinkle with ¼ cup chopped California walnuts. Chill. Cut in 10 or 12 squares.

Cherry Mallow Squares

RED LAYER: Dissolve one 3-ounce package raspberry-flavored gelatin in 1 cup boiling water; add ½ cup cold water and ½ cup cooking claret. Chill till partially set. Add one 1-pound can (2 cups) pitted dark sweet cherries, drained and halved. Pour into 9x9x2-inch pan. Chill till almost firm. FLUFFY GREEN LAYER: Drain 1 1-pound 4½-ounce can (2½ cups) crushed pineapple, *reserving syrup* (1 cup). To syrup add one 3-ounce package lime-flavored gelatin; heat and stir till gelatin dissolves. Add one 3-ounce package cream cheese, softened, and ½ cup mayonnaise; beat smooth with electric or rotary beater. Stir in ½ cup cold water, the drained pineapple, and ½ cup tiny marshmallows; chill till partially set. Whip ½ cup whipping cream; fold into lime mixture. Spread on red layer. Chill firm. Cut in 9 squares.

Ginger-y Citrus Mold

- 1 small grapefruit
- 1 medium orange
- 1 envelope (1 tablespoon) unflavored gelatin
- ¼ cup lemon juice
- ⅓ cup sugar
- ¼ teaspoon salt
- ⅔ cup orange juice
- 1 7-ounce bottle ginger ale, **well chilled**
- ½ cup broken pecans

Section grapefruit and orange, removing white membrane. Dice grapefruit and *all but 6 of the orange sections.* Soften gelatin in lemon juice; dissolve *over* hot water. In bowl, combine softened gelatin, sugar, salt, and orange juice. Slowly pour ginger ale down side of bowl; to keep bubbles in, mix *gently with up-and-down motion*. Chill till partially set. Arrange the whole orange sections and a few pecans in bottom of 3-cup ring mold. Pour *1 cup* of the gelatin over fruit; chill till firm. To remaining gelatin, add diced fruit and nuts, *stirring with up-and-down motion*. Pour over firm layer. Chill till firm. Turn out on greens. Serve with mayonnaise or salad dressing. Makes 4 or 5 servings.

Cranberry-Raspberry Ring

- 1 3-ounce package raspberry-flavored gelatin
- 1 3-ounce package lemon-flavored gelatin
- 2 cups boiling water
- 1 10-ounce package frozen red raspberries
- 1 cup cranberry-orange relish
- 1 7-ounce bottle (about 1 cup) lemon-lime carbonated beverage

Dissolve raspberry and lemon-flavored gelatin in boiling water. Stir in frozen raspberries, breaking up large pieces with fork. Add cranberry-orange relish. Chill till cold but not set. Resting bottle on rim of bowl, carefully pour in lemon-lime carbonated beverage; stir gently with up and down motion. Chill till partially set. Turn into a 5½-cup ring mold. Chill till firm, about 4 hours. Unmold on crisp greens. Makes 8 to 10 servings.

Frozen Orange-Pecan Molds

- 1 8-ounce package cream cheese, softened
- ¼ cup orange juice
- ½ cup chopped pecans
- 1 8¾-ounce can (1 cup) crushed pineapple, well drained
- ½ cup pitted dates, cut up
- ¼ cup chopped maraschino cherries
- ½ teaspoon grated orange peel
- 1 cup whipping cream, whipped

Combine cheese and orange juice, beating till fluffy. Stir in pecans, fruits, and peel. Fold in whipped cream. *Pack* into individual molds or into 8½x4½x2½-inch loaf pan. Freeze firm; let stand at room temperature about 15 minutes before serving. For a boost in height, unmold on orange slices. Makes 8 servings.

Sparkling Honeydew Maid

- 2 envelopes (2 tablespoons) unflavored gelatin
- 1 6-ounce (¾ cup) can frozen lemonade concentrate
- 1 7-ounce bottle (about 1 cup) ginger ale
- 2 tablespoons maraschino cherry juice
- ½ medium honeydew melon, cut in ½-inch cubes (2 cups)
- ¼ cup sliced maraschino cherries
- ¼ cup dairy sour cream
- ¼ cup mayonnaise or salad dressing

Soften gelatin in ½ cup cold water. Add 1¾ cups boiling water; stir till gelatin dissolves. Stir in thawed concentrate. Gently stir in ginger ale. Divide gelatin mixture in half. Stir cherry juice into first half. Chill till partially set; fold in fruits. Turn into 8½x4½x2½-inch baking dish; chill. Add sour cream and mayonnaise to remaining gelatin. Beat with rotary beater till smooth. Leave at room temperature till fruit layer is almost set. Slowly pour sour cream gelatin over fruit layer. Chill 3 to 4 hours. With narrow spatula, loosen sides of mold and invert onto platter. Makes 8 to 10 servings.

Melon Bowls–Honey Dressing

- ½ cup dairy sour cream
- ¼ teaspoon dry mustard
- 1½ to 2 tablespoons honey
- ½ teaspoon grated orange peel
- Dash salt
- 1 tablespoon orange juice
- 1 teaspoon lemon juice
- Honeydew melons
- Fresh blueberries
- Banana slices

Combine sour cream, mustard, and honey; beat well.* Add orange peel, salt; slowly beat in fruit juices. Chill at least 1 hour. Makes about ¾ cup. Spoon atop MELON BOWLS: Halve and seed melons. Fill with blueberries and sliced bananas.

*For fluffy dressing, beat with electric beater 5 to 7 minutes.

114 • FRUIT SALADS

Summer Fruit Bowl

In large bowl, arrange small pared watermelon wedges as dividers. Fill between with separate mounds of peach slices, banana cuts, halved avocado rings, cantaloupe and watermelon balls, orange sections, and halved pineapple rings. Center salad with flaked coconut. Tuck in mint sprigs. Pass favorite fruit dressing.

Fruit Freeze, Oriental

- 1 3-ounce package cream cheese
- 3 tablespoons mayonnaise
- 1 tablespoon lemon juice
- ¼ teaspoon salt
- ½ cup chopped preserved kumquats
- ½ cup dates, cut up
- ¼ cup quartered marschino cherries
- 1 8¾-ounce can (1 cup) crushed pineapple, drained
- 2 tablespoons finely chopped candied ginger, if desired
- 1 cup whipping cream, whipped
- ¼ cup slivered blanched almonds, toasted

Soften cream cheese; blend in mayonnaise, lemon juice, and salt. Stir in fruits and ginger. Fold in whipped cream. Pour into refrigerator tray. Sprinkle almonds over top. Freeze firm. Makes 6 to 8 servings.

Winter Orange Bowl with Walnut Croutons

- 1 small head lettuce
- ½ head curly endive
- 2 oranges, pared and sliced
- ½ mild white onion, sliced and separated into rings
- Walnut Croutons
- Italian dressing

Tear lettuce and endive (bite-size pieces) into bowl. Add orange slices, onion rings, and hot Walnut Croutons. Toss with enough Italian Dressing to coat greens. WALNUT CROUTONS: Melt 1½ teaspoons butter or margarine in skillet; add ¼ teaspoon salt. Add ⅓ cup California walnut halves; brown over medium heat, stirring constantly. Makes 6 to 8 servings.

Fresh Fruit Ambrosia

- 3 large oranges
- 1 fresh ripe pineapple
- 1 cup shredded coconut
- ¾ cup sugar
- Dash salt

Pare oranges with a sharp knife; remove sections by cutting close to membrane. Pare, core, and dice the pineapple. Combine fruit with coconut, sugar, and salt; toss lightly. Chill several hours. Spoon in serving bowl and decorate top with additional orange sections, coconut, and a few maraschino cherries and mint leaves. Makes 6 servings.

Peach Melba Mold

- 1 1-pound can (2 cups) sliced peaches
- 2 tablespoons lemon juice
- 1 3-ounce package lemon-flavored gelatin
- 2 teaspoons milk
- 2 tablespoons mayonnaise or salad dressing
- 1 3-ounce package cream cheese, softened
- 2 tablespoons finely chopped pecans
- 1 10-ounce package frozen red raspberries, thawed
- 2 tablespoons lemon juice
- 1 3-ounce package raspberry-flavored gelatin

PEACH LAYER: Drain peaches, reserving syrup. Combine syrup and 2 tablespoons lemon juice; add cold water to make 1 cup. Dissolve lemon gelatin in 1 cup *boiling* water; add syrup mixture. Chill till partially set. Add peaches. Pour into 6½-cup ring mold. Chill till almost set. Spread with CHEESE LAYER: Mix milk, mayonnaise, and cream cheese; stir in pecans. RASPBERRY LAYER: Drain raspberries, reserving syrup. Combine syrup and lemon juice; add cold water to make 1 cup. Dissolve raspberry gelatin in 1 cup *boiling* water; add syrup mixture. Chill till partially set; stir in raspberries. Pour over cheese. Chill till firm. Unmold. Makes 8 servings.

Frosty Mint Cubes

- 1 1-pound 4½-ounce can (2½ cups) crushed pineapple
- 2 **teaspoons** unflavored gelatin
- ½ cup mint jelly
  Dash salt
- 1 cup whipping cream, whipped
  Green food coloring

Drain pineapple, reserving syrup. Soften gelatin in syrup. Add jelly and salt; heat, stirring constantly, till gelatin dissolves and jelly melts. (If necessary, beat to blend in jelly.) Add pineapple. Chill till mixture is thick and syrupy. Fold in whipped cream. Tint with few drops food coloring. Freeze firm in 1-quart refrigerator tray, 6 hours or overnight. Cut in 1-inch cubes, or slice. Serve with fruit. Makes 8 to 10 servings.

Fluffy Pineapple-Cheese Salad

- 1 1-pound 4½-ounce can (2½ cups) pineapple chunks
- 2 8-ounce cartons (2 cups) cream-style cottage cheese
- 2 cups miniature marshmallows
- 1 tablespoon lemon juice
- ½ cup pitted dates, cut up
  Lettuce
  Whole pitted dates

Drain pineapple, reserving ¼ cup syrup. Combine reserved syrup, cottage cheese, marshmallows, lemon juice, and cut-up dates. Serve on crisp lettuce and frame with pineapple chunks. Top each serving with whole pitted dates. Makes 6 servings.

Or center a fresh-fruit tray with this salad mixture. Omit the whole dates and sprinkle the pineapple chunks over.

Fruit-and-Cheese Ring

- 1 1-pound 4½-ounce can (2½ cups) crushed pineapple
- 1 3-ounce package lemon-flavored gelatin
- 1 cup boiling water
- ½ cup mayonnaise or salad dressing
- 1 5-ounce jar pimento-cheese spread
- 1 cup grated carrots

Drain pineapple, reserving ¾ cup syrup. Dissolve gelatin in boiling water. Add mayonnaise and pimento cheese; beat smooth with electric or rotary beater. Stir in reserved pineapple juice. Chill till partially set. Fold in carrots and pineapple. Turn into a 5½-cup ring mold. Chill till firm. Unmold. Fill with grapes or other fruit. Makes 6 servings.

Red Raspberry Ring

- 1 10-ounce package frozen red raspberries, thawed
- 2 3-ounce packages raspberry-flavored gelatin
- 2 cups boiling water
- 1 pint vanilla ice cream
- 1 6-ounce can (¾ cup) frozen pink lemonade concentrate, thawed
- ¼ cup chopped pecans

Drain raspberries, reserving syrup. Dissolve gelatin in boiling water. Add ice cream by spoonfuls, stirring till melted. Stir in lemonade concentrate and reserved syrup. Chill till partially set. Add raspberries and pecans. Turn into a 6-cup ring mold. Chill till firm. Makes 8 to 10 servings.

Strawberry-Pineapple Freeze

- 1 8¾-ounce can (1 cup) crushed pineapple, drained
- 1 cup strawberries, crushed
- ⅓ cup sugar
- 1 8-ounce carton (1 cup) cream-style cottage cheese
- 2 teaspoons lemon juice
- ½ cup whipping cream, whipped

Combine pineapple, strawberries, and sugar; mix well. Combine cottage cheese and lemon juice; beat smooth with rotary or electric beater. Fold in whipped cream and fruit mixture. Turn into 1-quart refrigerator tray; freeze firm, about 2 hours. To serve, let stand at room temperature 15 minutes. Cut in squares. Makes 5 or 6 servings.

Macaroni-and-Cheese Salad

- ¾ cup elbow macaroni, cooked, drained, and cooled
- 1 12-ounce can chopped ham, cut in strips
- 1 cup cubed sharp Cheddar cheese
- ½ cup bias-cut celery slices
- ⅓ cup chopped green pepper
- ¼ cup sliced green onions and tops
- 2 tablespoons chopped canned pimiento
- ¼ cup drained pickle relish
- ½ cup mayonnaise
- 1 tablespoon prepared mustard
- ¼ teaspoon salt

Combine first 8 ingredients. Blend mayonnaise, mustard, and salt; add; toss lightly. Chill. Serve on greens. Serves 6.

Ham Salad

- 1½ cups diced cooked or canned ham
- 6 hard-cooked eggs, coarsely diced
- ½ cup diced celery
- ½ cup sliced sweet pickles
- ⅓ cup mayonnaise or salad dressing
- 2 tablespoons prepared mustard
- 1 tablespoon lemon juice
- Salt and pepper

Combine ham, eggs, celery, and sweet pickles. Blend mayonnaise, mustard, and lemon juice; add to ham mixture, and toss lightly. Season to taste with salt and pepper. Chill. Makes 6 servings.

Chicken and Ham in Tomatoes

- 2 cups diced cooked or canned chicken
- 1 cup diced cooked or canned ham
- 1 tablespoon finely chopped onion
- ¼ cup clear French dressing
- ½ cup mayonnaise or salad dressing
- 1 tablespoon prepared mustard
- ½ cup diced celery
- 6 medium tomatoes, chilled

Combine chicken, ham, onion, and French dressing; cover

and chill at least 1 hour. Mix mayonnaise and mustard; add with celery to salad; toss lightly. Season to taste with salt and pepper. Place tomatoes stem end down and cut each, *not quite through*, in 6 wedges. Spread tomato wedges apart; sprinkle with salt, fill with salad. Top with parsley or ripe olives. Serve on lettuce. Makes 6 servings.

Party Chicken Salad

- 1 envelope (1 tablespoon) unflavored gelatin
- 1 14-ounce can (1¾ cups) chicken broth
- 1 cup dairy sour cream
- 1 teaspoon grated onion
- ¼ teaspoon salt
  Dash pepper
- 1 cup diced cooked or canned chicken
- ¼ cup chopped stuffed green olives
- ¼ cup chopped celery

Soften gelatin in 1 *cup* chicken broth; heat and stir till gelatin dissolves. Add remaining broth. Beat in sour cream till smooth. Add onion, salt, and pepper. Chill till partially set; add chicken, olives, and celery. Turn into a 3½-cup mold. Chill till firm. Makes 4 to 6 servings.

Fruited Chicken Salad

- 3 cups diced cooked or canned chicken
- 1 cup diced celery
- 1 cup orange sections
- 1 8¾-ounce can (1 cup) pineapple tidbits, drained
- ½ cup slivered almonds, toasted
- 2 tablespoons salad oil
- 2 tablespoons orange juice
- 2 tablespoons vinegar
- ½ teaspoon salt
  Dash marjoram
- ½ cup mayonnaise or salad dressing

Combine first 5 ingredients. Blend salad oil, orange juice, vinegar, and seasonings. Add to chicken mixture. Chill 1 hour. Drain. Add mayonnaise; toss. Makes 8 to 10 servings.

Salami-Swiss Cheese Salad

- 1 head lettuce
- ¼ pound salami, cubed
- 4 ounces Swiss cheese, cut in strips
- ½ cup sliced ripe olives
- 1 4-ounce can (½ cup) chopped pimiento
- 2 tomatoes, cut in eighths
- 1 2-ounce can (3 tablespoons) anchovies, chopped
- ⅓ cup salad oil
- 3 tablespoons wine vinegar
- ½ teaspoon salt
- Dash pepper
- 1 clove garlic, minced

Break lettuce in bite-size chunks. Add salami, cheese, olives, pimiento, tomatoes, and anchovies. In jar, combine oil, vinegar, salt, pepper, and garlic for dressing. Shake well. Pour dressing over vegetables and toss lightly. Makes 8 to 10 servings.

Egg Salad

- 6 hard-cooked eggs, chopped
- ¼ cup chopped green pepper
- ¼ cup sliced green onions
- ¼ cup chopped ripe olives
- ⅓ cup mayonnaise or salad dressing

Combine first 4 ingredients. Blend mayonnaise with ½ *teaspoon salt* and *dash pepper*; add; toss lightly; chill. Makes 6 servings.

Use for stuffed tomatoes; *or* nest in lettuce—with ham, cucumber slices, olives.

Old-time Egg Salad   Break ½ small head lettuce and ½ bunch leaf lettuce in bite-size pieces in bowl. Top with 6 hard-cooked eggs, sliced, and 1 onion, sliced thin and separated in rings. Sprinkle with ½ cup shredded sharp process cheese; dash with paprika. Pour on VINEGAR OIL DRESSING: Combine ½ cup salad oil, 4 tablespoons vinegar, 2 teaspoons Worcestershire, 2 tablespoons minced parsley, ½ teaspoon salt, and ¼ teaspoon pepper. Toss lightly. Serves 8.

Shrimp Luncheon Molds

- 1 envelope (1 tablespoon) unflavored gelatin
- ⅔ cup cold water
- 1 cup dairy sour cream
- ¼ cup chili sauce
- ½ teaspoon salt
- ⅓ cup frozen lemonade concentrate, thawed
- 1 cup cleaned cooked or canned shrimp, cut up
- ½ cup diced celery
- ¼ cup diced green pepper

Soften gelatin in cold water. Heat and stir till gelatin dissolves. Beat in sour cream till smooth. Add chili sauce and salt. Stir in concentrate. Chill till partially set; add remaining ingredients. Pour into 5 or 6 individual molds or a 3½-cup mold. Chill till firm. Unmold on lettuce.

Crab Louis

- 1 cup mayonnaise or salad dressing
- ¼ cup whipping cream, whipped
- ¼ cup chili sauce
- ¼ cup chopped green pepper
- ¼ cup chopped green onion and tops
- 1 teaspoon lemon juice
- 1 large head lettuce
- 2 to 3 cups cooked crab meat, or 2 6½-ounce cans, chilled
- 2 large tomatoes, cut in wedges
- 2 hard-cooked eggs, cut in wedges

Combine mayonnaise, whipped cream, chili sauce, green pepper, green onion, and lemon juice. Salt to taste. Chill. Makes 2 cups of Louis Dressing. Line four large plates with lettuce leaves. Shred rest of lettuce, arrange on leaves. Remove bits of shell from crab meat. Reserve claw meat; leave remainder in chunks and arrange atop lettuce. Circle with wedges of tomato and egg. Sprinkle with salt. Pour ¼ cup Louis Dressing over each salad. Sprinkle with paprika. Top with claw meat. Pass remaining dressing. Makes 4 servings.

Luncheon Tuna Ring

- 1 envelope (1 tablespoon) unflavored gelatin
- ½ cup cold water
- 1 tablespoon sugar
- ½ teaspoon salt
- ¼ teaspoon paprika
- 1 teaspoon prepared mustard
- 2 beaten eggs
- 1 cup light cream
- ¼ cup lemon juice
- 1 6½- or 7-ounce can tuna, drained
- ½ cup chopped celery
- ¼ cup chopped stuffed green olives

Soften gelatin in cold water. In top of double boiler, combine seasonings, eggs, and cream; cook and stir over *hot, not boiling*, water till mixture thickens. Remove from heat; add gelatin, stirring to dissolve. Chill till partially set. Sprinkle *1 tablespoon* of the lemon juice over tuna; toss lightly. Fold tuna, celery, olives, and remaining lemon juice into gelatin mixture. Pour into a 3-cup ring mold. Chill till firm; unmold. Makes 4 or 5 servings.

French Dressing

- ½ cup salad oil
- 2 tablespoons vinegar
- 2 tablespoons lemon juice
- 1 teaspoon sugar
- ½ teaspoon salt
- ½ teaspoon dry mustard
- ½ teaspoon paprika
- Dash cayenne

Put ingredients in jar; cover and shake well before using. Makes ¾ cup.

Blue-cheese French Dressing Add 2 ounces blue cheese, crumbled (½ cup), to recipe above.

Garlic French Dressing Add ¼ teaspoon garlic powder with dry ingredients to recipe above.

Italian Dressing

- 1 cup salad oil
- ¼ cup vinegar
- 1 teaspoon salt
- ½ teaspoon white pepper
- ½ teaspoon celery salt
- ¼ teaspoon cayenne
- ¼ teaspoon dry mustard
- 1 clove garlic, minced
- Dash bottled hot pepper sauce

Combine ingredients in jar; cover and shake.

Thousand Island Dressing

To 1 cup mayonnaise or salad dressing, add ¼ cup chili sauce; 2 hard-cooked eggs, chopped or sieved; 2 tablespoons chopped green pepper; 2 tablespoons chopped celery; 1½ tablespoons finely chopped onion; 1 teaspoon paprika; and ½ teaspoon salt. Mix well. Makes 1½ cups dressing.

Sour Cream Special

- 1 cup dairy sour cream
- ½ cup finely chopped, well-drained cucumber
- ¼ cup finely chopped green onions
- ¼ cup finely chopped radishes
- 1 tablespoon tarragon vinegar
- 1 to 1½ teaspoons prepared horseradish
- ¾ teaspoon salt

Combine ingredients; chill. Makes about 1⅓ cups. Use as a dip for cucumber and celery sticks, or dressing for lettuce wedges. Top with extra horseradish, if desired.

Celery-seed Dressing

½ cup sugar
1 teaspoon celery seed
1 teaspoon salt
1 teaspoon dry mustard
1 teaspoon paprika
⅓ cup lemon juice
¾ cup salad oil

Combine all ingredients except salad oil. Gradually add salad oil, beating with an electric or rotary beater until thick. Makes about 1½ cups.

Nippy Nectar Dressing

1 3-ounce package cream cheese
2 tablespoons honey
1 teaspoon grated lemon peel
2 tablespoons lemon juice
½ teaspoon salt
Dash cayenne
½ cup salad oil

Soften cream cheese. Blend in remaining ingredients except salad oil. Add oil 1 tablespoon at a time, beating well after each addition. Chill. Beat again before serving over fruit salad. Makes 1 cup.

Glossy Fruit Dressing

½ cup sugar
1 teaspoon salt
1 teaspoon celery salt
1 teaspoon paprika
1 teaspoon dry mustard
1 teaspoon grated onion
1 cup salad oil
¼ cup vinegar

Mix dry ingredients; add onion. Add oil, a little at a time, alternately with vinegar, ending with vinegar. Beat with fork till well blended. Makes 1½ cups.

SECTION 4
Desserts

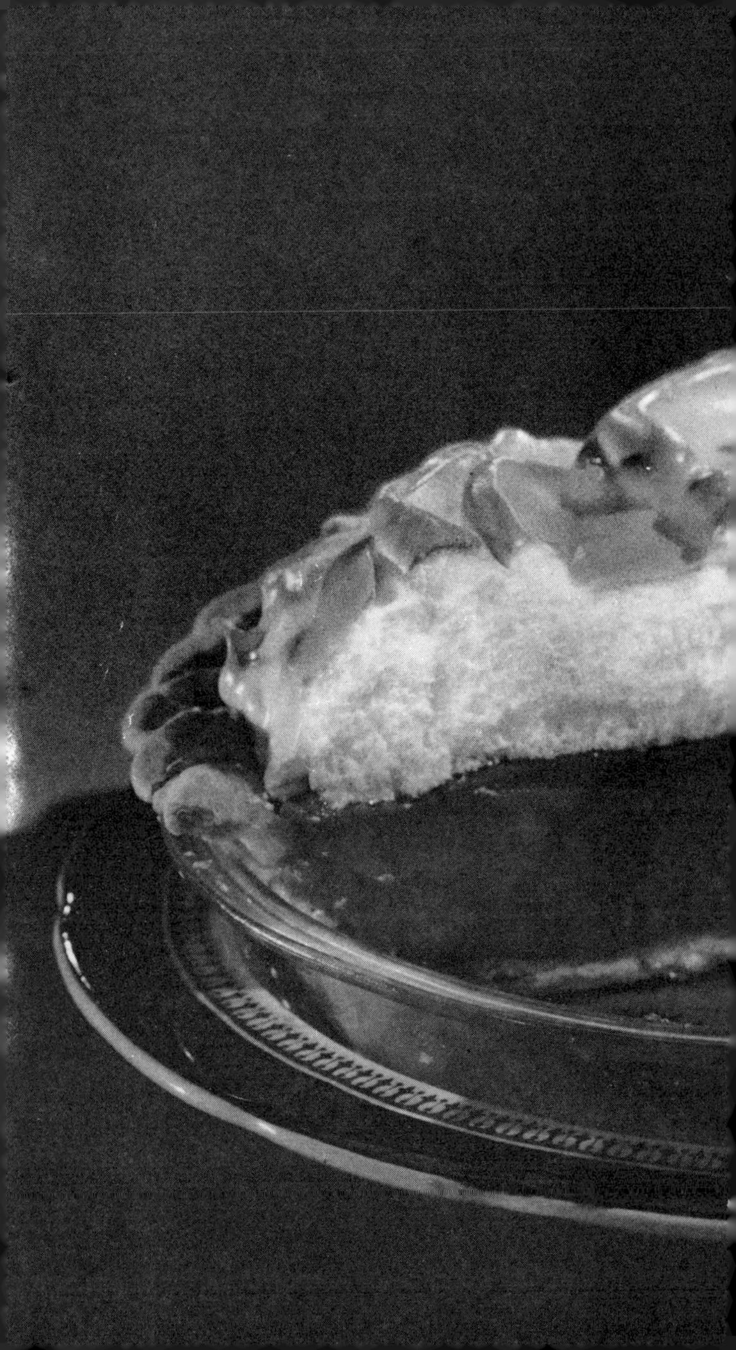

SECTION 4

Desserts

128 • CAKES

Baked Alaska

Trim a ¾-inch layer of sponge or layer cake 1 inch larger on all sides than a 1-quart brick of ice cream. Place on a wooden cutting board or a cooky sheet.

Keep ice cream in freezing compartment till just ready to use. Make MERINGUE: Beat 5 egg whites till soft peaks form. Gradually add ⅔ cup sugar, beating to stiff peaks. Center the brick of ice cream on the cake. (A strip of paper under cake will help you slip dessert onto plate later.)

Spread meringue over ice cream and cake, sealing carefully to edges of cake. Sprinkle with granulated sugar. Bake in extremely hot oven (500°) till golden, about 3 minutes. If desired, assemble Alaska ahead; freeze; then brown just before serving.

Melba Alaska

    1 pint vanilla ice cream
    1 pint raspberry sherbet
    1 9-inch round layer yellow
      cake

    Meringue
    1 1-pound can sliced peaches

Line 8-inch round cake pan with aluminum foil. Stir ice cream to soften slightly; pack in bottom of pan. On top, pack sherbet. Cover with foil; flatten top by smoothing with hands. Freeze *firm*. Place cake on cooky sheet or wooden cutting board. Prepare MERINGUE: Beat 4 egg whites, ½ teaspoon vanilla, and ¼ teaspoon cream of tartar till soft peaks form. Gradually add ½ cup sugar beating till stiff peaks form. Remove foil from ice cream; invert on cake. Remove pan; peel off foil. Completely cover dessert with meringue, sealing carefully to edges of cake. Sift confectioners' sugar over top of meringue. Bake at once or freeze till just before serving time. Bake in extremely hot oven (500°) about 3 minutes or till browned. Drain peaches. Trim Alaska; serve at once with remaining peaches. Makes 8 servings.

Ribbon Alaska Pie

    2 tablespoons butter
    2 1-ounce squares unsweetened
      chocolate
    1 cup sugar
    1 6-ounce can (⅔ cup)
      evaporated milk
    1 teaspoon vanilla

    2 pints vanilla ice cream,
      softened
    1 9-inch baked pastry shell
      Meringue
    ¼ cup crushed peppermint-
      stick candy

Make FUDGE SAUCE: Mix butter, chocolate, sugar, and evaporated milk in saucepan; cook and stir over medium heat till thick and blended. Remove from heat. Add vanilla. Cool thoroughly. Spread 1 *pint* ice cream in pastry shell; cover with *half* the cooled Fudge Sauce; freeze. Repeat layers; freeze *firm*. Prepare MERINGUE as for pie, using 3 egg whites. Reserve 2 teaspoons candy; fold remainder into meringue; spread over pie, sealing to edges. Top with candy. Bake at 475° about 3 to 4 minutes or till lightly browned. Serve at once or freeze.

130 • CAKES

Spiced Chocolate Cake

Melt four 1-ounce squares unsweetened chocolate; set aside to cool. Stir ⅔ cup shortening to soften. Sift in 2 cups sifted all-purpose flour, 2 cups sugar, 1 teaspoon *each* baking powder, soda, salt, cloves, cinnamon, and instant coffee powder. Add 1 cup buttermilk; mix till flour is dampened. Beat vigorously 2 minutes. Stir in ½ cup more buttermilk, 3 eggs, the chocolate, and 1 teaspoon vanilla. Beat 2 minutes longer. Bake in greased and floured 13x9x2-inch baking dish in 350° oven 40 minutes or till done. Cool. Frost with 7-minute frosting.

Rum Royale Cake

- 3 eggs
- 1 cup sugar
- 1 teaspoon rum flavoring
- 1 cup sifted all-purpose flour
- ¼ teaspoon salt
- 1 teaspoon baking powder
- 1 7½-ounce package chocolate frosting mix
- 1 cup whipping cream
- 1 teaspoon rum flavoring

Beat eggs till thick and lemon-colored; gradually beat in sugar. Blend in ¼ cup lukewarm water and 1 teaspoon flavoring. Sift together flour, salt, and baking powder; add to egg mixture; beat well. Pour into ungreased 9-inch tube pan. Bake at 350° 35 to 40 minutes. Invert; cool. Combine last 3 ingredients; beat till fluffy. Split cake in 2 layers. Spread ⅓ of frosting between layers and remaining on sides and top.

Butterscotch Upside-down Cake

BUTTERSCOTCH TOPPING: Mix ⅓ cup melted butter or margarine, 1 cup graham-cracker crumbs, one 6-ounce package (1 cup) miniature butterscotch or caramel pieces, ½ cup flaked coconut, ½ cup chopped walnuts, and dash salt; spread over bottom of buttered 13x9x2-inch baking dish. CAKE: Stir ½ cup shortening to soften. Gradually add 1½ cups sugar, creaming fluffy. Add 1 teaspoon vanilla. Add 3 eggs, 1 at a time, beating well after each. Sift 2 cups sifted all-purpose flour with 2½ teaspoons baking powder, and 1 teaspoon salt; add to creamed mixture alternately with 1 cup milk, beginning and ending with flour, and beating well after each addition. Beat 1 minute longer; pour over Topping. Bake in 350° oven 30 minutes or till done. Cut in squares. Serve warm, upside down.

Angel Cheesecake

- 1 cup zwieback crumbs
- 2 tablespoons sugar
- 2 tablespoons melted butter or margarine
- ½ cup sugar
- 1 teaspoon grated lemon peel
- 1 tablespoon lemon juice
- 1 teaspoon vanilla
- ¼ teaspoon salt
- 2 8-ounce packages cream cheese, softened
- 5 egg yolks
- 2 cups dairy sour cream
- 5 egg whites
- ½ cup sugar
- 1 recipe Raspberry Glaze

CRUST: Mix crumbs, 2 tablespoons sugar, and butter; press on bottom of ungreased 9-inch spring-form pan. FILLING: Beat next 5 ingredients into cheese. Blend in yolks, then sour cream. Beat whites to soft peaks; gradually add ½ cup sugar, beating to stiff peaks. Fold whites into cheese mixture. Gently pour into pan. Bake in slow oven (325°) 1¼ hours or till done. Cool about 10 minutes; run spatula around edge to loosen. Then cool thoroughly before removing sides of pan. Top with RASPBERRY GLAZE: Thaw one 10-ounce package frozen red raspberries; drain, reserving syrup. Add water to syrup to make 1 cup; blend in 4 teaspoons cornstarch and dash salt. Cook and stir till mixture thickens. Add raspberries; cool. Chill glazed cheesecake, if desired.

Tropical Cheesecake

- ½ cup graham-cracker crumbs
- 2 tablespoons butter or margarine, melted
- 1 8-ounce package cream cheese, softened
- ½ cup sifted confectioners' sugar
- 1 1-pound 4½-ounce can (2½ cups) crushed pineapple, well drained
- 1 2-ounce package dessert-topping mix

Mix crumbs and butter; reserving 2 tablespoons, press on bottom of 8-inch round cake pan; chill. Whip cream cheese and confectioners' sugar till fluffy; stir in pineapple. Prepare topping according to package directions; fold into pineapple mixture. Spread over crust. Sprinkle with reserved crumbs; chill well. Makes 6 to 8 servings.

Pudding-and-Pineapple Cake

GRAHAM CRUST: Combine 1¼ cups fine graham-cracker crumbs, 2 tablespoons sugar, and ⅓ cup melted butter or margarine; press onto bottom and sides of 11x7x1½-inch baking pan. PINEAPPLE FILLING: Drain 1 12-ounce carton (1½ cups) cream-style cottage cheese, reserving liquid; add milk to liquid to measure 2¼ cups. Beat the cheese till fluffy. In saucepan, mix 1 package lemon pudding-and-pie filling and 1 envelope (1 tablespoon) unflavored gelatin. Prepare according to *label directions for pie filling*, using the 2¼ cups milk instead of water. Stir in one 8¾-ounce can (1 cup) crushed pineapple (with syrup) and the cheese. Beat 2 egg whites to soft peaks. Gradually add ¼ cup sugar, beating to stiff peaks; fold into pudding. Pour into crust. Chill till set. Cut in 10 or 12 squares; trim with strawberries.

Strawberry Meringue Cake

1 package 2-layer-size yellow-cake mix	4 egg whites
1⅓ cups orange juice	¼ teaspoon cream of tartar
4 egg yolks	1 cup sugar
1½ teaspoons grated orange peel	1 pint fresh strawberries
	2 tablespoons sugar
	1 cup whipping cream

Combine first 4 ingredients; beat 4 minutes at medium speed on electric mixer. Pour into 2 greased and floured 9x1½-inch round cake pans. Beat egg whites with cream of tartar to soft peaks; gradually add the 1 cup sugar, beating to stiff peaks. Spread meringue evenly over batter. Bake at 350° for 35 minutes; cool. Remove from pans, meringue side up. Mash ½ cup strawberries with 2 tablespoons sugar; add cream; whip till stiff. *To assemble:* spread ⅔ of cream mixture over bottom meringue. Reserving a few whole berries, slice remainder and place over cream mixture. Add top layer; garnish with remaining cream mixture and reserved berries.

Easy Daffodil Cake

1 package angel-cake mix	1 cup sugar
¼ teaspoon yellow food coloring	¼ teaspoon cream of tartar
1 teaspoon water	Dash salt
2 egg whites	1 cup miniature marshmallows
2 tablespoons lemon juice	½ teaspoon grated lemon peel

Prepare cake mix according to package directions: Divide batter in half. Combine coloring and water; fold into half the batter. Spoon batters alternately into ungreased 10-inch tube pan. Bake as directed on package. Invert; cool. Frost with LEMON FROSTING: Combine next 5 ingredients in top of double boiler; beat 1 minute with electric or rotary beater. Cook over boiling water, beating till stiff peaks form. Fold in marshmallows and peel.

Pineapple Topper

- ¼ cup butter or margarine
- 1 cup brown sugar
- 1 3½-ounce can (1⅓ cups) flaked coconut
- ½ cup chopped California walnuts
- 1 8¾-ounce can (1 cup) crushed pineapple, drained

Melt butter; blend in remaining ingredients. Spread on hot or cool 13x9-inch cake. Broil about 3 inches from the heat for 2 minutes or till frosting is bubbly and browned.

Peanut Cake Quick

1 package 1-layer-size
   yellow-cake mix
¼ cup peanut butter
¼ cup light cream
1 cup brown sugar
½ cup flaked coconut

Prepare and bake batter from cake mix according to package directions. Blend peanut butter, cream, and brown sugar; spread over warm cake. Sprinkle with coconut. Broil 4 to 5 inches from heat about 4 minutes or till frosting is lightly browned.

Marmalade Upside-down Cake

¼ cup butter or margarine
½ cup brown sugar
   Walnut halves
   Pitted dates, halved
¼ cup chopped California
   walnuts
½ cup sliced pitted dates
½ cup orange juice
1 package 1-layer-size
   yellow-cake mix
2 teaspoons grated orange peel

Melt butter in a 9x1½-inch round pan. Blend in sugar, spreading mixture evenly over bottom. Arrange walnut and date halves in center; sprinkle chopped walnuts and sliced dates around edge. Pour orange juice over all. Prepare cake mix according to package directions; stir in orange peel. Carefully spoon over date-nut mixture. Bake in moderate oven (350°) 40 minutes or till done. Cool slightly; invert on plate. Serve with whipped cream.

Pineapple Crunch Cake

- 1 8¾-ounce can (1 cup) crushed pineapple
- ⅓ cup shortening
- ½ cup sugar
- 1 teaspoon vanilla
- 1 egg
- 1¼ cups sifted all-purpose flour
- 1½ teaspoons baking powder
- ¼ teaspoon salt
- 1 recipe Coconut Topper
- 3 tablespoons melted butter or margarine

Drain pineapple *well*, reserving ½ cup syrup. Thoroughly cream shortening, sugar, and vanilla. Add egg; beat well. Sift together dry ingredients; add to creamed mixture alternately with reserved syrup, beating after each addition. Pour *half* of the batter into greased and floured 8¼x1¾-inch round ovenware cake dish; spoon pineapple over. Cover with remaining batter, then Coconut Topper. Drizzle all with butter. Bake in moderate oven (350°) about 35 minutes or till done. Top with pineapple chunks. Serve warm with whipped cream.
COCONUT TOPPER: Mix ½ cup flaked coconut, ⅓ cup brown sugar, ⅓ cup chopped walnuts.

Vanilla Wafer Coconut Cake

- ½ cup butter or margarine
- 1 cup sugar
- 1½ cups vanilla-wafer crumbs
- ½ teaspoon baking powder
- 3 eggs
- 1 cup chopped pecans
- 1 3½-ounce can (1⅓ cups) flaked coconut

Cream butter and sugar till fluffy. Blend in next 2 ingredients. Beat in eggs, one at a time. Stir in pecans and coconut. Turn into greased and floured 9x1½-inch round baking pan. Bake at 325° 40 minutes; cool. Cut in 6 to 8 wedges.

Banana Cream Cake

- ½ cup shortening
- 2 cups sifted all-purpose flour
- 1⅓ cups granulated sugar
- 1½ teaspoons baking powder
- 1 teaspoon soda
- 1 teaspoon salt
- ½ teaspoon nutmeg
- 1 cup mashed **ripe** banana
- ¼ cup milk
- 1 teaspoon vanilla
- 2 eggs
- ½ cup finely chopped California walnuts
- 1 cup dairy sour cream
- ⅓ cup brown sugar
- ¼ cup broken California walnuts

Stir shortening just to soften. Sift in dry ingredients. Add banana, milk, and vanilla. Mix till all flour is dampened. Then beat vigorously 2 minutes. Add eggs and beat 2 minutes longer. Stir in finely chopped nuts. Bake in a greased and floured 12x7½x2-inch baking dish in moderate oven (325°) 30 to 35 minutes or till done. For SOUR-CREAM FROSTING: Mix sour cream and brown sugar; spread over warm cake in pan. Sprinkle with broken nuts. Bake 2 minutes longer or till frosting is set. Cut cake in squares; trim with sliced bananas.

Frosty Ribbon Loaf

- 1 3-ounce package cream cheese, softened
- ¼ cup sugar
- 1 cup whipping cream, whipped
- 1 1-pound can (2 cups) whole-cranberry sauce
- ½-inch-thick slices angel cake

Combine softened cheese, sugar, and dash salt; beat fluffy; fold in whipped cream. Break up cranberry sauce with a spoon; fold into cream mixture. Spoon *half* this mixture over bottom of 8½x4½x2½-inch loaf dish. Arrange cake slices, in a single layer, over cranberry mixture (trim cake, if necessary, to fit pan). Repeat layers once. Freeze firm, about 8 hours. Slice. Makes 8 servings.

Prune Spice Cake

- ½ pound (1½ cups) dried prunes
- 2 cups sifted all-purpose flour
- 1½ cups sugar
- 1¼ teaspoons soda
- 1 teaspoon salt
- 1 teaspoon cinnamon
- 1 teaspoon nutmeg
- ¼ to ½ teaspoon cloves
- ½ cup salad oil
- 3 eggs
- 1 recipe Crumb Top
- ½ cup broken California walnuts

Cover prunes with water. Cover and simmer 20 minutes or till tender. (Do not sweeten.) Drain, reserving *⅔ cup of the liquid* (add water, if necessary.) Pit and chop prunes. Sift together dry ingredients; add reserved prune liquid and the salad oil. Mix to blend. Beat vigorously 2 minutes. Add eggs; beat 1 minute longer. Stir in prunes. Pour into greased and floured 13x9x2-inch baking dish. Sprinkle with Crumb Top, then nuts. Bake in moderate oven (350°) 35 minutes or till done. Serve warm. CRUMB TOP: Mix ½ cup sugar and 2 tablespoons all-purpose flour; cut in 2 tablespoons butter till crumbly.

Caramel Ginger Cake

Cream ½ cup butter or margarine. Gradually add 1½ cups brown sugar, creaming well. Add 1 teaspoon vanilla. Add 2 eggs, 1 at a time, beating well after each. Sift 2½ cups sifted all-purpose flour with 2 teaspoons baking powder, 1 teaspoon salt, 1 teaspoon ground ginger, ¼ teaspoon soda; add to creamed mixture alternately with 1½ cups milk, beginning and ending with flour, and beating well after each addition. Bake in greased and floured 13x9x2-inch pan in 350° oven 35 to 40 minutes or till done. Cool thoroughly. Frost with

TUTTI-FRUTTI FROSTING: In double boiler, combine 1 egg white, ¾ cup sugar, 1 teaspoon light corn syrup, 3 tablespoons cold water, and dash salt. Beat 1 minute with electric or rotary beater to blend. Place over boiling water and cook, beating constantly, till stiff peaks form, *about* 4 minutes. Remove from water; add ½ teaspoon vanilla and 3 drops almond extract; beat to spreading consistency. Fold in ½ cup *each* plumped golden raisins and chopped walnuts, and 1 tablespoon chopped candied ginger.

Butter-nut Cake

- ½ cup chopped almonds
- 1 tablespoon butter
- 2 cups sifted all-purpose flour
- 1 cup sugar
- 2½ teaspoons baking powder
- ½ teaspoon salt
- ⅓ cup **soft** butter
- 1 egg
- 1 cup milk
- ½ teaspoon vanilla
- ½ teaspoon maple flavoring

In skillet, toast almonds in 1 tablespoon butter; set aside. Sift together dry ingredients. Add ⅓ cup soft butter, the egg, milk, and flavorings; mix till all the flour is dampened. Beat vigorously 2 minutes. *Reserve ¼ cup of the toasted almonds* for Frosting; fold remainder into batter. Bake in a greased and floured 9x9x2-inch pan in moderate oven (350°) 30 minutes or till done. Cool thoroughly. Spread top with NUT FROSTING: Cream 3 tablespoons soft butter, ½ teaspoon vanilla, and dash salt. Gradually add 1 cup sifted confectioners' sugar, creaming till fluffy. Add 1 cup sifted confectioners' sugar, and enough milk to make of spreading consistency; beat smooth. Stir in reserved almonds.

Sour Cream Velvet Frosting

- 1 6-ounce package (1 cup) semisweet chocolate pieces
- ¼ cup butter or margarine
- ½ cup dairy sour cream
- 1 teaspoon vanilla
- ¼ teaspoon salt
- 2½ to 2¾ cups sifted confectioners' sugar

Melt chocolate pieces and butter over hot (not boiling) water; remove from hot water and blend in sour cream, vanilla, and salt. Gradually beat in enough confectioners' sugar to make a frosting of spreading consistency. Makes enough frosting for tops and sides of 2 9-inch layers or a 10-inch tube cake.

Creamy Lemon Frosting

- ¼ cup butter or margarine
- ¼ cup hydrogenated vegetable shortening
- 1 egg
- ¼ teaspoon salt
- 3 cups sifted confectioners' sugar
- ¼ cup light corn syrup
- 3 tablespoons lemon juice

Stir butter and shortening to soften; with electric mixer beat in egg and salt. Gradually add confectioners' sugar. Slowly add corn syrup and lemon juice, beating till fluffy. Makes enough frosting for 3 dozen medium cupcakes or 1 10-inch angel cake.

Chocolate Pudding Frosting

- 1 4-ounce package dark chocolate pudding mix
- 1¼ cups milk
- ½ cup butter or margarine
- ½ cup hydrogenated vegetable shortening
- 1 cup sifted confectioners' sugar
- 1 teaspoon vanilla
- ¼ teaspoon salt

Cook pudding according to package directions, *using 1¼ cups milk*. Cover surface of pudding with waxed paper or clear plastic wrap; cool to room temperature. Cream together butter, shortening, and sugar till light and fluffy; stir in vanilla and salt. Gradually beat in chocolate pudding. Makes enough frosting for tops and sides of 2 9-inch layers.

How to Make Perfect Pastry

For one single-crust pie or 4 to 6 tart shells:

1½ cups sifted all-purpose flour
½ teaspoon salt
½ cup shortening
4 to 5 tablespoons cold water

For one 8-, 9-, or 10-inch double-crust or lattice-top pie, two 8-, 9-, or 10-inch single-crust pies, or 6 to 8 tart shells:

2 cups sifted all-purpose flour
1 teaspoon salt
⅔ cup shortening
5 to 7 tablespoons cold water

Sift together flour and salt; cut in shortening with pastry blender or blending fork till pieces are the size of small peas. (For extra tender pastry, cut in *half* the shortening till mixture looks like corn meal. Then cut in remaining till like small peas.) Sprinkle 1 tablespoon water over part of mixture. Gently toss with fork; push to side of bowl. Sprinkle next tablespoon over dry part; mix lightly; push to moistened part at side. Repeat till all is moistened. Form into ball. (For double-crust and lattice-top pies, divide dough for lower and upper crust. Form each portion into ball.) Flatten ball on lightly floured surface. Roll from center to edge till dough is ⅛ inch thick.

To bake single-crust pie shells: Fit pastry into pie plate, trim ½ to 1 inch beyond edge; fold under and flute. Prick bottom and sides well with fork. Bake in a very hot oven (450°) for 10 to 12 minutes or till golden.

For lattice-top pie: Trim lower crust ½ inch beyond edge of pie plate. Roll remaining dough ⅛ inch thick. Cut strips of pastry ½ inch to ¾ inch wide with pastry wheel or knife. Lay strips on filled pie at 1-inch intervals. Fold back alternate strips as you weave cross-strips. Trim lattice even with outer rim of pie plate; fold lower crust over strips. Seal and flute.

For double-crust pie: Trim lower crust even with rim of pie plate. Cut slits in upper crust. Fit loosely over filling; trim ½ inch beyond edge; tuck under edge of lower crust. Flute.

Pumpkin Meringue Pie

- ¾ cup sugar
- 3 tablespoons cornstarch
- ½ teaspoon salt
- 1 teaspoon cinnamon
- ½ teaspoon nutmeg
- ½ teaspoon ginger
- ¼ teaspoon cloves
- 1 cup canned or mashed cooked pumpkin
- 2 cups milk
- 3 slightly beaten egg yolks
- 1 baked 9-inch pastry shell
- 1 recipe Meringue

In saucepan, mix sugar, cornstarch, salt, and spices; gradually stir in pumpkin and milk. Cook and stir till mixture thickens and comes to boiling. Cook 2 minutes longer; remove from heat. Stir small amount hot mixture into egg yolks; return to hot mixture. Cook and stir 2 minutes. Cool to room temperature. Pour into cooled pastry shell. Top with MERINGUE: Beat 3 egg whites with ½ teaspoon vanilla and ¼ teaspoon cream of tartar till soft peaks form. Gradually add 6 tablespoons sugar, beating till stiff peaks form and sugar has dissolved. Spread over filling, *sealing* meringue to edge of pastry. Bake in moderate oven (350°) 12 to 15 minutes. Cool pie thoroughly before cutting.

Banana-Apricot Meringue Pie

- 2 cups snipped dried apricots
- 1½ cups water
- 1¼ cups sugar
- 3 tablespoons all-purpose flour
- ¼ teaspoon salt
- 3 beaten egg yolks
- 2 tablespoons butter or margarine
- 2 medium bananas, sliced (2 cups)
- 1 baked 9-inch pastry shell, cooled
- 3 egg whites
- ½ teaspoon vanilla
- ¼ teaspoon cream of tartar
- 6 tablespoons sugar

Combine apricots and water. Cover; simmer 10 minutes or till tender. Combine the 1¼ cups sugar, the flour, and salt; stir into apricot mixture. Cook till boiling and boil 2 minutes, stirring constantly. Blend some of hot mixture into egg yolks; return to hot mixture. Cook and stir till boiling. Add butter or margarine; cool. Place bananas in bottom of pastry shell; top with apricot filling. Beat egg whites with vanilla and cream of tartar to soft peaks. Gradually add the 6 tablespoons sugar, beating to stiff peaks. Spread meringue over filling, *sealing* to edge of pastry. Bake at 350° for 12 to 15 minutes.

Pineapple Sour-cream Pie

- ¾ cup sugar
- ¼ cup all-purpose flour
- ½ teaspoon salt
- 1 1-pound 4½-ounce can (2½ cups) crushed pineapple (undrained)
- 1 cup dairy sour cream
- 1 tablespoon lemon juice
- 2 slightly beaten egg yolks
- 1 baked 9-inch pastry shell
- 2 egg whites
- ½ teaspoon vanilla
- ¼ teaspoon cream of tartar
- ¼ cup sugar

In saucepan, combine ¾ cup sugar, flour, and salt. Stir in next 3 ingredients. Cook and stir till mixture thickens and comes to boiling; cook 2 minutes. Stir small amount hot mixture into egg yolks;.return to hot mixture, stirring constantly. Cook and stir 2 minutes. Cool to room temperature; spoon into pie shell. Beat egg whites with vanilla and cream of tartar to soft peaks. Gradually add ¼ cup sugar, beating till stiff and glossy; spread atop pie, *sealing* to edge of pastry. Bake at 350° 12 to 15 minutes.

Peach Petal Pie

> 1 1-pound 5-ounce can (2½ cups) peach-pie filling
> About 10 ¼-inch slices refrigerated slice-and-bake sugar cookies

Heat pie filling and pour into 8-inch pie plate. Overlap cooky slices around edge of pie plate. Sprinkle cookies with a mixture of 1 teaspoon sugar and dash cinnamon. Bake in moderate oven (350°) 35 to 40 minutes or till cookies are done. Serve warm in saucedishes with ice cream. Makes 5 servings.
FRESH PEACH FILLING: Mix ¼ cup sugar and 1 tablespoon flour. Add to 2½ cups sliced fresh peaches; mix lightly. Turn into pie plate; continue as above.

Pear-Apple Crumb Pie

> 1 1-pound 13-ounce can (3½ cups) pear halves, drained
> 3 to 4 tart apples
> ⅓ to ½ cup sugar
> 2 tablespoons flour
> ¼ teaspoon salt
> ½ teaspoon cinnamon
> ½ cup raisins
> ½ teaspoon grated lemon peel
> 1 tablespoon lemon juice
> 1 unbaked 9-inch pastry shell
> 2 tablespoons butter or margarine
> Crumb Topper

Slice pears. Pare and dice apples (2 cups). Combine sugar, flour, salt, and cinnamon; mix with fruits, lemon peel and juice. Pile into pastry shell. Dot with butter. Top with CRUMB TOPPER: Combine ¼ cup flour with ½ cup brown sugar and ¼ teaspoon salt. Cut in one 3-ounce package cream cheese (chilled) till crumbly; add ½ cup chopped walnuts and toss; sprinkle over pie. Bake at 450° 10 minutes; cover pie with foil and bake at 350° 40 to 45 minutes more. Serve warm.

Cocoa-crust Lime Pie

Cocoa Crust: Sift together 1 cup sifted all-purpose flour, ¼ cup instant cocoa (dry), and ½ teaspoon salt; cut in ⅓ cup shortening. Combine 3 tablespoons milk and ½ teaspoon vanilla; stir into dry ingredients till mixture is moistened and forms a ball. Roll out between waxed paper (do not add extra flour). Line 9-inch pie plate; flute edge. Prick bottom and sides. Bake at 400° 10 minutes; cool. Filling: Thaw one 6-ounce can frozen limeade concentrate; add 2 juice cans water and 6 drops green food coloring. In saucepan, mix 1¼ cups sugar, ½ cup all-purpose flour, and ¼ teaspoon salt. Slowly stir in limeade. Cook and stir till mixture thickens and boils; cook 2 minutes. Stir a little hot mixture into 3 slightly beaten egg yolks; return to hot mixture. Stir and cook till mixture boils; add 3 tablespoons butter or margarine. Cool; turn into crust. Meringue: Beat 3 egg whites with ½ teaspoon vanilla and ¼ teaspoon cream of tartar to soft peaks. Gradually add 6 tablespoons sugar, beating to stiff peaks. Spread on filling, *sealing* to pastry. Bake pie at 350° 12 to 15 minutes.

Fruit Medley Pie

- ½ cup sugar
- 3 tablespoons quick-cooking tapioca
- Dash salt
- 1 10-ounce package frozen red raspberries, thawed and drained
- 1 1-pound 14-ounce can (3½ cups) fruit cocktail, drained
- 1 ripe banana, sliced
- 1 tablespoon lemon juice
- 1 recipe plain pastry (based on 2 cups flour)

Combine sugar, tapioca, and salt. Mix in fruits and lemon juice. Spoon into a 9-inch pastry-lined pie plate. Adjust top crust; flute edge. Bake at 450° 10 minutes, then at 350° 40 to 45 minutes more. Serve warm.

Christmas Cran-Mince Pie

- 2 cups prepared mincemeat
- ¾ cup canned jellied cranberry sauce
- 1½ cups diced pared tart apples
- ¼ teaspoon grated lemon peel
- 1 tablespoon lemon juice
- 1 recipe plain pastry (based on 2 cups flour)

Combine mincemeat and cranberry sauce. Stir in apples, lemon peel, and juice. Pour into 9-inch pastry-lined pie plate; top with lattice crust. Flute edge. Bake in hot oven (400°) 35 to 40 minutes. Serve warm.

Pumpkin Pecan Pie

- 3 slightly beaten eggs
- 1 cup canned or mashed cooked pumpkin
- 1 cup sugar
- ½ cup dark corn syrup
- 1 teaspoon vanilla
- ½ teaspoon cinnamon
- ¼ teaspoon salt
- 1 unbaked 9-inch pastry shell
- 1 cup chopped pecans

In small mixing bowl, combine eggs, pumpkin, sugar, corn syrup, vanilla, cinnamon, and salt; mix well. Pour into unbaked pastry shell. Top with chopped pecans. Bake in moderate oven (350°) about 40 minutes or till knife inserted halfway between center and edge comes out clean. Chill; serve topped with whipped cream. Makes 1 9-inch pie.

Ambrosia Chiffon Pie

- ½ cup sugar
- ½ teaspoon salt
- 1 envelope (1 tablespoon) unflavored gelatin
- 1 cup orange juice
- 3 slightly beaten egg yolks
- 1 teaspoon shredded orange peel
- ½ teaspoon shredded lemon peel
- 3 egg whites
- ⅓ cup sugar
- 1 cup diced orange sections
- ⅓ cup flaked coconut
- 1 baked 9-inch pastry shell
- 1 cup whipping cream, whipped

In top of double boiler, thoroughly mix ½ cup sugar, the salt, and gelatin; stir in orange juice and egg yolks. Cook and stir over *hot, not boiling*, water till gelatin dissolves and mixture thickens slightly. Stir in peels. Chill, stirring occasionally, till partially set. Beat egg whites till soft peaks form. Gradually add ⅓ cup sugar, beating to stiff peaks. Fold in gelatin mixture, then oranges and coconut. Chill till mixture mounds *slightly* when spooned; pile into cooled pastry shell. Chill till firm. Top with whipped cream and halved orange slices.

Chocolate Dream Pie (Low-Calorie)

COCONUT CRUST: In oven, toast ½ cup flaked coconut. Butter a 9-inch pie plate with ½ teaspoon soft butter. Reserve 2 tablespoons coconut; lightly press remainder *just on sides*

of plate. FILLING: Soften 1 envelope (1 tablespoon) unflavored gelatin in ¼ cup cold water. Into saucepan, measure noncaloric sweetener to equal 3 tablespoons sugar;* and 1¾ cups skim milk, 1 to 2 teaspoons instant coffee powder, and 2 envelopes chocolate-flavored low-calorie pudding. Cook and stir till mixture comes to a boil. Remove from heat. Add gelatin, stirring to dissolve. Chill; beat fluffy. Fold in 2 stiff-beaten egg whites. Pour into crust. Prepare one 2-ounce package dessert-topping mix according to label, *but making it with skim milk and using 1 teaspoon vanilla.* Spread 1 cup of the topping over filling; swirl through. (Save rest for another use.) Sprinkle coconut around edge. Chill. One serving (⅛ of pie): 110 calories.

* Follow label directions for amount.

Blueberry Strata Pie

- 1 1-pound can (2 cups) blueberries
- 1 8¾-ounce can (1 cup) crushed pineapple
- 1 8-ounce package cream cheese, softened
- 3 tablespoons sugar
- 1 tablespoon milk
- ½ teaspoon vanilla
- 1 baked 9-inch pastry shell
- ¼ cup sugar
- 2 tablespoons cornstarch
- ¼ teaspoon salt
- 1 teaspoon lemon juice
- ½ cup whipping cream, whipped

Drain fruits, reserving syrups. Blend cream cheese and next 3 ingredients. Set aside 2 tablespoons pineapple; stir remaining into cheese mixture. Spread over bottom of pastry shell; chill. Blend the ¼ cup sugar, the cornstarch, and salt. Combine reserved syrups; measure 1½ cups; blend into cornstarch mixture. Cook and stir till thickened. Stir in blueberries, lemon juice; cool. Pour over cheese layer; chill. Top with whipped cream, reserved pineapple.

Raspberry Ribbon Pie

- 1 3-ounce package raspberry-flavored gelatin
- ¼ cup sugar
- 1¼ cups boiling water
- 1 10-ounce package frozen red raspberries
- 1 tablespoon lemon juice
- 1 3-ounce package cream cheese, softened
- ⅓ cup sifted confectioners' sugar
- 1 teaspoon vanilla
- Dash salt
- 1 cup whipping cream, whipped
- 1 baked 9-inch pastry shell, cooled

RED LAYERS: Dissolve gelatin and granulated sugar in boiling water. Add frozen berries and lemon juice; stir till berries thaw. Chill till partially set. WHITE LAYERS: Meanwhile blend cheese, confectioners' sugar, vanilla, and salt. Fold in a small amount of whipped cream, then fold in remainder. Spread *half* the white cheese mixture over bottom of pastry shell. Cover with *half* the red gelatin mixture. Repeat layers; chill till set.

Easy Strawberry Frozen Pie

- 1 8-ounce package cream cheese, softened
- 1 cup dairy sour cream
- 2 10-ounce packages frozen sliced strawberries, thawed
- 1 recipe Graham-cracker Crust

Blend cream cheese and sour cream. Reserve ½ cup berries (and syrup); add remaining to cheese mixture. Pour into Graham-cracker Crust. Freeze firm. Remove from freezer 5 minutes before serving. Cut in wedges; spoon reserved berries over. GRAHAM-CRACKER CRUST: Combine 1 cup fine graham-cracker crumbs, 2 tablespoons sugar, and 3 tablespoons melted butter or margarine. Press firmly into unbuttered 9-inch pie plate; chill till firm, about 45 minutes.

Rhubarb-Cherry Pie

3 cups ½-inch slices rhubarb (1 pound)
1 1-pound can (2 cups) pitted tart red cherries, drained
1¼ cups sugar
¼ cup quick-cooking tapioca
5 drops red food coloring
1 recipe plain pastry (based on 2 cups flour)

Combine ingredients, except pastry; let stand 15 minutes. Line 9-inch pie plate with pastry; add filling Adjust top crust; flute edge. Bake in 400° oven 40 to 50 minutes. Serve warm.

Citrus Chiffon Tarts

- ⅔ cup sugar
- 1 envelope (1 tablespoon) unflavored gelatin
- ½ teaspoon salt
- 3 slightly beaten egg yolks
- ½ cup fresh lime juice (about 5 limes)
- ¼ cup water
- 1 teaspoon grated lime peel
- 4 drops green food coloring
- ¼ cup light rum
- 3 egg whites
- ⅓ cup sugar
- 6 to 8 baked tart shells

In medium saucepan, combine the ⅔ cup sugar, the gelatin, and salt. Stir in egg yolks; mix well. Add lime juice and water. Cook and stir over medium heat till mixture is boiling and gelatin dissolves. Remove from heat; stir in lime peel and food coloring. Cool to room temperature; stir in rum. Chill till mixture begins to thicken. Beat egg whites to soft peaks. Gradually add the ⅓ cup sugar; beat to stiff peaks. Fold in gelatin mixture. Chill till mixture holds soft mounds. Spoon into baked tart shells. Chill 4 to 6 hours before serving. Garnish with maraschino cherries, if desired. Makes 6 to 8 tarts or 1 9-inch pie.

Glazed Strawberry Tartlets

TART SHELLS: For 12, make pastry based on 3 cups all-purpose flour (or use 3 sticks pastry mix); roll to ⅛ inch. Cut twelve 5-inch circles. Lightly press a pastry round atop same-size circle of heavy-duty foil. Prick pastry with fork. Holding pastry and foil together, flute edges to form tart shells—it will take about 5 crimps. Bake on cooky sheet in very hot oven (450°) 10 minutes or till done. Cool on rack. Remove foil.

FILLING: Gradually add 2 *cups milk* to one 2¼-ounce package custard-flavor dessert mix. Cook and stir over medium heat till mixture comes to a *full* boil and cook 3 minutes. Remove from heat; stir in one 8-ounce package cream cheese, cubed, and ½ teaspoon vanilla, beating smooth with rotary beater. Cool 10 minutes, stirring occasionally. Spoon into tart shells. Chill firm. GLAZE: Crush 1 cup fresh strawberries. Mix ½ cup sugar, 1 tablespoon cornstarch, dash salt, and ¼ cup orange juice; add crushed berries. Cook and stir till mixture thickens and comes to boiling. Sieve and cool. Slice 1 cup berries; arrange atop tarts. Spoon glaze over berries. Chill.

Strawberry-Cheese Tarts

Mix 1¼ cups graham-cracker crumbs, ¼ cup sugar, and ⅓ cup melted butter or margarine. Press into eight 3½-inch tart pans; chill. Sprinkle ¼ cup sugar over 2 cups sliced fresh strawberries; let stand. Drain, *reserving* ¼ cup syrup. Soften ½ envelope (1½ teaspoons) unflavored gelatin in reserved syrup; dissolve over hot water. Beat one 3-ounce package cream cheese with ¼ cup sugar till fluffy; add dissolved gelatin. Have one 6-ounce can (⅔ cup) evaporated milk *chilled icy-cold*. In chilled bowl, whip milk till fluffy; add 2 tablespoons lemon juice and beat to stiff peaks. Fold into cheese mixture; fold in berries. Spoon into tart shells. Chill firm, about 2 hours.

Cran-Apple Tarts

  1 cup cranberries, cut in half
  ½ cup sugar
  1 stick pastry mix
  1 1-pound 5-ounce can (2½ cups) apple-pie filling
  ½ teaspoon vanilla
  2 tablespoons butter or margarine

Mix cranberries and sugar; let stand 1 hour. Prepare pastry according to package directions, roll it to ⅛ inch. Cut in 6 circles, 1 inch larger in diameter than your baking cups. Combine pie filling and vanilla; stir in cranberries. Pour into six 6-ounce custard cups or tart pans. Dot with butter. Top with pastry rounds; crimp edges of pastry to edges of baking cups. Bake in hot oven (425°) about 25 minutes or till done.

Pumpkin Date Torte

½ cup chopped dates
½ cup chopped California walnuts
2 tablespoons all-purpose flour
¼ cup butter or margarine
1 cup brown sugar
⅔ cup canned pumpkin
1 teaspoon vanilla
2 eggs
½ cup sifted all-purpose flour
½ teaspoon baking powder
½ teaspoon cinnamon
½ teaspoon nutmeg
¼ teaspoon ginger
¼ teaspoon baking soda

Mix dates, nuts, and 2 tablespoons flour; set aside. Melt butter over low heat; blend in brown sugar. Remove from heat; stir in pumpkin and vanilla. Beat in eggs, one at a time. Sift together dry ingredients; add to pumpkin mixture, mixing thoroughly. Stir in floured dates and nuts; turn into greased 9x1½-inch round baking pan. Bake in moderate oven (350°) 20 to 25 minutes. Serve warm with whipped cream. Makes 8 servings.

Almond Peach Torte

2½ cups sifted all-purpose flour
½ cup finely chopped toasted almonds
⅓ cup sugar
½ teaspoon salt
¾ cup butter or margarine
2 cups whipping cream
¼ cup sugar
¼ teaspoon almond extract
1 1-pound 13-ounce can (3½ cups) sliced peaches, drained and chilled
1 8¾-ounce can (1 cup) crushed pineapple, drained and chilled
2 tablespoons toasted slivered almonds

Combine first 4 ingredients; cut in butter. Gradually add ⅓ cup cold water; gently toss with fork to moisten. Form dough in ball; divide dough in thirds. Roll each third ⅛ inch thick on an ungreased baking sheet; trim to 8-inch circles. Prick well. Bake at 375° till lightly browned, 10 to 12 minutes; cool. Whip cream with sugar and extract; set aside 1½ cups for frosting. Reserve 6 peach slices; chop remaining and fold, with pineapple, into whipped cream. To assemble, spread half of mixture on one crust, top with second crust, remaining filling and third crust. Frost with reserved whipped cream; garnish with the peach slices and slivered almonds.

Bridge Meringue Torte

6 egg whites
2 teaspoons vanilla
½ teaspoon cream of tartar
Dash salt
2 cups sugar
6 ¾-ounce chocolate-coated English toffee bars, chilled and crushed
Dash salt
2 cups whipping cream, whipped

Have egg whites at room temperature. Add vanilla, cream of tartar, and dash salt; beat to soft peaks. Gradually add sugar, beating to very stiff peaks. Cover 2 cooky sheets with plain ungreased paper. Draw a 9-inch circle on each and spread meringue evenly within circles. Bake in very slow oven (275°) 1 hour. Turn off heat; let dry in oven (door closed) at least

2 hours. Fold crushed candy and dash salt into whipped cream. Spread ⅓ of the whipped cream between the layers; frost top and sides with remainder. Chill 8 hours or overnight. Garnish with additional crushed candy. Makes 16 servings.

Red-letter Day Torte

CRUST: Sift 2 cups sifted all-purpose flour and 1 teaspoon salt; cut in 1 cup shortening. Add 1 slightly beaten egg; stir till a soft dough. Pat over bottom of 11x7x1½-inch baking pan. Bake at 425° about 20 minutes. FILLING: Drain one 1-pound can (2 cups) pitted tart red cherries (water pack), reserving juice. Add water to juice to make 1 cup. Combine juice with ¾ cup sugar, 3 slightly beaten egg yolks, 3 tablespoons quick-cooking tapioca, and ¼ teaspoon red food coloring; let stand 5 minutes. Cook and stir till mixture thickens and comes to boiling. Add cherries and 2 teaspoons lemon juice; cool slightly. MERINGUE: Beat 3 egg whites with 1 teaspoon vanilla, ¼ teaspoon cream of tartar, and dash salt till soft peaks form. Slowly add ¾ cup sugar, beating to stiff peaks. Fold in 1 cup broken walnuts. Pour Filling over baked crust; top with Meringue. Bake in moderate oven (350°) about 20 minutes or till lightly browned. Cool. Cut in 9 or 12 squares.

Peach-a-berry Cobbler

- 1 tablespoon cornstarch
- ¼ cup brown sugar
- ½ cup cold water
- 2 cups sugared sliced fresh peaches*
- 1 cup fresh blueberries*
- 1 tablespoon butter or margarine
- 1 tablespoon lemon juice
- 1 recipe Cobbler Crust
- 1 recipe Nutmeg Topper

Mix first 3 ingredients; add fruits. Cook and stir till mixture thickens. Add butter and lemon juice. Pour into 8¼x1¾-inch round ovenware cake dish. COBBLER CRUST: Sift together 1 cup sifted all-purpose flour, ½ cup granulated sugar, 1½ teaspoons baking powder, ½ teaspoon salt. Add ½ cup milk and ¼ cup soft butter or margarine all at once. Beat smooth. Spread over fruit. Sprinkle with NUTMEG TOPPER: Mix 2 tablespoons sugar and ¼ teaspoon nutmeg. Bake cobbler in moderate oven (350°) 30 minutes or till done. Serve warm with cream. Makes 6 servings.

*Or use canned or frozen fruits. Drain, using ½ cup syrup in place of the water.

Fruit Cocktail Cobbler

- 1 1-pound 13-ounce can (3½ cups) fruit cocktail
- ¼ cup sugar
- 2 tablespoons cornstarch
- ½ teaspoon grated orange peel
- ¾ cup diced orange sections (2 oranges)
- 1 cup packaged biscuit mix
- ⅓ cup light cream
- 1 tablespoon butter or margarine, melted
- 2 teaspoons sugar

Drain fruit cocktail, reserving syrup. Combine the ¼ cup sugar and the cornstarch; add reserved syrup. Cook and stir till thickened. Add fruit cocktail, orange peel, and orange sections; heat till boiling. Pour into 8x8x2-inch baking dish. Combine biscuit mix, cream, and butter; stir just to moisten. Drop by spoonfuls onto hot fruit; sprinkle with the 2 teaspoons sugar. Bake at 400° about 20 minutes, or till biscuits are golden brown. Serve with cream or ice cream. Makes 5 or 6 servings.

Perfect Peach Cobbler

- 3 cups sliced fresh or canned peaches
- 1 tablespoon lemon juice
- 1 cup sifted all-purpose flour
- 1 cup sugar
- ½ teaspoon salt
- 1 beaten egg
- 6 tablespoons butter or margarine, melted
- 1 pint vanilla ice cream, softened
- ¾ teaspoon cinnamon

Place peaches on bottom of 10x6x1½-inch baking dish. Sprinkle with lemon juice. Sift together dry ingredients; add egg, tossing with fork till crumbly. Sprinkle over peaches. Drizzle with butter. Bake at 375° for 35 to 40 minutes. Top with CINNAMON ICE CREAM: Combine vanilla ice cream with cinnamon. Makes 6 servings.

Hawaiian Dazzler

- ½ cup granulated sugar
- ¼ cup brown sugar
- 3 tablespoons cornstarch
- 1 1-pound 14-ounce can (3½ cups) crushed pineapple
- 1 3½-ounce can (1⅓ cups) flaked coconut
- 2 cups sifted all-purpose flour
- 1 teaspoon soda
- 1 teaspoon salt
- ½ cup shortening
- 1 slightly beaten egg
- ⅓ cup granulated sugar
- ½ cup dairy sour cream
- 1 teaspoon vanilla

Combine first 3 ingredients; mix in undrained pineapple. Cook and stir till mixture is thick and boiling; cool. Stir in coconut. Sift together flour, soda, and salt; cut in shortening. Combine remaining ingredients; add to flour mixture; beat thoroughly. Chill about 1 hour. Press ⅔ of dough on bottom and sides of 9x9x2-inch baking dish. Top with pineapple filling. Roll out remaining dough and cut in desired shapes; arrange over filling. Bake at 350° about 30 minutes. Cut in 9 squares. Serve warm.

Deep-dish Grapefruit Dessert

- 1 1-pound can grapefruit sections*
- ½ cup brown sugar*
- 2 tablespoons all-purpose flour
- 2 tablespoons butter or margarine
- 1 cup sifted all-purpose flour
- 1 tablespoon granulated sugar
- 1½ teaspoons baking powder
- ¼ teaspoon salt
- ¼ cup butter or margarine
- 1 egg plus milk to equal ½ cup

Place fruit (with syrup) in 10x6x1½-inch baking dish. Mix brown sugar and 2 tablespoons flour; sprinkle over fruit. Dot with 2 tablespoons butter; heat in 425° oven 15 minutes. Sift together dry ingredients; cut in ¼ cup butter. Stir in egg-milk mixture all at once. Drop 6 biscuits onto hot fruit; dash with cinnamon. Bake in 425° oven 25 to 30 minutes or till biscuits are done. Serve warm with cream. Makes 6 servings.

 * *Or* use 3 cups fresh fruit and ¾ *cup* brown sugar.

Coffee-Crunch Dessert

- 1 cup vanilla-wafer crumbs (24 wafers)
- 2 tablespoons melted butter or margarine
- ½ cup butter or margarine
- 1 cup sifted confectioners' sugar
- 3 egg yolks
- 2 teaspoons instant coffee powder
- 1 1-ounce square unsweetened chocolate, melted and cooled
- ½ teaspoon vanilla
- 3 stiff-beaten egg whites
- 3 ¾-ounce chocolate-coated English toffee bars, chilled and crushed (½ cup)

Blend crumbs and melted butter; press into bottom of 8x8x2-inch baking pan. Cream butter and sugar till fluffy. Blend in next 4 ingredients. Fold in egg whites; spread mixture over crust. Top with crushed candy. Freeze till firm. Makes 6 to 8 servings.

Walnut Crunch Pudding

- 1 cup sugar
- 1 cup chopped California walnuts
- 1 beaten egg
- 1 3¾- or 3⅝-ounce package instant vanilla pudding mix
- 1 cup dairy sour cream
- 1 cup milk
- 2 medium bananas, sliced

Combine sugar, walnuts, and egg. Spread thinly on greased baking sheet. Bake in moderate oven (350°) for 18 to 20 minutes, or till golden brown; cool to room temperature. Crush baked nut mixture; sprinkle half of the crumbs in bottom of 8x8x2-inch baking pan. Combine pudding mix, sour cream, and milk; beat on low speed of electric mixer or with rotary beater 1 to 2 minutes or till well blended. Fold in sliced bananas. Spoon over crumbs in pan; top with remaining crumbs. Chill several hours before serving. Cut in squares; garnish each square with a walnut half. Makes 9 servings.

Hawaiian Fruit Crumble

- 2 cups sliced pared tart apples
- 1 tablespoon lemon juice
- 1 8¾-ounce can (1 cup) crushed pineapple, drained
- 1 1-pound can (2 cups) whole-cranberry sauce
- 1 cup quick-cooking rolled oats
- ¾ cup brown sugar
- ½ cup sifted all-purpose flour
- ½ teaspoon cinnamon
- Dash salt
- ⅓ cup butter or margarine

Toss apple slices with lemon juice; place in 10x6x1½-inch baking dish. Spoon pineapple evenly over apples, then cover with cranberry sauce. For topping, mix next 5 ingredients; cut in butter till crumbly. Sprinkle over fruit. Bake at 350° 30 minutes or till apples are tender. Serve warm. Six servings.

Lemon Tea "Cakes"

1½ teaspoons vinegar	1 teaspoon shredded lemon peel
½ cup milk	1¾ cups sifted all-purpose flour
½ cup butter or margarine	1 teaspoon baking powder
¾ cup sugar	¼ teaspoon soda
1 egg	¼ teaspoon salt

Stir vinegar into milk. Cream butter and ¾ cup sugar till fluffy. Add egg and peel; beat well. Sift together dry ingredients; add to creamed mixture alternately with the milk, beating smooth after each addition. Drop from teaspoon, 2 inches apart, on ungreased baking sheet. Bake in moderate oven (350°) 12 to 14 minutes or till done. Remove at once from pan and immediately brush tops with Lemon Glaze; cool. Makes about 4 dozen. LEMON GLAZE: Mix ¾ cup sugar and ¼ cup lemon juice.

Lemon Crisp

- 6 tablespoons butter or margarine
- ¾ cup brown sugar
- 1 cup sifted all-purpose flour
- ½ teaspoon soda
- ½ teaspoon salt
- ½ cup flaked coconut
- ¾ cup finely crushed saltines (18 crackers)
- ¾ cup granulated sugar
- 2 tablespoons cornstarch
- ¼ teaspoon salt
- 1 cup hot water
- 2 beaten egg yolks
- ½ teaspoon grated lemon peel
- ½ cup lemon juice

Cream butter and brown sugar; stir in next 5 ingredients. Press *half* the mixture into 8x8x2-inch baking pan. Bake at 350° for 10 minutes. Meanwhile, in saucepan, combine granulated sugar, cornstarch, and the ¼ teaspoon salt; gradually stir in water. Cook and stir till mixture is thick and boiling; boil about 2 minutes. Remove from heat; stir small amount of hot mixture into egg yolks; return to remaining mixture in pan. Bring to boiling, stirring constantly; remove from heat. Gradually stir in lemon peel and juice. Pour over baked crumb crust; top with reserved crumbs. Bake at 350° for 30 minutes or till crumbs are lightly browned. Top with whipped cream. Makes 8 servings.

Coconut-Oatmeal Cookies

- 2 cups quick-cooking rolled oats
- ⅔ cup flaked coconut
- 1 cup butter, margarine, or shortening
- 1 cup sugar
- 2 eggs
- 3 tablespoons milk
- 1½ teaspoons vanilla
- 1½ cups sifted all-purpose flour
- ½ teaspoon soda
- ½ teaspoon salt

In oven, toast oats and coconut till golden brown. Thoroughly cream butter and sugar; add eggs, milk, and vanilla, beating well. Sift together dry ingredients; add to creamed mixture, blending well. Stir in oats and coconut. Drop from teaspoon, 2 inches apart, on ungreased baking sheet. Flatten with a tumbler dipped in sugar. If desired, sprinkle tops with untoasted coconut. Bake in a hot oven (400°) 8 to 10 minutes or till lightly browned. Remove at once from pan; cool. Makes 4 dozen.

Chocolate-raisin Drops

Cream ¾ cup butter or margarine and ¾ cup sugar till fluffy. Beat in 1 egg and 1 teaspoon vanilla. Sift together 2 cups sifted all-purpose flour, 1½ teaspoons baking powder, and ½ teaspoon salt; add to creamed mixture alternately with ½ cup milk. Stir in 1½ cups (one 9-ounce package) chocolate-covered raisins and ½ cup chopped California walnuts. Drop from teaspoon, 2 inches apart, on ungreased baking sheet. Bake in hot oven (400°) 10 to 12 minutes or till lightly browned. Remove at once from pan; cool. Makes 4 dozen.

Frosted Cashew Drops

- ½ cup butter or margarine
- 1 cup brown sugar
- 1 egg
- ½ teaspoon vanilla
- 2 cups sifted all-purpose flour
- ¾ teaspoon soda
- ¾ teaspoon baking powder
- ¼ teaspoon salt
- ½ teaspoon cinnamon
- ¼ teaspoon nutmeg
- ⅓ cup dairy sour cream
- 1 cup salted cashew nuts, broken

Cream butter and sugar. Add egg and vanilla; beat well. Sift together dry ingredients; add to creamed mixture, alternately with sour cream. Stir in nuts. Drop from teaspoon, 2 inches apart, on greased baking sheet. Bake in hot oven (400°) 8 to 10 minutes or till lightly browned. Remove at once from pan; cool. Frost with GOLDEN BUTTER ICING: Heat and stir 3 tablespoons butter till browned. Slowly beat in 2 cups sifted confectioners' sugar, 2 tablespoons milk, 1 teaspoon vanilla. Makes 4 dozen.

Butterscotch Meringue Bars

Combine ¼ cup butter or margarine and 1 cup brown sugar; cook and stir over low heat till mixture begins to bubble;

cool. Add 1 egg and ½ teaspoon vanilla; beat well. Sift together ¾ cup sifted all-purpose flour, ½ teaspoon salt, and ¼ teaspoon nutmeg; stir into sugar mixture. Spread in greased 8x8x2-inch baking pan. Beat 1 egg white to soft peaks; gradually add 1 tablespoon light corn syrup. Then gradually add ½ cup granulated sugar, beating to *very stiff peaks*. Fold in ½ cup chopped California walnuts; spread over dough. Bake in moderate oven (350°) about 30 minutes. Cut in bars.

Chocolate-Peanut Bars

½ cup light corn syrup
¼ cup brown sugar
Dash salt
1 cup peanut butter
1 teaspoon vanilla

2 cups crisp rice cereal
1 cup corn flakes, slightly crushed
1 6-ounce package (1 cup) semisweet chocolate pieces

Combine syrup, sugar, and salt in saucepan; bring to a full boil. Stir in peanut butter. Remove from heat. Stir in vanilla, cereals, and chocolate pieces. Press into buttered 9x9x2x-inch pan. Chill about 1 hour. Cut in small bars or squares. (For easy serving, store in refrigerator.) Makes about 2 dozen.

Bran Apricot Squares

- ½ cup dried apricots
- 1 cup water
- 1 recipe Bran Layer
- 2 eggs
- 1 cup brown sugar
- ½ teaspoon vanilla
- ½ cup sifted all-purpose flour
- ½ teaspoon baking powder
- ½ teaspoon salt
- ½ cup chopped California walnuts

Dice apricots; add water; simmer covered 10 minutes; drain. Set aside to cool. Prepare and bake Bran Layer. Meanwhile, beat eggs till thick and lemon colored. Stir in brown sugar and vanilla. Sift together dry ingredients; add to egg mixture. Stir in apricots and walnuts. Pour over the baked Bran Layer. Bake in moderate oven (350°) 25 to 30 minutes or till done. Cool; cut in squares or bars. Makes 1½ dozen. BRAN LAYER: Cream together ½ cup butter or margarine and ¼ cup granulated sugar. Stir in ½ cup sifted all-purpose flour and ¾ cup whole bran. Press over bottom of 9x9x2-inch pan. Bake in 350° oven 15 minutes.

Pineapple-Chocolate Squares

- ¾ cup shortening
- 1½ cups sugar
- 1 teaspoon vanilla
- 3 eggs
- 1 cup sifted all-purpose flour
- 1 teaspoon baking powder
- ½ teaspoon salt
- ½ teaspoon cinnamon
- ¼ cup chopped pecans
- 2 1-ounce squares unsweetened chocolate, melted and cooled
- 1 8¾-ounce can (1 cup) crushed pineapple, well drained

Cream first 3 ingredients till fluffy; beat in eggs. Sift together dry ingredients; stir into creamed mixture. Divide batter; to one half add nuts and chocolate. Spread in greased 9x9x2-inch baking pan. Add pineapple to remaining batter; spread *carefully* over chocolate layer. Bake in 350° oven about 35 minutes. Sprinkle with confectioners' sugar, if desired. Cut in squares.

Apple-Date Squares

- ½ cup shortening
- ¾ cup granulated sugar
- 1 egg
- 1½ cups sifted all-purpose flour
- 1 teaspoon soda
- ¼ teaspoon salt
- 2 cups finely chopped pared tart apples
- 1 8-ounce package (1 cup) pitted dates, cut up
- ¼ cup brown sugar
- 1 teaspoon cinnamon
- ½ cup chopped nuts

Cream together shortening and granulated sugar; add egg and beat well. Sift together flour, soda, and salt; add to creamed mixture and blend. Stir in fruits; spread in a greased 11x7x1½-inch baking dish. Combine brown sugar, cinnamon, and nuts; sprinkle evenly over the apple mixture. Bake in moderate oven (350°) 30 to 35 minutes or till done. Cut in 8 to 12 squares. Serve warm with vanilla ice cream.

Double Chocolate Brownies

- ¼ cup butter or margarine
- ¾ cup sugar
- 1 teaspoon vanilla
- ¼ cup corn syrup
- 2 eggs
- 2 1-ounce squares unsweetened chocolate, melted and cooled
- 1 cup sifted all-purpose flour
- ½ teaspoon salt
- ½ teaspoon baking powder
- ½ 6-ounce package (½ cup) semisweet chocolate pieces
- ½ cup chopped California walnuts

Cream together first 3 ingredients till fluffy; add syrup and continue creaming. Beat in eggs and chocolate. Sift together dry ingredients; stir into batter. Fold in chocolate pieces and walnuts. Spread in greased 9x9x2-inch baking pan; bake in moderate oven (350°) about 25 minutes. Cut in squares or bars.

Chocolate Malt Bars

- 1 1-ounce square unsweetened chocolate
- ½ cup shortening
- ¾ cup sugar
- ½ teaspoon vanilla
- 2 eggs
- 1 cup sifted all-purpose flour
- ½ cup chocolate-flavored malted-milk powder
- ½ teaspoon baking powder
- ½ teaspoon salt
- ½ cup chopped California walnuts

Melt chocolate; cool. Cream together next 3 ingredients till fluffy; beat in eggs. Blend in melted chocolate. Sift together dry ingredients; stir into creamed mixture. Fold in nuts. Spread in greased 8x8x2-inch baking pan. Bake in moderate oven (350°) 20 to 25 minutes; cool. Frost with MALT FROSTING: Cream 2 tablespoons soft butter or margarine, ¼ cup chocolate-flavored malted-milk powder, and dash salt. Slowly beat in 1 cup sifted confectioners' sugar and enough light cream to make of spreading consistency (about 1½ tablespoons). Makes 32 bars.

Holiday Fig Squares

- ½ cup butter or margarine
- 1¾ cups brown sugar
- 4 well-beaten eggs
- 1 teaspoon grated lemon peel
- 1 teaspoon grated orange peel
- 2 cups snipped dried figs or dates
- 1 cup chopped California walnuts
- 1½ cups sifted all-purpose flour
- 1 teaspoon baking powder
- ½ teaspoon salt

Melt butter or margarine; stir in brown sugar. Add eggs; mix well. Stir in lemon and orange peel, *half* the figs and *half* the walnuts. Sift together dry ingredients. Blend into batter. Pour into greased 13x9x2-inch baking pan. Sprinkle with remaining figs and walnuts. Bake in slow oven (325°) 50 to 55 minutes. Cut in squares and serve warm with softened ice cream or CREAMY HARD SAUCE: Thoroughly cream together 4 tablespoons butter or margarine and 2 cups sifted confectioners' sugar. Add 3 tablespoons milk and 1 teaspoon vanilla; mix well. Whip ½ cup whipping cream; fold into creamed mixture. Makes 12 servings.

Frosty Strawberry Squares

- 1 cup sifted all-purpose flour
- ¼ cup brown sugar
- ½ cup chopped California walnuts
- ½ cup butter or margarine, melted
- 2 egg whites
- 1 cup granulated sugar
- 2 cups sliced fresh strawberries*
- 2 tablespoons lemon juice
- 1 cup whipping cream, whipped

Stir together first 4 ingredients; spread evenly in shallow baking pan. Bake in 350° oven 20 minutes, stirring occasionally. Sprinkle ⅔ *of the nut mixture* in 13x9x2-inch baking pan. Combine egg whites, sugar, berries, and lemon juice in large bowl; with electric beater, beat at high speed to stiff peaks, about 10 minutes. Fold in whipped cream. Spoon over nut mixture; top with remaining nut mixture. Freeze 6 hours or overnight. Cut in 10 or 12 squares. Trim with whole strawberries.

* *Or* use 1 10-ounce package frozen berries, partially thawed; reduce granulated sugar to ⅔ cup.

Chocolate Cloud Souffle

- ⅓ cup light cream
- 1 3-ounce package cream cheese
- ½ cup semisweet chocolate pieces
- 3 egg yolks
  Dash salt
- 3 egg whites
- 4 tablespoons sifted confectioners' sugar

Blend cream and cream cheese over very *low* heat. Add chocolate pieces; heat and stir till melted. Cool. Beat egg yolks and salt till thick and lemon-colored. Gradually blend into chocolate mixture. Beat egg whites till soft peaks form. Gradually add sugar, beating to stiff peaks; fold in chocolate mixture. Pour into *ungreased* 1-quart souffle dish or casserole. Bake in slow oven (300°) 50 minutes or till knife inserted comes out clean. Makes 5 or 6 servings.

Golden Souffle

- ½ cup sugar
- 6 slightly beaten egg yolks
- ½ teaspoon grated lemon peel
- 3 tablespoons lemon juice
  Dash salt
- ½ cup butter or margarine
- 6 egg whites

In top of double boiler, combine first 6 ingredients. Cook over hot water; stir constantly till butter melts and sauce *begins* to thicken, 4 to 5 minutes. Cool 15 minutes, beating occasionally with electric or rotary beater. Beat egg whites to stiff peaks; fold in lemon mixture. Transfer to ungreased 1½-quart soufflé dish or casserole; set in shallow pan. Place on oven rack; pour hot water into pan to 1-inch depth. Bake at 325° for 45 to 50 minutes or till knife, inserted halfway between center and edge, comes out clean. Serve at once. Makes 4 to 6 servings.

Swiss Pudding Mold

- ¾ cup sugar
- 1 envelope (1 tablespoon) unflavored gelatin
- Dash salt
- 1¼ cups cold water
- 2 egg whites
- ¼ teaspoon shredded lemon peel
- 2 tablespoons lemon juice
- 1 cup dairy sour cream
- 1 cup whipping cream

Thoroughly mix sugar, gelatin, salt, and cold water. Place over medium heat, stirring constantly, till gelatin dissolves. Chill till partially set. Add egg whites, lemon peel, and juice; beat till fluffy. Chill till partially set. Fold sour cream into gelatin mixture. Whip cream and fold in. Pile into a 6-cup mold or 9 or 10 individual molds. Chill till firm, 6 hours or overnight. Unmold. Serve with sweetened fresh berries, peaches, or other fruit. Makes 9 or 10 servings.

Mocha Mousse

- 1 envelope (1 tablespoon) unflavored gelatin
- 1 10½-ounce jar (1 cup) chocolate-flavored syrup
- 1½ teaspoons instant coffee powder
- 1 cup whipping cream, whipped
- Peppermint stick candy

Soften gelatin in ¼ cup water; set aside. Combine chocolate syrup, coffee powder, and another ¼ cup water in saucepan. Cook over low heat; do not boil. Add softened gelatin, stirring to dissolve. Cool mixture about 15 minutes. Fold in whipped cream. Pour into 3-cup mold. Chill till firm, about 4 hours. Unmold; garnish with additional whipped cream and crushed peppermint candy. Makes 6 servings.

Tangerine-Apricot Mold

- 2 envelopes (2 tablespoons) unflavored gelatin
- ½ cup sugar
  Dash salt
- 1¾ cups tangerine juice*
- 1 12-ounce can (1½ cups) apricot nectar
- 3 egg whites
- ½ cup whipping cream, whipped

Combine first 4 ingredients. Cook and stir over medium heat till gelatin dissolves. Stir in apricot nectar; chill till partially set. Add egg whites; beat till fluffy. Chill till partially set; fold in whipped cream. Pile into 6-cup mold; chill till firm. Unmold; trim with tangerine sections, canned apricots. Serves 10.

* Reconstitute one 6-ounce can frozen tangerine-juice concentrate; measure out 1¾ cups.

Chocolate Chiffon Dessert

- 1 envelope (1 tablespoon) unflavored gelatin
- ¼ cup cold water
- ⅔ cup chocolate-flavored syrup
- ½ teaspoon vanilla
- 1 cup evaporated milk, chilled **icy cold**
- 1 recipe Crust

Soften gelatin in cold water. Heat syrup; add gelatin and stir till gelatin dissolves. Cool to room temperature. Add vanilla. In chilled bowl, whip milk; fold in chocolate mixture. Chill till mixture mounds *slightly* when spooned. Pour over Crust. Chill firm. Cut in 9 squares. CRUST: Mix 1 cup vanilla-wafer crumbs, ¼ cup chopped walnuts, and 3 tablespoons melted butter; press in 8x8x2-inch pan. Chill.

Red and White Delight

- 1 1-pound 4½-ounce can (2½ cups) crushed pineapple
- 1 envelope (1 tablespoon) unflavored gelatin
- ½ cup sugar
- ¼ teaspoon salt
- ¼ cup water
- 2 egg whites
- ½ teaspoon vanilla
- 1 6-ounce can (⅔ cup) evaporated milk, chilled **icy cold** and whipped
- 1 tablespoon lemon juice

Drain pineapple, reserving ¾ cup syrup. Mix gelatin, sugar, salt, water, and the reserved syrup. Heat, stirring till gelatin dissolves. Chill till partially set. Add egg whites and vanilla. Beat fluffy. Combine whipped milk, lemon juice, and pineapple; fold into gelatin. Pile into 6-cup mold. Chill till firm; unmold. Serve with CRANBERRY SAUCE: Mix ½ cup sugar and 1½ tablespoons cornstarch; add 1½ cups cranberry-juice cocktail. Cook and stir till mixture thickens; cook 2 minutes. Chill. Makes 8 to 10 servings.

Strawberry Charlotte Russe

Dissolve one 3-ounce package strawberry-flavored gelatin and ¼ cup sugar in 1¼ cups boiling water. Stir in 1 cup miniature marshmallows; cool. Add ¼ cup sugar to 2 cups fresh strawberries*; crush; add to gelatin along with 2 tablespoons lemon juice and 2 unbeaten egg whites. Chill till partially set. Beat till fluffy. Whip ½ cup whipping cream; fold into gelatin mixture. Cut 3 individual jelly rolls (one 9½-ounce package) in ½-inch slices; arrange on bottom and sides of oiled 3-quart bowl or mold. *Carefully* spoon mixture over jelly roll. Chill overnight. Makes 8 to 10 servings.

* *Or* 10-ounce package frozen berries; do not sugar.

Jewel Squares

- 1 1-pound 4½-ounce can (2½ cups) crushed pineapple
- 1 3-ounce package strawberry-flavored gelatin
- 1 cup boiling water
- 2 tablespoons lemon juice
- 1 cup whipping cream
- 2 tablespoons sugar
- ½ teaspoon vanilla
- ⅓ cup chopped California walnuts
- 18 graham-cracker squares
- Canned pineapple tidbits

Drain crushed pineapple, reserving syrup. For top layer, dissolve gelatin in boiling water; add syrup and lemon juice. Chill till partially set. For cream layer, whip cream with sugar and vanilla; fold in crushed pineapple and nuts. For crust, line bottom of 8x8x2-inch baking dish with 9 graham crackers; spread with cream layer. Gently press remaining crackers over top. Arrange halved pineapple tidbits on each cracker. Spoon gelatin over. Chill firm. Top with whipped cream. Cut between crackers.

Chocolate-Mint Dessert

- ½ cup graham-cracker crumbs
- 2 tablespoons butter or margarine, melted
- ½ cup sugar
- 1 envelope (1 tablespoon) unflavored gelatin
- 2 tablespoons cornstarch
- 2 cups milk
- 3 slightly beaten egg yolks
- 3 egg whites
- ¼ cup sugar
- ½ cup whipping cream, whipped
- 1½ teaspoons crème de menthe syrup
- 2 squares (2 ounces) unsweetened chocolate, melted

Blend first 2 ingredients. Reserve 1 tablespoon crumbs; spread remainder in 10x6x1½-inch baking dish. Combine next 3 ingredients; add milk; cook and stir till boiling. Add small amount hot mixture to egg yolks; return to hot mixture; cook 1 minute. Cool till partially thickened. Beat egg whites to soft peaks; gradually add the ¼ cup sugar; beat to stiff peaks. Fold into custard; then fold in whipped cream. Remove 1½ cups mixture; add syrup to it. Stir chocolate into remaining mixture. Spread half the chocolate mixture over crumbs; cover with mint layer, then remaining chocolate. Top with reserved crumbs. Chill till firm. Six servings.

Pumpkin Ice Cream Squares

- 1 cup fine ginger-snap crumbs
- ¼ cup sugar
- ¼ cup butter or margarine, melted
- 1 envelope (1 tablespoon) unflavored gelatin
- ¼ cup cold water
- ½ cup cooked pumpkin
- ½ teaspoon salt
- 1 teaspoon cinnamon
- ¼ teaspoon ginger
- ¼ teaspoon nutmeg
- 1 teaspoon vanilla
- 1 quart vanilla ice cream

Combine crumbs, sugar, and butter; reserving ⅓ cup, press in bottom of 8x8x2-inch baking pan. Soften gelatin in cold water; combine in a saucepan with next 6 ingredients. Stir over low heat till gelatin dissolves; cool. In chilled bowl, stir ice cream to soften; fold in pumpkin mixture, spoon over crust. Sprinkle crumbs over top. Freeze firm. Cut in 9 squares.

Pineapple Jewel Squares

- 1 cup fine graham-cracker crumbs
- 2 tablespoons sugar
- ¼ cup butter or margarine, melted
- 1 8¾-ounce can (1 cup) crushed pineapple
- 1 3-ounce package orange-pineapple-flavored gelatin
- 1¼ cups boiling water
- 1 3-ounce package cream cheese, softened
- 3 tablespoons sugar
- ½ teaspoon vanilla
- ¼ teaspoon grated orange peel
- 1 cup dairy sour cream

Mix crumbs, 2 tablespoons sugar, and the butter; press into bottom of 8x8x2-inch baking dish. Chill. *Thoroughly* drain pineapple, reserving ½ cup syrup. Dissolve gelatin in boiling water. Add pineapple syrup; cool. Blend cream cheese with 3 tablespoons sugar, the vanilla, and orange peel. Stir *½ cup gelatin* into drained pineapple, set aside. Gradually blend remaining gelatin into cream-cheese mixture; stir in sour cream. Pour into crust; chill till firm. Spoon pineapple mixture evenly over cream-cheese layer. Chill 4 to 6 hours. Makes 6 to 9 servings.

Pumpkin Chiffon Pudding

- 1 envelope (1 tablespoon) unflavored gelatin
- 1⅓ cups cooked pumpkin
- 1 cup brown sugar
- ½ teaspoon salt
- 1 teaspoon cinnamon
- ¼ teaspoon ginger
- ¼ teaspoon nutmeg
- 3 slightly beaten egg yolks
- ½ cup milk
- 3 egg whites
- ⅓ cup sugar

Soften gelatin in ¼ cup cold water. Mix pumpkin, brown sugar, salt, and spices in saucepan. Combine egg yolks and milk; add to pumpkin mixture. Cook and stir till mixture boils. Remove from heat; stir in gelatin. Chill till mixture mounds slightly when spooned. Beat egg whites to soft peaks; gradually add ⅓ cup sugar, beating to stiff peaks. Fold into pumpkin mixture. Spoon into sherbet glasses. Chill at least 2 hours. Top with whipped cream and nutmeg. Makes 6 to 8 servings.

Blueberry Rice Bavarian

- 1 envelope (1 tablespoon) unflavored gelatin
- ⅓ cup sugar
- Dash salt
- ½ cup water
- 1 7-ounce bottle (about 1 cup) lemon-lime carbonated beverage
- 1 tablespoon lemon juice
- 1½ cups cooked long-grain rice
- 1 cup whipping cream, whipped
- 2 cups fresh blueberries (or well-drained frozen)*

In saucepan, combine gelatin, sugar, and salt. Add water and heat till gelatin dissolves; remove from heat and cool. Stir in lemon-lime carbonated beverage, lemon juice, and cooked long-grain rice. Chill till partially set. Carefully fold in the whipped cream and the blueberries. Spoon into sherbet glasses; chill till set. Makes about 8 servings.

*Or with fresh nectarines, or with fresh or well-drained frozen peaches.

Choc-o-date Dessert

- 12 packaged cream-filled chocolate cookies, crushed
- 1 8-ounce package (1 cup) pitted dates, cut up
- ¾ cup water
- ¼ teaspoon salt
- 2 cups miniature marshmallows or 16 regular marshmallows
- ½ cup chopped California walnuts
- 1 cup whipping cream
- ½ teaspoon vanilla
- Walnut halves

Reserve ¼ cup cooky crumbs; spread remainder in 10x6x1½-inch baking dish. In saucepan, combine dates, water, and salt; bring to boiling, reduce heat and simmer 3 minutes. Remove from heat, add marshmallows and stir till melted. Cool to room temperature. Stir in chopped nuts. Spread date mixture over crumbs in dish. Combine cream and vanilla; whip, swirl over dates. Sprinkle with reserved crumbs; top with walnuts. Chill overnight. Cut in squares. Makes 8 servings.

Java Tapioca Parfait

- 1 egg yolk
- ⅓ cup sugar
- 2 teaspoons instant coffee powder
- 2 cups milk
- 3 tablespoons quick-cooking tapioca
- Dash salt
- ½ teaspoon vanilla
- 1 stiff-beaten egg white
- ½ cup whipping cream, whipped

Combine first 6 ingredients; cook and stir over medium heat till mixture boils. Remove from heat; stir in vanilla. Slowly pour hot mixture over egg white, mixing well. Cover; chill. Alternate layers of tapioca and whipped cream in parfait glasses. Makes 4 or 5 servings.

Lemondown Fancy

    4 tablespoons butter or
       margarine
    ½ cup brown sugar
    1½ cups wheat flakes cereal
    ½ cup chopped California
       walnuts

    3 egg whites
    ½ cup granulated sugar
    3 egg yolks
    1 cup whipping cream
    1 teaspoon grated lemon peel
    ¼ cup lemon juice

Combine butter and brown sugar. Cook over low heat till mixture is boiling; cook about 1 minute more. Remove from heat; stir in cereal and nuts. Spread mixture on baking sheet; cool. Beat egg whites to soft peaks; gradually add granulated sugar; beat to stiff peaks. Beat egg yolks till thick and lemon colored; fold into meringue. Combine remaining ingredients; beat till stiff. Fold into egg mixture. Crumble the cereal-nut crunch; sprinkle 2 cups of the crunch into a buttered 9-inch pie pan. Spoon in filling; sprinkle with remaining crunch. Freeze till firm, 6 to 8 hours. Makes 8 to 10 servings.

Cherry Creme Parfaits

    1 cup whipping cream
    3 tablespoons sugar
    1 teaspoon vanilla
       Dash salt

    1 cup dairy sour cream
    1 1-pound 5-ounce can (2½ cups)
       cherry-pie filling

Whip cream with sugar, vanilla, and salt. Fold in the sour cream. Alternate layers of cherry filling and whipped-cream mixture in parfait or sherbet glasses, beginning with a red layer and ending with a white one. Top each with a single cherry. Chill till serving time. Makes 8 to 10 servings.

Coffee-Nut Tortoni

- 1 cup whipping cream
- ¼ cup sugar
- 1 tablespoon instant coffee powder
- 1 teaspoon vanilla
- Few drops almond extract
- 1 egg white
- 2 tablespoons sugar
- ¼ cup finely chopped almonds, toasted
- ¼ cup flaked coconut, toasted and crumbled

Whip cream; fold in ¼ cup sugar, the instant coffee, and flavorings. Beat egg white till soft peaks form; gradually add 2 tablespoons sugar and beat to stiff peaks. Mix almonds and coconut. Fold egg white and *half* the nut mixture into whipped cream. Spoon into 8 souffle cups or paper bake cups set in muffin pan. Sprinkle remaining nut mixture over top; freeze firm. Top with maraschino cherries.

Cherry Angel Dessert

- 8 cups ½-inch cubes angel cake
- 1 1-pound 5-ounce can (2½ cups) cherry-pie filling
- 1 package instant vanilla pudding-mix
- 1½ cups milk
- 1 cup dairy sour cream

Place *half* the cake pieces in a 9x9x2-inch pan. Reserve ⅓ cup cherry filling; spoon remainder over cake. Top with remaining cake. Combine pudding mix, milk, and sour cream; beat smooth; spoon over cake. Chill 5 hours. Cut in 9 squares. Garnish with filling.

Carioca Cups

- 1 6¼-ounce package (4 cups) miniature marshmallows
- ¼ teaspoon salt
- ¼ cup milk
- 1 6-ounce package (1 cup) semisweet chocolate pieces
- 2 teaspoons instant coffee powder
- ¼ teaspoon cinnamon
- 1 cup whipping cream, whipped
- 8 sponge cake dessert cups
- 1 cup finely chopped California walnuts

Combine first 3 ingredients in top of double boiler. Cook and stir over boiling water till marshmallows melt. Remove from heat; stir in chocolate pieces, coffee powder, and cinnamon. Fold ½ cup chocolate mixture into whipped cream; cover and chill. Frost sides and top edge of dessert cups with remaining chocolate mixture; roll in chopped nuts. Spoon in cream filling; chill. Makes 8 servings.

Luscious Lemon Frost

- 1 egg white
- ⅓ cup water
- ⅓ cup nonfat dry milk
- 1 slightly beaten egg yolk
- ⅓ cup sugar
- ¼ teaspoon grated lemon peel
- 2 to 3 tablespoons lemon juice
- Dash salt
- 3 tablespoons graham-cracker crumbs

Combine egg white, water, and dry milk; beat to stiff peaks. Mix next 5 ingredients; gradually beat into egg whites. Sprinkle 2 *tablespoons* of the crumbs into refrigerator tray. Spoon in lemon mixture; dust with crumbs. Freeze. Cut in 6 wedges.

Pot de Creme

Combine one 6-ounce package (1 cup) semisweet chocolate pieces and 1¼ cups light cream in heavy saucepan. Stir over low heat till blended, *satin-smooth*.

The mixture should be *slightly thick*—but don't let it boil. Beat 2 egg yolks with dash of salt till airy and thick. Gradually stir in chocolate-cream mixture.

Spoon the rich dessert into 6 or 7 traditional cups or into small sherbets, filling ⅔ full. Cover and chill at least 3 hours or till mixture becomes like pudding.

Raspberry Cream Pudding

- 1 10-ounce package frozen red raspberries, thawed
- 1 3- or 3¼-ounce package vanilla pudding mix
- ½ cup whipping cream, whipped
- ¼ cup vanilla-wafer crumbs (6 or 7 wafers)

Drain berries thoroughly, reserving syrup. Chill berries. Add water to the syrup to make 1½ cups. In saucepan, combine pudding mix and the 1½ cups liquid. Cook and stir over medium heat till mixture comes to a full boil. Cover and chill thoroughly till thick, about 2 hours. Beat smooth with rotary beater; fold in whipped cream. Spoon into sherbet glasses; chill about 2 hours. Just before serving, wreathe puddings with wafer crumbs; top with the raspberries. Makes 4 to 6 servings.

Lemonade Pudding

- 2 slightly beaten egg yolks
- 1½ cups milk
- 1 3- or 3¼-ounce package vanilla pudding mix
- 1 3-ounce package cream cheese, softened
- 1 6-ounce can frozen lemonade concentrate, thawed
- 2 egg whites
- ¼ cup sugar
- ½ cup vanilla-wafer crumbs
- 2 tablespoons chopped California walnuts
- 2 tablespoons butter or margarine, melted

Combine egg yolks and milk. Prepare pudding according to package directions, *using the egg-milk mixture as the liquid.* Add cream cheese and beat smooth with electric or rotary beater; stir in lemonade concentrate. Cover and cool 10 minutes; beat smooth again. Beat egg whites to soft peaks; gradually add sugar beating to stiff peaks. Fold egg whites into pudding. Combine crumbs, nuts, and butter. Sprinkle *half* the crumb mixture into 6 sherbet glasses. Spoon in pudding; top with remaining crumbs. Chill. Just before serving, stand a vanilla wafer in each. Makes 6 servings.

Chocolate Nut Pudding

- 2 cups soft bread crumbs (3 slices)
- 1½ cups milk, scalded
- ¾ cup sugar
- 2 beaten egg yolks
- 2 envelopes (2 ounces) no-melt unsweetened chocolate
- 1 teaspoon grated orange peel
- ¼ cup orange juice
- ½ teaspoon salt
- ½ cup chopped California walnuts
- 2 stiff-beaten egg whites

Stir bread crumbs into hot milk. Combine next 6 ingredients; thoroughly blend into milk mixture. Add nuts; fold in egg whites. Turn into six buttered 6-ounce custard cups. Place custard cups in shallow pan on oven rack; pour hot water around them, 1 inch deep. Bake at 350° about 35 minutes or till knife inserted halfway between center and edge comes out clean. (Pudding will have custard layer at bottom.) Serve warm. Makes 6 servings.

Baked Fruit Compote

- 1 1-pound can (2 cups) **each** apricot halves, peach halves, and purple plums
- 3 or 4 thin orange slices, halved
- ½ cup orange juice
- ¼ cup brown sugar
- ½ teaspoon shredded lemon peel
- 2 tablespoons melted butter or margarine
- ½ cup flaked coconut

Drain canned fruits well. Arrange with orange slices in a shallow baking dish. Mix orange juice, sugar, and peel; pour over fruit. Drizzle butter over the plums; sprinkle coconut over all. Bake in 425° oven 15 minutes or till hot. Serve warm. Makes 8 servings.

Ruby Fruit Compote

- 1 1-pound 4-ounce can (2½ cups) frozen pitted tart red cherries, thawed
- 1 10-ounce package frozen red raspberries, thawed
- 1½ tablespoons cornstarch
- 1 tablespoon lemon juice
- 2 cups fresh whole strawberries
- Dairy sour cream

Drain frozen fruits, reserving syrup. Add enough water to syrup to measure 2½ cups. Blend cornstarch, dash salt, and syrup. Cook and stir till thick and clear. Add lemon juice. Stir in fruits. If desired, sweeten. Chill thoroughly. Spoon into sherbets. Top with sour cream. Makes 8 servings.

Lemon Angel Frost

- 2 egg whites
- ½ cup sugar
- 2 egg yolks
- ½ teaspoon grated lemon peel
- ¼ cup lemon juice
- ½ cup whipping cream, whipped
- Semisweet-chocolate curls

Beat egg whites till soft peaks form; gradually add sugar, beating to stiff peaks. Beat egg yolks till thick and lemon colored. Fold egg yolks, lemon peel, and lemon juice into egg whites. Fold in whipped cream. Pour into refrigerator tray; freeze firm. Serve in sherbets. Top with shaved semisweet chocolate. Makes 6 to 8 servings.

Maple-Almond Ice Cream

- 3 egg yolks
- 1 cup maple-flavored syrup
  Dash salt
- 1 6-ounce can (⅔ cup) evaporated milk, chilled **icy cold** and whipped
- 3 stiff-beaten egg whites
- ½ cup chopped blanched almonds, toasted

Beat egg yolks well. Mix in syrup and salt. Cook and stir over low heat till mixture thickens. Cool thoroughly. Fold in whipped milk, egg whites, and almonds. Pour into refrigerator trays; freeze firm. Top with additional almonds. Makes 8 to 10 servings.

Lime Refresher—Low Cal

- 1 3-ounce package lime-flavored gelatin
- ¾ cup boiling water
- ½ cup sugar
- 3 tablespoons lemon juice
- 1½ teaspoons grated lemon peel
- 1½ cups buttermilk
- 1 stiff-beaten egg white

Dissolve gelatin in boiling water. Add sugar; stir to dissolve. Stir in juice, peel, and buttermilk. Pour into refrigerator tray; freeze firm. Break in chunks; beat with electric beater till smooth.* Fold in egg white. Freeze firm. Makes 5 or 6 servings.

* *Or* partially freeze; beat with rotary beater.

Marshmallow Fudge Topping

1 cup brown sugar
¼ cup cocoa (dry)
½ cup milk
1 tablespoon butter or margarine
1 teaspoon vanilla
1 cup miniature marshmallows

Mix brown sugar and cocoa in 1-quart saucepan; stir in milk. Cook and stir till mixture comes to boiling; cook rapidly 5 minutes longer. Remove from heat; stir in butter and vanilla. Cool 5 minutes; fold in marshmallows. Makes about 1¼ cups. Serve warm over vanilla ice cream.

Mincemeat Sundae Sauce

½ cup sugar
½ cup orange juice
½ cup diced pared apple
1 cup prepared mincemeat
¼ cup chopped California walnuts
¼ cup chopped maraschino cherries

Combine all ingredients in a small saucepan. Bring to boiling point; simmer gently, uncovered, 10 minutes. Serve warm over vanilla ice cream.

Ginger Sundae Sauce

⅓ cup light corn syrup
¼ cup **finely** chopped candied or preserved ginger
Dash salt
½ cup light cream
¼ cup butter or margarine
½ teaspoon vanilla

In 1-quart saucepan, mix corn syrup, ginger, salt, and *half* the cream. Simmer 5 minutes. *Gradually* stir in remaining cream. Heat through (do not boil). Remove from heat; stir in butter and vanilla. Makes ¾ cup. Serve warm over vanilla ice cream.

Coffee Dot Fudge

- 3 cups sugar
- 1 cup milk
- ½ cup light cream
- 2 tablespoons instant coffee powder
- 1 tablespoon light corn syrup
- Dash salt
- 3 tablespoons butter or margarine
- 1 teaspoon vanilla
- ½ 6-ounce package (½ cup) semisweet chocolate pieces
- ½ cup broken pecans

Butter sides of heavy 3-quart saucepan. In it combine sugar, milk, light cream, instant coffee, corn syrup, and salt. Heat over medium heat, stirring constantly, till sugar dissolves and mixture comes to boiling. Then cook to soft-ball stage (234°), stirring only if necessary. Immediately remove from heat; add butter and cool to lukewarm (110°) without stirring. Add vanilla. Beat vigorously till fudge becomes very thick and starts to lose its gloss. At once stir in chocolate pieces and pecans. Quickly spread in buttered shallow pan or small platter. Score in squares while warm and, if desired, top each with a pecan half; cut when firm.

Marshmallow-Nut Puffs

Dip marshmallows in hot cream, flavored with vanilla, until outsides of marshmallows are soft. Roll in finely ground pecans, flaked coconut, or chocolate decorettes; flatten slightly. Chill.

Caramel Fudge

- 2 cups sugar
- 1 6-ounce can (⅔ cup) evaporated milk
- 2 tablespoons light corn syrup
- 1 10-ounce jar vanilla caramel sauce
- 1 teaspoon vanilla
- ¼ teaspoon maple flavoring
- ½ cup chopped California walnuts

Butter sides of heavy 2-quart saucepan. In it combine sugar, milk, corn syrup, and caramel sauce. Heat and stir over medium heat till sugar dissolves and mixture comes to boiling. Then cook to soft-ball stage (235°), stirring occasionally. Remove from heat. Stir in vanilla and maple flavoring; beat just till mixture begins to lose its gloss. Stir in nuts. Pour into buttered 8x8x2-inch pan. Score while warm; cut when firm.

Marshmallow-road Fudge

- ¾ cup broken California walnuts
- 2 cups sugar
- 1 cup evaporated milk
- ¼ teaspoon salt
- 1 12-ounce package (2 cups) semisweet chocolate pieces
- 1 teaspoon vanilla
- 2 cups miniature marshmallows

Sprinkle walnuts evenly over bottom of buttered 9x9x2-inch pan; set aside. Butter sides of heavy 2-quart saucepan. In it combine sugar, milk, and salt. Heat and stir till sugar is dissolved. Bring to rolling boil and boil 2 minutes (222°), stirring frequently to prevent sticking. Remove from heat; immediately stir in chocolate and vanilla. Beat until chocolate is melted and blended. Cover walnuts with *half* of fudge mixture. Top with tiny marshmallows, pressing them gently into fudge. Spread with remaining fudge. Chill. Cut in squares.

Orange-Butter Fondant

Cream 3 cups sifted confectioners' sugar with 3 tablespoons butter; add orange juice to moisten (about 6 tablespoons). Fill pitted dates or prunes, topping each with a thin slice of candied orange peel or a perfect walnut or pecan half.

Frosty Stuffed Figs

Slit side of soft whole dried figs and fill center with broken California walnuts or pecans; press closed. Dip bottom of figs in sifted confectioners' sugar.

Peanut-Butter Fudge

    2 cups sugar
    ⅔ cup milk
    ½ of pint jar marshmallow créme
    1 cup chunk-style peanut butter
    1 6-ounce package (1 cup) semisweet chocolate pieces
    1 teaspoon vanilla

Butter sides of heavy 2-quart saucepan. In it combine sugar and milk. Heat and stir over medium heat till sugar dissolves and mixture comes to boiling. Then cook to soft-ball stage (234°). Remove from heat; add remaining ingredients and stir till blended. Pour into buttered 9x9x2-inch pan. Score in squares while warm; cut when firm.

Iced Almonds

    1 cup whole blanched almonds
    ½ cup sugar
    2 tablespoons butter or margarine
    ½ teaspoon vanilla
    ¾ teaspoon salt

Heat almonds, sugar, and butter in heavy skillet over medium heat, stirring constantly, till almonds are toasted and sugar is golden brown, about 15 minutes. Stir in vanilla. Spread nuts on a sheet of aluminum foil; sprinkle with salt. Cool, break into 2- or 3-nut clusters.

Candied Orange Peel

    3 oranges
    1 tablespoon salt
    4 cups water
    2 cups sugar
    ½ cup water

Cut peel of each orange in sixths; loosen from pulp with bowl of spoon. (Save orange sections for breakfast.) Add salt to 4 cups water; add peel. Weight with a plate to keep peel under water; let stand overnight. Drain; wash thoroughly. Cover with cold water; heat to boiling. Drain. Repeat three times. This helps remove bitter taste. With kitchen scissors, cut peel in strips. In saucepan, combine 2 cups peel, sugar, and ½ cup water. Heat and stir till sugar dissolves. Cook slowly till peel is translucent. Drain; roll in granulated sugar. Dry on rack.

SECTION 5

Breads, Sandwiches, Pancakes and Waffles

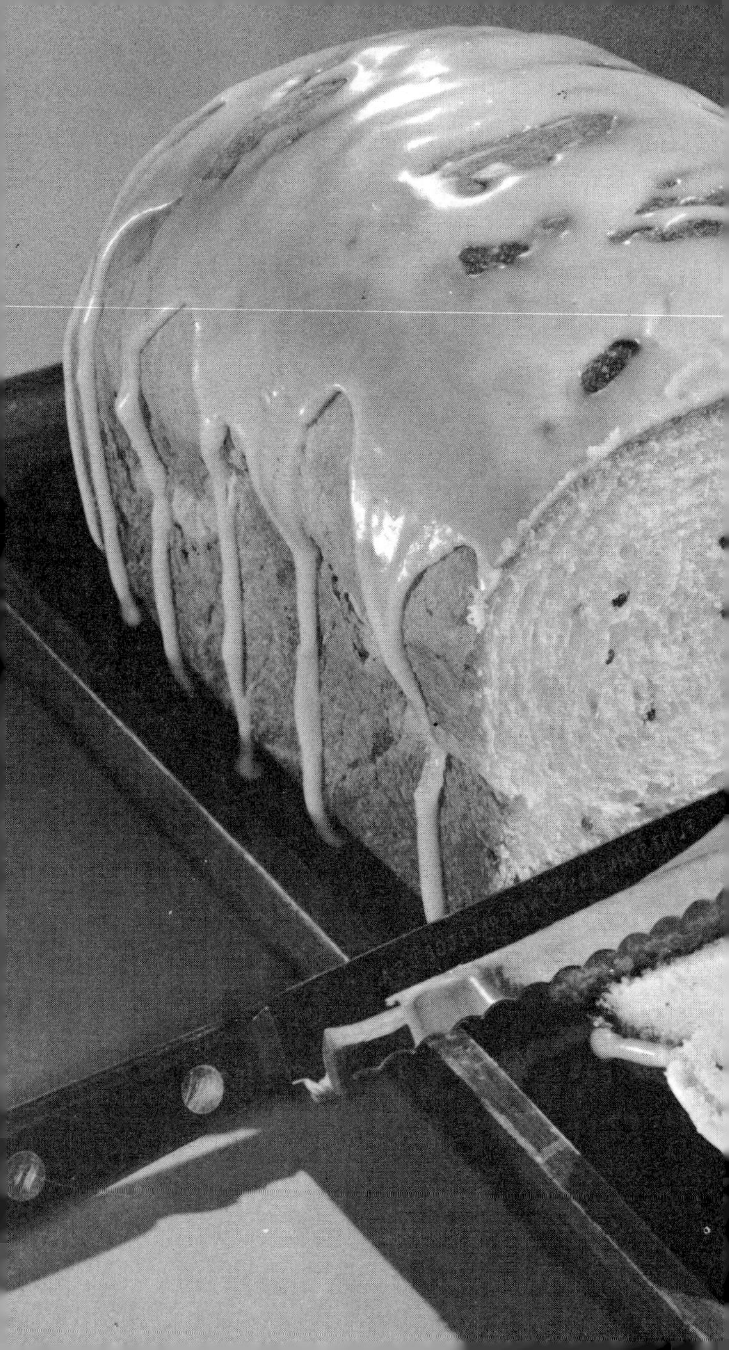

SECTION 5

Breads, Sandwiches, Pancakes and Waffles

Easter Anise Bread

Soften 1 package active dry yeast in ¼ cup *warm* water. Combine ⅓ cup *each* butter, sugar, and milk, and ½ teaspoon salt; scald, stirring till butter melts. Cool to lukewarm. Add 1 cup sifted all-purpose flour; beat well. Add yeast, 1 slightly beaten egg, 2 tablespoons lemon juice, 1 teaspoon shredded lemon peel, 2 to 3 teaspoons anise seed; beat well. Add 2½ cups sifted flour (or enough to make a soft dough). On lightly floured surface, knead till smooth and elastic (8 to 10 minutes). Place in lightly greased bowl, turning once to grease surface. Cover; let double in warm place (about 1½ hours). Punch down; let rest 10 minutes. Shape in loaf. Place in greased 8½x4½x2½-inch loaf pan. Cover; let double (about 45 minutes). Bake at 375° 35 to 40 minutes (place foil over top last 20 minutes). Remove from pan; cool. Glaze with icing.

Walnut Graham Bread

- ¼ cup shortening
- ¾ cup sugar
- ½ teaspoon vanilla
- 2 eggs
- 1 cup sifted all-purpose flour
- 2 teaspoons baking powder
- ½ teaspoon salt
- ½ teaspoon cinnamon
- ¼ teaspoon nutmeg
- ¼ teaspoon allspice
- ½ cup stirred wholewheat flour
- ⅔ cup milk
- ½ cup chopped California walnuts

Cream the shortening, sugar, and vanilla. Add eggs, one at a time, beating after each. Sift together next 6 ingredients; stir in wholewheat flour; then add to creamed mixture alternately with milk, beating smooth after each addition. Add nuts. Turn into greased 8½x4½x2½-inch loaf pan. Bake in 350° oven 55 minutes. Remove from pan; cool.

Prune Nut Bread

- 1 cup dried prunes, pitted and chopped
- 2 teaspoons shredded orange peel
- 1 cup orange juice
- 2 cups sifted all-purpose flour
- ¾ cup sugar
- 3 teaspoons baking powder
- ½ teaspoon salt
- ½ teaspoon cinnamon
- 2 beaten eggs
- 2 tablespoons salad oil
- ½ cup chopped California walnuts

Combine prunes, orange peel, and juice; let stand ½ hour. Sift together dry ingredients. Combine eggs, salad oil, and prune mixture; add to dry ingredients mixing well. Add nuts. Turn into greased 9x5x3-inch loaf pan. Bake at 350° 55 minutes. Remove from pan; cool.

Oatmeal Banana Bread

- 2 cups packaged biscuit mix
- 1 cup quick-cooking rolled oats
- ½ cup chopped California walnuts
- ¼ cup butter or margarine
- ½ cup sugar
- 2 eggs
- 2 large ripe bananas, mashed (1 cup)
- ¼ cup milk

Combine first 3 ingredients; set aside. Cream butter and sugar till light and fluffy. Beat in eggs, one at a time; stir in bananas and milk. Add dry ingredients, all at once, stirring just till all are moistened. Turn into greased 9x5x3-inch loaf pan. Bake in moderate oven (350°) about 40 minutes or till done. Remove from pan; cool.

Poppy-dot Cheese Bread

3¾ cups packaged biscuit mix
5 ounces sharp process American cheese, shredded (1¼ cups)
1 tablespoon poppy seed
1 beaten egg
1½ cups milk

Combine biscuit mix, cheese, and poppy seed. Add egg and milk; mix just to blend. Beat vigorously 1 minute. Turn into well-greased 9x5x3-inch loaf pan. Sprinkle with additional poppy seed. Bake in moderate oven (350°) 50 to 60 minutes or till done. Remove from pan; cool.

Onion Supper Bread

½ cup chopped onion
2 tablespoons butter or margarine
1 package corn-muffin or corn-bread mix
½ cup dairy sour cream
½ cup shredded sharp process American cheese

Cook onion in butter till tender but not brown. Prepare mix according to package directions. Pour into greased 8x8x2-inch pan. Sprinkle with cooked onion. Mix sour cream and cheese; spoon over the top. Bake in hot oven (400°) 25 minutes or till done. Let stand a few minutes; cut in 9 squares.

Bacon Spoon Bread

¾ cup corn meal
1½ cups cold water
8 ounces sharp natural Cheddar cheese, shredded (2 cups)
¼ cup soft butter or margarine
2 cloves garlic, crushed
½ teaspoon salt
1 cup milk
4 well-beaten egg yolks
½ pound sliced bacon, crisp-cooked and drained
4 stiff-beaten egg whites

Combine corn meal and water; cook, stirring constantly, till the consistency of mush. Remove from heat; add cheese, butter, garlic, and salt; stir to melt cheese. Gradually add milk. Stir in egg yolks. Crumble bacon, reserving some for garnish if desired, and add to corn meal mixture. Fold in egg whites. Pour into greased 2-quart souffle dish or casserole. Bake in slow oven (325°) about 65 minutes or till done. Spoon into warm dishes; top with butter and serve with spoons. Makes 6 servings.

Glazed Lemon-Nut Bread

- ¼ cup butter or margarine
- ¾ cup sugar
- 2 eggs
- 2 teaspoons grated lemon peel
- 2 cups sifted all-purpose flour
- 2½ teaspoons baking powder
- 1 teaspoon salt
- ¾ cup milk
- ½ cup chopped California Walnuts
- 2 teaspoons lemon juice
- 2 tablespoons sugar

Cream together butter and ¾ cup sugar until light and fluffy. Add eggs and lemon peel; beat well. Sift together flour, baking powder, and salt; add to creamed mixture alternately with milk, beating till smooth after each addition. Stir in walnuts. Pour into greased 8½x4½x2½-inch loaf pan. Bake in moderate oven (350°) 50 to 55 minutes or till done. Let cool in pan 10 minutes, then spoon mixture of lemon juice and 2 tablespoons sugar over top. Remove from pan and cool.

French Onion Bread

- 1 package active dry yeast or 1 cake compressed yeast
- ¼ cup water
- 1 envelope onion-soup mix
- 2 cups water
- 2 tablespoons sugar
- 1 teaspoon salt
- 2 tablespoons grated Parmesan cheese
- 2 tablespoons shortening or salad oil
- 6 to 6½ cups sifted all-purpose flour
- Corn meal

Soften dry yeast in ¼ cup *warm* water or compressed yeast in *lukewarm* water. Combine soup mix and 2 cups water; simmer covered 10 minutes; add sugar, salt, cheese, and shortening; stir. Cool to lukewarm. Stir in *2 cups* of the flour; beat well. Stir in yeast. Add enough of the remaining flour to make a moderately stiff dough. Turn out on lightly floured surface. Cover; let rest 10 minutes. Knead till smooth and elastic (8 to 10 minutes). Place in a lightly greased bowl, turning once to grease surface. Cover; let double in warm place (1¼ to 1½ hours). Punch down; divide in half. Cover; let rest 10 minutes. Shape in 2 long loaves, tapering ends. Place on greased baking sheet sprinkled with corn meal. Gash tops diagonally, ⅛ to ¼ inch deep. Cover; let almost double (about 1 hour). Bake in moderate oven (375°) 20 minutes. Brush with mixture of 1 egg white and 1 tablespoon water. Bake 10 to 15 minutes longer or till done.

Cheese Bread Sticks

- 1 package hot-roll mix
- 4 ounces sharp process American cheese, shredded (1 cup)
- 1 tablespoon poppy seed
- ¼ cup butter or margarine, melted

Prepare hot-roll dough according to package directions; add cheese and poppy seed. After dough has risen, divide in half. On lightly floured surface, roll each half to a 10x6-inch rectangle, about ½ inch thick. Cut each in twenty 6-inch-long sticks. (For a smoother shape, roll sticks under hand pencil fashion.) Place on greased baking sheet. Brush with melted butter. Let rise till double (30 to 45 minutes). Bake in hot oven (400°) 10 minutes or till done. Makes 40.

Molasses Corn Bread

- ½ cup shortening
- ½ cup sugar
- 2 eggs
- ½ cup molasses
- 1 cup milk
- 1 cup sifted all-purpose flour
- 3 teaspoons baking powder
- ½ teaspoon salt
- ½ cup yellow corn meal
- 1½ cups whole bran

Cream shortening and sugar. Beat in eggs, one at a time; stir in molasses and milk. Sift together flour, baking powder, and salt; stir in corn meal and bran; add to creamed mixture, stirring just till blended. Pour into greased 9x9x2-inch baking pan. Bake at 375° about 30 minutes. Cut in squares.

Old-time Herb Loaf

    1 package hot-roll mix   ½ teaspoon basil
    1 teaspoon sage   ¼ teaspoon nutmeg

Prepare hot-roll mix according to package directions, adding sage, basil, and nutmeg to dry mix. Turn out on generously floured surface (use about ¼ cup all-purpose flour). Knead till smooth and satiny, 5 to 7 minutes. Place in a greased bowl, turning once to grease top. Cover; let double in warm place (about 1 hour). Shape in loaf. Place in greased 9x5x3-inch loaf pan. Cover; let rise till almost double (about 45 minutes). Bake in a moderate oven (375°) 40 to 45 minutes or until done. Remove from pan; brush with butter, if desired.

Glazed Raisin Loaf

    1 package active dry yeast or   1 teaspoon salt
      1 cake compressed yeast   ½ cup buttermilk or milk,
    ¼ cup water   scalded
    1 cup raisins   3¼ to 3½ cups sifted all-
    ¼ cup soft butter or margarine   purpose flour
    ¼ cup sugar   2 beaten eggs

Soften active dry yeast in *warm* water or compressed yeast in *lukewarm* water. Combine next 4 ingredients. Add hot milk; stir to dissolve sugar. Cool to lukewarm. Add *1 cup* of the flour; mix well. Add yeast and eggs; beat well. Stir in remaining flour, mixing well. Turn out on lightly floured surface. Cover; let rest 10 minutes. Knead till smooth and elastic (8 to 10 minutes). Place in lightly greased bowl, turning once to grease surface. Cover; let double (1½ to 2 hours) in warm place. Punch down; cover and let rest 10 minutes. Shape in loaf. Place in greased 9x5x3-inch loaf pan. Cover; let almost double (45 to 60 minutes). Bake in moderate oven (375°) about 25 minutes; place foil over top last 10 minutes, if necessary. Remove from pan; cool. Glaze with confectioners' sugar icing.

Spring Flower Rolls

    1 package active dry yeast   ½ teaspoon salt
    ¼ cup **warm** water   2¾ to 3¼ cups sifted all-
    ½ cup milk, scalded   purpose flour
    ¼ cup butter or margarine   1 slightly beaten egg
    2 tablespoons sugar

Soften yeast in water. Mix hot milk, butter, sugar, and salt; cool to lukewarm. Add 1 *cup* flour; beat smooth. Beat in softened yeast and egg. Stir in enough remaining flour to make a soft dough. Turn out on floured surface; knead till smooth and elastic (8 to 10 minutes). Place in lightly greased bowl, turning once to grease surface. Cover; let rise in warm place till double (about 1 hour). Punch down. Cover; let rest 10 minutes. On lightly floured surface, roll dough to ¼ inch; cut with floured 1¼-inch biscuit cutter. Grease muffin cups (about 2½ inches across); arrange 5 circles of dough around sides of each cup and 1 in center. Cover; let almost double (about 30 minutes). Lightly poke down center of each roll and fill with various colors of jams or preserves. Bake in hot oven (400°) 10 to 15 minutes. Brush with melted butter. Makes about 16.

Golden Pumpkin Hi-lighters

Soften 1 package active dry yeast in ¼ cup *warm* water. Scald 1 cup milk; stir in 2 tablespoons *each* shortening and sugar, 1 teaspoon salt, and ½ cup canned pumpkin; cool to lukewarm. Add 2 cups sifted all-purpose flour; beat smooth. Beat in yeast and 1 slightly beaten egg. Stir in 3 to 3½ cups sifted all-purpose flour (enough for soft dough). On lightly floured surface, knead 8 to 10 minutes. Place in lightly greased bowl, turning to grease surface. Cover; let double in warm place, about 1¾ hours. Punch down. Cover; let rest 10 minutes. Form in 32 balls. Place in 2 greased 9x9x2-inch baking pans. Cover; let double, about 50 minutes. Bake in hot oven (400°) 15 minutes or till done. Makes 32.

Airy Cheese Rolls

1 package active dry yeast	¼ cup sugar
¼ cup **warm** water	2 tablespoons shortening
1¾ cups milk, scalded	1 teaspoon salt
4 ounces sharp process American cheese, shredded (1 cup)	4 cups sifted all-purpose flour
	1 beaten egg
	½ cup corn meal

Soften yeast in warm water. In large bowl of electric mixer, combine milk, cheese, sugar, shortening, and salt. Stir till cheese melts; cool to lukewarm. Add 2 *cups* of the flour; beat 2 minutes at medium speed. Add egg, softened yeast, corn meal, and remaining flour. Beat 2 minutes. Cover; let rise in warm place till double, about 1¼ hours; stir down. Fill greased 2½-inch muffin pans ½ full. Cover and let rise till double, about 45 minutes. Bake in moderate oven (375°) 15 to 20 minutes. Makes 2 dozen rolls.

Butterscotch Swirls

Soften 1 package active dry yeast in ¼ cup *warm* water. Scald ½ cup milk; stir in ¼ cup shortening, ¼ cup sugar, and 1 teaspoon salt; cool to lukewarm. Add 1 cup sifted all-purpose flour; beat well. Beat in yeast. Stir in 1¼ to 1¾ cups sifted flour (enough for soft dough). On lightly floured surface, knead 8 to 10 minutes. Place in greased bowl, turning to grease surface. Cover; let double in warm place, about 1½ hours. Punch down; let rest 10 minutes. Roll to 16x8-inch rectangle. Spread with 2 tablespoons soft butter or margarine; sprinkle with ¼ cup sugar mixed with ½ teaspoon cinnamon. Roll lengthwise; seal. Cut in 1-inch slices. Place, cut side down, in greased 9x9x2-inch baking pan. Drizzle with BUTTERSCOTCH TOPPING: Combine one 6-ounce package (1 cup) butterscotch pieces, ¼ cup light corn syrup, 2 tablespoons *each* butter and water. Melt over low heat, stirring; cool. Add ½ cup chopped California walnuts. Cover rolls; let double, about 40 minutes. Bake at 350° 30 minutes or till done. Cool 2 to 3 minutes; invert on board or rack. Makes 16.

Hot Cross Muffins

- 2 cups packaged biscuit mix
- ¼ cup sugar
- ¼ teaspoon salt
- 1 teaspoon cinnamon
- 2 slightly beaten eggs
- ¾ cup milk
- 2 tablespoons salad oil
- 2 teaspoons shredded orange peel
- ½ cup currants or raisins, plumped

Mix first 8 ingredients; beat vigorously 30 seconds. Add currants. Grease muffin pans or line with paper bake cups; fill ⅔ full. Bake at 400° 15 to 18 minutes. Cool slightly. Pipe on crosses of confectioners' frosting. Serve warm. Makes 12.

Peanut-butter Muffins

    2 cups sifted all-purpose flour
    ½ cup sugar
    2½ teaspoons baking powder
    ½ teaspoon salt
    ½ cup chunk-style peanut butter

    2 tablespoons butter or margarine
    2 well-beaten eggs
    ¾ cup milk
    ¼ cup currant jelly, melted
    ⅓ cup finely chopped peanuts, toasted

Sift together dry ingredients. Cut in peanut butter and butter till mixture resembles coarse crumbs. Add eggs and milk, all at once, stirring just till flour is moistened. Grease 2-inch muffin pans or line with paper bake cups; fill ⅔ full. Bake in hot oven (400°) 15 to 17 minutes or till done. *Immediately* brush tops of muffins with melted jelly; dip tops in peanuts. Serve warm. Makes 20 small muffins.

Orange-blossom Muffins

    1 slightly beaten egg
    ¼ cup sugar
    ½ cup orange juice
    2 tablespoons salad oil or melted shortening

    2 cups packaged biscuit mix
    ½ cup orange marmalade
    ½ cup chopped pecans
    1 recipe Spicy Topping

Combine egg, ¼ cup sugar, the orange juice, and salad oil; add biscuit mix; beat vigorously 30 seconds. Stir in marmalade and pecans. Grease muffin pans or line with paper bake cups; fill ⅔ full. Sprinkle with SPICY TOPPING: Combine ¼ cup sugar, 1½ tablespoons all-purpose flour, ½ teaspoon cinnamon, and ¼ teaspoon nutmeg; cut in 1 tablespoon butter until crumbly. Bake muffins in hot oven (400°) 20 to 25 minutes or till done. Makes 1 dozen.

Spicy Fruit Puffs

- 2 cups sifted all-purpose flour
- 3 teaspoons baking powder
- 1 teaspoon salt
- ½ teaspoon cinnamon
- ¼ teaspoon nutmeg
- 1 cup shredded pared apple or ½ cup raisins
- ⅔ cup brown sugar
- ¼ cup chopped California walnuts
- 2 beaten eggs
- ⅔ cup milk
- ¼ cup shortening, melted and cooled
- 1 cup whole wheat or bran flakes

Sift together first 5 ingredients. Stir in apple *or* raisins, brown sugar, and walnuts. Combine eggs, milk, and shortening; add all at once, stirring just to blend. Fold in cereal flakes. Fill greased muffin pans ⅔ full. Bake at 400° for 15 to 20 minutes. Makes 12 muffins.

Applesauce Puffs

Combine 2 cups packaged biscuit mix, ¼ cup sugar, and 1 teaspoon cinnamon. Add ½ cup applesauce, ¼ cup milk, 1 slightly beaten egg, and 2 tablespoons salad oil. *Beat vigorously* 30 seconds. Fill greased 2-inch muffin pans ⅔ full. Bake in hot oven (400°) 12 minutes or till done. Cool slightly; remove. Dip tops in 2 tablespoons melted butter or margarine, then in ¼ cup sugar mixed with ¼ teaspoon cinnamon. Makes 24 small muffins.

Cheddar Bran Muffins

1¼ cups buttermilk or sour milk	1½ teaspoons baking powder
1 cup whole bran	½ teaspoon salt
¼ cup shortening	¼ teaspoon soda
⅓ cup sugar	4 ounces sharp natural
1 egg	Cheddar cheese, shredded
1½ cups sifted all-purpose flour	(1 cup)

Pour buttermilk or sour milk over bran in small bowl; let stand till softened. Meanwhile, cream shortening and sugar till light and fluffy. Beat in egg. Sift together flour, baking powder, salt, and soda. Add to creamed mixture alternately with milk-bran mixture. Stir in shredded cheese. Fill greased muffin pans ⅔ full. Bake in hot oven (400°) about 30 minutes. Serve warm. Makes 12 muffins.

Dixie Corn-Meal Biscuits

1½ cups sifted all-purpose flour	¼ cup shortening
1 tablespoon sugar	1 slightly beaten egg
2 teaspoons baking powder	¾ cup dairy sour cream
¾ teaspoon salt	1 tablespoon sesame seed
½ teaspoon soda	2 tablespoons butter or
½ cup corn meal	margarine

Sift together first 5 ingredients; stir in corn meal. Cut in shortening till mixture resembles coarse crumbs. Add egg and sour cream; *mix just till dough follows fork around bowl.* Turn out on lightly floured surface; knead gently ½ minute. Roll or pat to about ¼ inch and cut with floured 2½-inch biscuit cutter. Crease just off center with back of knife; fold over so top overlaps. Seal edges. In skillet, lightly brown sesame seed in butter; brush over biscuits. Bake on ungreased baking sheet in hot oven (425°) 10 minutes or till done. Makes about 2 dozen.

Quick Parmesan Biscuits

1 clove garlic, minced
2 tablespoons finely chopped parsley
¼ cup butter or margarine melted
2 packages refrigerated biscuits
¼ cup shredded Parmesan cheese

Add garlic and parsley to butter; dip biscuits in mixture. Overlap 13 biscuits around outer edge of 9x1½-inch round metal cake pan. Overlap remaining biscuits in center. Drizzle remaining butter over top; sprinkle with cheese. Bake in hot oven (425°) 15 to 20 minutes. Makes 20.

Banana Ambrosia Ring

- 1 recipe Coconut Topper
- 2 cups packaged biscuit mix
- 3 tablespoons sugar
- ½ cup mashed ripe banana
- 1 slightly beaten egg
- 3 tablespoons melted butter or margarine
- 2 tablespoons sugar
- 1 teaspoon cinnamon
- 2 tablespoons butter or margarine

Spread Coconut Topper over bottom of 5-cup ring mold. Combine biscuit mix and 3 tablespoons sugar. Stir in banana, egg, and melted butter. Beat vigorously 1 minute. Spoon *half* the batter over coconut in mold. Mix 2 tablespoons sugar with the cinnamon; sprinkle over batter; dot with butter. Cover with remaining batter. Bake in moderate oven (375°) 20 minutes or till done. Invert to unmold. Serve warm.
COCONUT TOPPER: Mix ½ cup flaked coconut with ⅓ cup maple-flavored syrup and 2 tablespoons melted butter or margarine.

Easter Nest Coffeecake

Soften 1 package active dry yeast in ¼ cup *warm* water. Scald ½ cup milk; stir in ¼ cup shortening, ¼ cup sugar, and 1 teaspoon salt; cool to lukewarm. Add 1 cup sifted all-purpose flour; beat smooth. Add yeast and 1 slightly beaten egg; beat well. Add 2 cups sifted flour (or enough for soft dough). On floured surface, knead till smooth and elastic (8 to 10 minutes). Place in greased bowl, turning once to grease surface. Cover; let double in warm place (about 1 hour). Punch down; divide in thirds. Cover; let rest 10 minutes. Shape *a third* of the dough in 6 "eggs"; place close together in center of greased baking sheet. For nest, shape remaining dough in two 26-inch ropes; twist together. Coil around eggs; seal ends. Cover; let double (about 1 hour). Bake at 375° 15 to 20 minutes. Cool. Frost with confectioners' icing; sprinkle eggs with candy decorettes, nest with green shredded coconut.

COFFEE CAKES • 213

Kugelhoff

- 1 package active dry yeast
- ¼ cup **warm** water
- ½ cup milk, scalded
- ¼ cup butter or margarine
- ½ cup sugar
- 2 eggs
- 2½ cups sifted all-purpose flour
- 1 teaspoon salt
- ½ cup golden raisins
- 1 teaspoon grated lemon peel
- 1 tablespoon melted butter
- 3 tablespoons fine dry bread crumbs
- Blanched whole almonds

Soften yeast in *warm* water. Cool milk to lukewarm. In mixing bowl, cream butter and sugar till light; add eggs, one at a time, beating after each. Add yeast and milk. Sift together flour and salt; add to creamed mixture. Beat at medium speed on mixer till smooth, 2 minutes. Stir in raisins and lemon peel. Cover; let rise in a warm place till double (2 hours). Meanwhile, prepare a 1½-quart Turk's Head Mold: Brush liberally with butter; sprinkle with bread crumbs, coating well. Arrange almonds in a design in bottom of mold. Stir down batter; spoon carefully into mold. Let rise till almost double (1 hour). Bake at 350° for 25 minutes or till done. Cool 10 minutes. Remove mold.

William Tell Coffeecake

- ¼ cup butter or margarine
- ¾ cup sugar
- 1 egg
- 1 teaspoon vanilla
- 1½ cups sifted all-purpose flour
- 2 teaspoons baking powder
- ½ teaspoon nutmeg
- ¼ teaspoon salt
- ⅔ cup milk
- 1 recipe Apple Top

Stir butter to soften. Cream together butter and sugar till fluffy. Add egg and vanilla; beat well. Sift together dry ingredients; add to creamed mixture alternately with milk, beating smooth after each addition. Pour into greased 9x9x2-inch pan. Sprinkle with Apple Top. Bake in moderate oven (375°) 25 to 30 minutes or till done. Cool 15 minutes; cut in squares and serve warm. APPLE TOP: Combine 1 cup finely chopped pared tart apple, ⅓ cup sugar, and 1 teaspoon cinnamon.

Flaky Danish Crescent

- 1 package active dry yeast
- ¼ cup **warm** water
- 2 cups sifted all-purpose flour
- 1 tablespoon sugar
- ½ teaspoon salt
- ½ cup chilled butter or margarine
- ¼ cup milk, scalded
- 1 slightly beaten egg yolk
- 1 recipe Meringue Filling
- ½ cup chopped almonds or pecans

Soften yeast in water. Sift together dry ingredients; cut in butter till some of the mixture is like corn meal and some the size of peas. Mix cooled milk and egg yolk; add with yeast to flour, stirring to make a soft dough. Cover; chill a few hours or overnight. Halve dough (keep half chilled). On floured surface, roll one piece in 12x9-inch rectangle, about ⅛ inch thick. Reserve 2 tablespoons Meringue Filling for glaze; spread dough with *half* of remainder. Sprinkle with *half* the nuts. Roll as for jelly roll (start at long side). Seal edges and ends. Place roll, seam down, on baking sheet. Shape in crescent; flatten slightly. Repeat with remaining dough. Cover; let rise in warm place till almost double (about 1 hour). Brush with reserved Meringue. To garnish, sprinkle with additional almonds, thinly sliced. Bake in moderate oven (375°) 20 minutes or till done. Serve warm. Makes 2. MERINGUE FILLING: Fold ½ cup sugar and 1 teaspoon cinnamon into 1 stiff-beaten egg white.

SANDWICHES • 215

Cheese Buns Deluxe

- 4 ounces sharp process American cheese, shredded (1 cup)
- ¼ cup mayonnaise or salad dressing
- ¼ cup chopped ripe olives
- 2 tablespoons chopped green onion
- ¼ teaspoon curry powder
- 4 hamburger buns, split and toasted

Mix first 5 ingredients; spread on toasted buns. Broil 4 inches from heat about 2 minutes or till cheese melts. Makes 8 open-faced sandwiches.

All-in-a-Roll Supper

- ¾ pound ground beef
- ¼ cup chopped onion
- 2 large brown-and-serve French rolls, each about 8 inches long*
- 1 beaten egg
- 3 tablespoons snipped parsley
- 1 to 2 tablespoons prepared mustard
- 2 tablespoons water
- ¾ teaspoon salt
- ¼ teaspoon oregano
- Dash pepper
- 2 tablespoons butter or margarine, melted
- 1 clove garlic, minced

Brown ground beef. Add onion; cook till tender but not brown. Drain off excess fat. Cut off one end of each roll; reserve. With a fork, hollow out roll centers and pull apart enough bread to make 1 cup crumbs. Mix crumbs with meat and next 7 ingredients. Fill rolls, replacing ends; tack with toothpicks. Mix butter and garlic; brush over rolls. Heat on baking sheet in moderate oven (375°) 20 minutes or till hot. Cut in 4 or 6 servings.

*Or 6 frankfurter buns. Fill, wrap each in foil; heat.

Grilled Crab Sandwiches

- 1 6½- or 7½-ounce can (about 1 cup) crab meat, drained and flaked
- ½ cup shredded sharp process American cheese
- ¼ cup chopped celery
- 2 tablespoons drained sweet-pickle relish
- 2 tablespoons chopped green onions and tops
- 1 hard-cooked egg, chopped
- 3 tablespoons salad dressing or mayonnaise
- ½ teaspoon lemon juice
- ½ teaspoon prepared horseradish
- 10 slices bread, buttered generously
- 5 tomato slices

Combine first 9 ingredients; spread on *unbuttered* side of 5 bread slices. Add tomato slices; season with salt and pepper. Top with bread slices, buttered side up. Grill on griddle, sandwich grill, or in skillet till sandwiches are golden brown. Makes 5.

Hot Avocado-Crab Sandwiches

- 1 10½-ounce can condensed cream of mushroom soup
- ¼ cup milk
- ½ teaspoon Worcestershire sauce
- Dash bottled hot pepper sauce
- 4 ounces sharp process American cheese, shredded (1 cup)
- 4 large English muffins, split, toasted, and buttered
- 1 6½- or 7½-ounce can (about 1 cup) crab meat, drained and flaked
- 2 avocados, peeled and sliced
- ½ cup shredded sharp process American cheese

Combine first 4 ingredients; heat, stirring occasionally. Add 1 cup cheese; stir till melted. Place muffins on baking sheet. Spread rounded tablespoon sauce on each muffin; top with crab meat, then avocado slices. Drizzle with remaining sauce. Sprinkle with ½ cup cheese. Broil 4 inches from heat 3 to 4 minutes or till golden brown and bubbly. Makes 8.

Hong Kong Hamburgers

- 1 pound ground beef
- 1 8½-ounce can sliced pineapple (4 slices)
- ⅓ cup brown sugar
- 2 teaspoons cornstarch
- 3 tablespoons red wine vinegar
- 1 tablespoon soy sauce
- 1 tablespoon Worcestershire sauce
- 4 green-pepper rings
- 4 hamburger buns, split and toasted

Shape meat in 4 patties; sprinkle with salt and pepper. Broil about 4 inches from heat 10 minutes, turning once. Meanwhile drain pineapple, reserving ¼ cup syrup. Mix brown sugar and cornstarch; blend in reserved pineapple syrup and next 3 ingredients. Cook and stir in small skillet till mixture comes to boiling. Add pineapple slices; top with green-pepper rings. Cover; heat through. Place burgers on buns; top with pineapple and green peppers. Spoon a little sauce over each burger; pass extra sauce.

Corned-beef Stag Sandwiches

- 1 cup packaged biscuit mix
- 1 12-ounce can corned beef, chilled
- 1 tablespoon mayonnaise or salad dressing
- 1 tablespoon prepared mustard
- ½ cup pitted ripe olives, sliced
- 1 large tomato, thinly sliced
- 4 slices sharp process American cheese

Prepare biscuit mix according to package directions for rolled biscuits. Roll to a 12x7-inch rectangle, about ⅜ inch thick. Place on ungreased baking sheet. Cut corned beef in 10 slices; arrange over dough. Mix mayonnaise and mustard; spread over meat. Sprinkle with olives. Bake in hot oven (425°) 10 minutes. Top with tomato slices, dash with freshly ground pepper. Halve cheese slices diagonally; arrange over tomatoes. Return to oven till cheese melts, about 5 minutes. Cut in 6 squares.

Dad's Denvers

- 6 hamburger buns, split and toasted
- 1 4½-ounce can deviled ham
- 4 eggs
- ¼ cup milk
- ¼ teaspoon salt
- Dash pepper
- ¼ cup chopped green onions
- 2 tablespoons butter, margarine, or bacon drippings
- 6 thin tomato slices
- 6 slices sharp process American cheese

Spread lower half of buns with deviled ham. Combine eggs, milk, salt, and pepper. Beat slightly for gold-and-white effect, thoroughly for all-yellow eggs. Add onions. Heat butter in skillet till just hot enough to make a drop of water sizzle. Pour in egg mixture. Reduce heat and cook, lifting and folding occasionally, till eggs are set; but still moist. Pile eggs atop deviled ham and add tomato and cheese slices. Place on baking sheet; broil about 4 inches from heat *just* till cheese melts. Cover with bun tops. Makes 6.

Chef's Salad in a Roll

Brown big brown-and-serve French rolls (about 8 inches long) according to package directions. Split rolls in half, but *not quite through.* (If you like, scoop out some of centers to make room for filling.) For *each* supersize sandwich, line bottom half of roll with romaine lettuce; drizzle with 1 teaspoon French dressing. Pile on slices of chicken; dash with salt, pepper. Add 1 or 2 slices boiled ham and Swiss cheese, halved to fit roll. Top with hard-cooked egg slices; salt. Cover with romaine and tomato slices; season. Drizzle with 2 teaspoons more dressing. Add roll tops, anchor with picks.

Hot Cheese-Salami Sandwiches

8 ounces process American cheese, shredded (2 cups) or 2 5-ounce jars spreading cheese	⅔ cup chopped ripe olives
	1 unsliced sandwich loaf, about 11 inches long
¼ cup mayonnaise or salad dressing	18 to 20 thin slices large salami (about ½ pound)
1 teaspoon prepared mustard	2 tablespoons butter or margarine, melted
1 teaspoon grated onion	

Blend first 4 ingredients; stir in olives. Cut crusts from top and sides of loaf. Make ½-inch slices, cutting to, *but not through,* bottom crust. Spread facing sides of first cut with cheese filling. Repeat with *every other* cut. Insert 2 salami slices in each "cheese sandwich." Carefully spread remaining cheese mixture over top of loaf. Tie loaf together with string. Brush sides with butter. Toast on baking sheet in moderate oven (350°) 25 to 30 minutes or till hot. To serve, snip string and cut through bottom crust in sections without filling. Makes 9 or 10 sandwiches.

Peanut-and-Apple Sandwiches

½ cup peanut butter	½ cup finely diced pared tart apple
2 tablespoons mayonnaise or salad dressing	6 slices bacon, crisp-cooked and crumbled
2 teaspoons lemon juice	Buttered bread slices

Blend peanut butter, mayonnaise, and lemon juice. Stir in apple and bacon. Use as a filling between buttered slices of bread. Add lettuce, if desired. Makes 1 cup filling—enough for 4 or 5 sandwiches.

Champion Roast Beef Sandwiches

- 8 slices dark rye bread
  Butter or margarine
- ½ cup dairy sour cream
- 2 teaspoons dry onion-soup mix
- 2 teaspoons prepared horseradish, well drained
  Dash freshly ground pepper
  Thinly sliced cold roast beef
  Leaf lettuce

Spread bread slices with butter. Combine sour cream, onion-soup mix, horseradish, and pepper. Spread about 1 tablespoon of the sour-cream mixture on each slice of bread. Top 4 slices with roast beef, then lettuce; cover with remaining bread. Makes 4 sandwiches.

Double-beef Sandwiches

- 12 slices rye bread, buttered
- 2 tablespoons prepared mustard
  Leaf lettuce
- 4 ounces dried beef, pulled apart
- 4 ounces sliced Muenster or brick cheese
- 4 ounces cooked or canned corned beef, sliced very thin*
- 2 large dill pickles, thinly sliced
- 1 onion, thinly sliced
- 1 tablespoon prepared horseradish

Spread *half* the bread slices with mustard and add layers of lettuce, dried beef, cheese, corned beef, pickle, and onion. Top each stack-up with more lettuce. Spread remaining bread slices with horseradish, and complete sandwiches. Anchor each with toothpick topped with a ripe olive. Makes 6.

* For easy slicing, have corned beef chilled.

Double-corn Cakes

- 1 cup packaged pancake mix
- 1 cup corn meal
- 1 teaspoon baking powder
- 2 slightly beaten eggs
- 1 1-pound can (2 cups) cream-style corn
- 1 cup milk
- 2 tablespoons salad oil or melted shortening

Stir together dry ingredients. Combine eggs, corn, milk, and oil; add to dry ingredients, stirring just till all is moistened. Drop batter from ¼-cup measure onto hot, lightly greased griddle or skillet. Turn once. Makes about sixteen 4-inch pancakes.

Easy Sourdough Flapjacks

- 1 package active dry yeast or 1 cake compressed yeast
- ¼ cup water
- 1 egg
- 2 cups milk
- 2 cups packaged biscuit mix

Soften dry yeast in *warm* water or compressed yeast in *lukewarm* water. Beat egg; add milk and biscuit mix. Beat with rotary beater until blended. Stir in softened yeast. Allow batter to stand at room temperature 1 to 1½ hours. *Do not stir.* Bake on a hot, lightly greased griddle or in skillet. (For uniform pancakes, pour from a ¼-cup measure.) Turn cakes when bubbles on surface break. Makes 2 dozen 4-inch cakes.

Blintz Pancakes

1 cup sifted all-purpose flour	1 8-ounce carton (1 cup) small-curd cream-style cottage cheese
1 tablespoon sugar	
½ teaspoon salt	
1 cup dairy sour cream	4 well-beaten eggs

Sift dry ingredients into bowl. Add sour cream, cottage cheese, and beaten eggs; fold only till flour is barely moistened. Bake on a hot, lightly greased griddle or in skillet. (For uniform pancakes, use a ¼-cup measure.) Turn cakes when bubbles on surface break. Stack pancakes and serve with warm maple-flavored syrup or BLUEBERRY SAUCE: Combine one 1-pound can (2 cups) blueberries and 2 teaspoons cornstarch. Cook and stir till thick and clear. Add 1 teaspoon lemon juice. Makes sixteen 4-inch pancakes.

Golden Apricot Roll-ups

1 cup packaged pancake mix	½ cup corn-flake crumbs
½ cup apricot jam	2 tablespoons butter or margarine
2 slightly beaten eggs	

Prepare pancake mix according to package directions, but using 1 *cup milk*, 1 egg, and 1 tablespoon salad oil or melted shortening. Bake on griddle as directed on package. Spread about a tablespoon jam over each hot cake. Roll up. Dip rolls in egg, then in corn-flake crumbs. Place, seam side down, in skillet. Brown on all sides in butter over low heat. Serve hot. Pass melted butter, if desired. Makes 8.

Peanut-butter Waffles

1 cup packaged pancake mix
2 tablespoons sugar
⅓ cup chunk-style peanut butter
1 egg

1 cup milk
2 tablespoons salad oil or melted shortening

Combine all ingredients. Beat with rotary or electric beater just till almost smooth. (There will be a few lumps.) Bake in preheated waffle baker. Makes eight 4-inch waffles. Pass butter, jelly, or maple-flavored syrup.

Everyday Waffles

1¾ cups sifted all-purpose flour
  or 2 cups sifted cake flour
3 teaspoons baking powder
½ teaspoon salt
2 beaten egg yolks

1¼ cups milk
½ cup salad oil or melted shortening
2 stiff-beaten egg whites

Sift together dry ingredients. Combine egg yolks and milk; stir into dry ingredients. Stir in oil. Fold in egg whites, leaving a few little fluffs—don't overmix. Bake in preheated waffle baker. Makes about 8 waffles.

Buttermilk Waffles Substitute buttermilk for sweet milk. Add ½ teaspoon soda and cut baking powder to 2 teaspoons.

224 • PANCAKES AND WAFFLES

Ham Waffles   Sprinkle 2 tablespoons finely diced cooked ham over, before closing baker.

Cheese Waffles   Cut shortening to 2 tablespoons; add ½ cup shredded process cheese.

Maple Waffles

- 1¾ cups sifted all-purpose flour
- 3 teaspoons baking powder
- ½ teaspoon salt
- 2 beaten egg yolks
- 1 cup milk
- ½ cup maple-flavored syrup
- ½ teaspoon maple flavoring
- ¼ cup salad oil
- 2 stiff-beaten egg whites

Sift together dry ingredients. Combine next 5 ingredients; stir into dry mixture. Fold in egg whites; do not overmix. Bake. Serve with butter and confectioners' sugar sprinkled over. Makes 4 to 6 waffles.

"Oh Boy" Waffles

- 2¼ cups sifted all-purpose flour
- 4 teaspoons baking powder
- ¾ teaspoon salt
- 1½ tablespoons sugar
- 2 beaten eggs
- 2¼ cups milk
- ¼ cup salad oil

Sift together dry ingredients. Combine eggs, milk, and oil; add just before baking, beating only till moistened. (Batter is thin.) Bake in preheated baker. Makes 10 to 12.

Spicy Party Waffles

- ½ cup shortening
- 1 cup brown sugar
- 2 eggs
- 1½ cups sifted all-purpose flour
- 2 teaspoons baking powder
- ½ teaspoon salt
- 1 teaspoon cinnamon
- 1 teaspoon allspice
- ½ teaspoon cloves
- ½ cup milk
- ½ cup broken California walnuts
- 2 to 3 tablespoons chopped candied ginger
- 1 cup whipping cream, whipped

Cream together shortening and sugar. Add eggs, one at a time, beating well after each. Sift together flour, baking powder, salt, and spices; add to creamed mixture alternately with milk. Stir in walnuts. Bake in preheated waffle baker. Fold candied ginger into whipped cream, serve atop waffles. Makes 2 to 3 large waffles.

Crisp Corn-meal Waffles

- 1 cup sifted all-purpose flour
- 2 teaspoons baking powder
- 1 teaspoon soda
- 1 teaspoon sugar
- ½ teaspoon salt
- 1 cup yellow corn meal
- 2 beaten eggs
- 2 cups buttermilk
- ¼ cup salad oil

Sift first 5 ingredients; stir in corn meal. Combine remaining ingredients; add, mixing just till moistened. Bake. Makes 8 to 10.

Date Dessert Waffles

Sift together 2 cups sifted all-purpose flour, 3 teaspoons baking powder, 1 teaspoon salt; stir in ¼ cup brown sugar. Combine 1¾ cups milk, ½ cup salad oil, and 2 slightly-beaten egg yolks. Add to dry mixture; blend well. Fold in 2 stiff-beaten egg whites. Finely chop enough dates to make 1 cup. Pour batter into preheated waffle baker; sprinkle with ⅛ cup of the dates; bake. Serve with LEMON TOPPING (see page 226). Makes 3.

Corn Waffles

- 1¾ cups sifted all-purpose flour **or** 2 cups sifted cake flour
- 1 to 2 tablespoons sugar
- 3 teaspoons baking powder
- ½ teaspoon salt
- 2 beaten egg yolks
- 1 cup milk
- 2 cups canned cream-style corn
- ½ cup salad oil **or** melted shortening
- 2 stiff-beaten egg whites

Sift together dry ingredients. Combine next 4 ingredients; stir into dry mixture. Fold in egg whites; leave a few little fluffs—don't overmix. Bake. Makes about 9 waffles.

Sour-cream Waffles

- 1 cup sifted all-purpose flour
- ½ tablespoon sugar
- 1 teaspoon baking powder
- ¼ teaspoon soda
- ¼ teaspoon salt
- 1 well-beaten egg yolk
- 1 cup dairy sour cream
- ¼ cup milk
- 3 tablespoons butter, melted
- 1 stiff-beaten egg white

Sift together dry ingredients. Combine egg yolk, sour cream, milk and butter; add to flour mixture and beat smooth. Fold in beaten egg white. Bake. Makes 4.

Toppers for Pancakes, Waffles

Maple Syrup　　Combine 1 cup light corn syrup, ½ cup brown sugar, ½ cup water; cook and stir till sugar dissolves. Add few drops maple flavoring, 1 tablespoon butter.

Lemon Topping　　Combine 1 cup dairy sour cream, ¼ cup sugar, 2 tablespoons lemon juice, ½ teaspoon grated lemon peel. Makes 1 cup.

Cranberry-Orange Butter　　Put 1 small unpeeled orange (diced), ¼ cup raw cranberries, and ¼ cup sugar in electric blender. Blend 40 seconds; fold into Whipped Butter.

Orange Sauce　　Combine ½ cup butter, 1 cup sugar, ½ cup frozen orange-juice concentrate. Bring just to boil; stir occasionally.

Whipped Butter

Let ¼ pound (½ cup) butter stand at room temperature for 1 hour. Place in mixing bowl and run mixer at lowest speed until large chunks smooth out. Gradually increase mixer speed to fastest position and whip until butter is fluffy (takes about 8 minutes). Cover butter until ready to use. (If made ahead and refrigerated, remove from refrigerator an hour before using.) Makes about 1½ cups spread.

SECTION 6

Casseroles and One-dish Meals

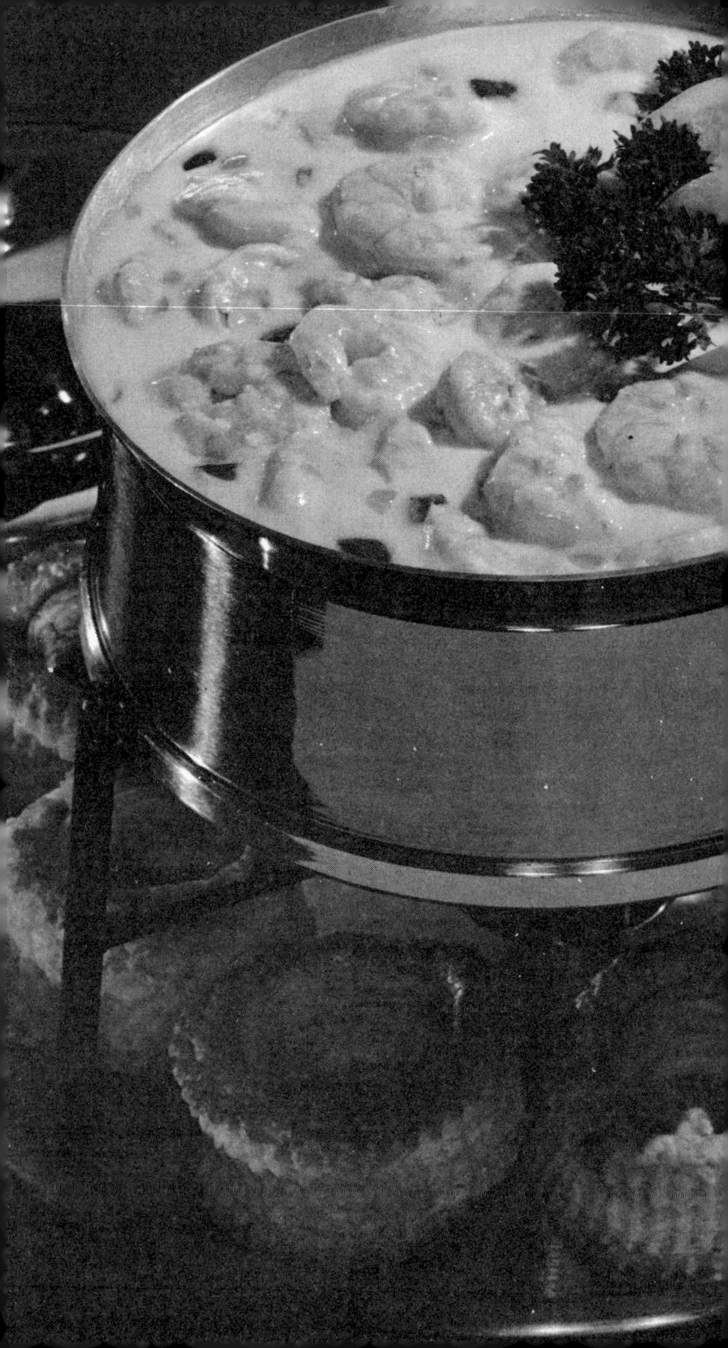

SECTION 6
Casseroles and One-dish Meals

For-the-Crowd Casserole

- 1½ pounds ground beef
- 1 cup chopped onion
- 1 12-ounce can (1½ cups) golden whole kernel corn, drained
- 1 10½-ounce can condensed cream of chicken soup
- 1 10½-ounce can condensed cream of mushroom soup
- 1 cup dairy sour cream
- ¼ cup chopped canned pimiento
- ¾ teaspoon salt
- ½ teaspoon monosodium glutamate
- ¼ teaspoon pepper
- 3 cups medium noodles, cooked
- 1 cup buttered soft bread crumbs

Brown meat. Add onion; cook till tender but not brown. Add next 8 ingredients; mix well. Stir in noodles. Pour into a 2-quart casserole. Sprinkle crumbs over top. Bake in moderate oven (350°) 30 minutes or till hot. Makes 8 to 10 servings.

Saucy Meat Loaves

- 2 pounds ground beef
- ½ cup chopped onion
- ½ cup chopped celery
- ½ cup chopped green pepper
- 1 envelope dry tomato-soup mix
- 1 teaspoon salt
  Dash pepper
- ½ cup dry bread crumbs
- ½ cup milk
- 2 eggs
- 1 1-pound can (2 cups) tomato sauce
- 1 6-ounce can (1⅓ cups) chopped broiled mushrooms, undrained
- ⅔ cup water
- 2 tablespoons brown sugar
- 1 teaspoon salt

Combine first 10 ingredients. Shape in 12 loaves, using ½ cup mixture each. Place in 13x9x2-inch baking dish. Combine remaining ingredients; pour over meat. Bake, uncovered, at 350° for 50 to 60 minutes, basting occasionally.

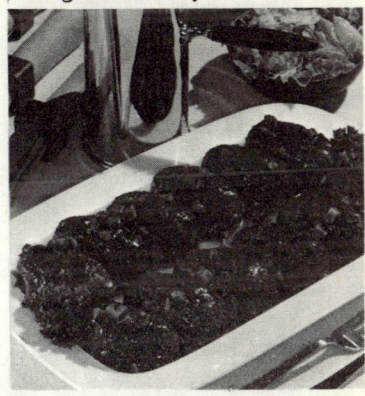

Italian Hamburger Bake

- 1 pound ground beef
- ½ cup chopped onion
- 1 envelope dry tomato-soup mix
- 1 cup milk
- 1 8-ounce carton (1-cup) large-curd cottage cheese
- Dash garlic powder
- ¼ teaspoon crushed basil
- ¼ teaspoon oregano
- ¼ teaspoon salt
- ¼ cup shredded Parmesan cheese
- 1 package refrigerated biscuits

Cook meat and onion together till browned. Stir in soup mix, milk, cottage cheese, and seasonings; heat to boiling. Pour into 10x6x1½-inch baking dish. Sprinkle with Parmesan cheese. Halve 6 biscuits; arrange on *hot* meat mixture. (Bake remainder on baking sheet.) Bake in moderate oven (375°) 20 minutes or till biscuits are done. Makes 4 servings.

Big-biscuit Hamburger Bake

1 pound ground beef
½ cup chopped onion
1 10¾-ounce can condensed cream of vegetable soup
½ teaspoon crushed oregano
Dash freshly ground pepper
1 recipe Big Biscuit

Cook ground beef and onion till meat is brown; drain off excess fat. Stir in soup and seasonings; heat to bubbling. Turn into an 8¼x1¾-inch round ovenware cake dish. Top with Big Biscuit: Add ½ cup milk, all at once, to 1 cup packaged biscuit mix. Stir with fork into a soft dough; beat 15 strokes. Spread over *hot* meat mixture. Bake in very hot oven (450°) 15 minutes or till browned. Spread biscuit with ½ cup dairy sour cream. Sprinkle with ½ cup shredded Parmesan cheese, then snipped parsley. Bake 2 minutes. Makes 6 servings.

German Caraway Meat Balls

1 recipe Meat Balls
2 tablespoons fat
1 10½-ounce can condensed beef broth
1 3-ounce can chopped mushrooms, drained (½ cup)
½ cup chopped onion
1 cup dairy sour cream
1 tablespoon all-purpose flour
½ to 1 teaspoon caraway seed
1 recipe Spaetzle

MEAT BALLS: Combine 1 pound ground beef, ¼ cup fine dry bread crumbs, 1 teaspoon salt, dash pepper, ¼ teaspoon poultry seasoning, 1 tablespoon snipped parsley, ¼ cup milk, and 1 egg; mix lightly. Shape in about twenty-four 1½-inch balls. Brown slowly on all sides in hot fat, shaking frequently. Add broth, mushrooms, and onion. Simmer covered 30 minutes. Blend sour cream, flour, and caraway seed; stir into broth. Cook and stir till mixture thickens. Serve with SPAETZLE: Sift together 2 cups sifted all-purpose flour and 1 teaspoon salt. Add 2 slightly beaten eggs and ¾ cup milk; beat well. Place mixture in coarse-sieved colander. Hold over large kettle of rapidly boiling salted water. Press batter through colander. Cook and stir 5 minutes; drain. Sprinkle with mixture of ¼ cup fine dry bread crumbs, 2 tablespoons melted butter. Makes 5 or 6 servings.

Italian Sauce—Spinach Squares

ITALIAN SAUCE: Cook 1 pound ground beef and 1 cup chopped onion in 2 tablespoons hot olive oil till meat is brown. Add one 1-pound can (2 cups) tomatoes, one 8-ounce can (1 cup) seasoned tomato sauce, one 3-ounce can broiled sliced mushrooms, drained (½ cup), 2 cloves garlic, minced, 1 teaspoon *each* salt and sugar, ½ teaspoon rosemary, crushed, and ¼ teaspoon pepper. Cover; simmer 1½ hours, stirring occasionally. Serve over hot spaghetti or SPINACH SQUARES: Cook and drain one 10-ounce package frozen chopped spinach. Combine with ½ cup chopped onion, 2 ounces sharp process American cheese, shredded (½ cup), ¼ cup snipped parsley, ¼ teaspoon salt, 1 clove garlic, minced, 2 slightly beaten eggs, and 2 cups soft bread crumbs; shape in 10x3-inch rectangle. Chill. Cut in 6 servings; brown slowly in butter on both sides.

Inside-out Ravioli Casserole

- 1 pound ground beef
- 1 medium onion, chopped (½ cup)
- 1 clove garlic, minced
- 1 tablespoon salad oil
- 1 10-ounce package frozen chopped spinach
- 1 1-pound can spaghetti sauce with mushrooms
- 1 8-ounce can (1 cup) tomato sauce
- 1 6-ounce can (⅔ cup) tomato paste
- ½ teaspoon salt
- Dash pepper
- 1 7-ounce package (2 cups) shell or elbow macaroni, cooked
- 4 ounces sharp process American cheese, shredded (1 cup)
- ½ cup soft bread crumbs
- 2 well-beaten eggs
- ¼ cup salad oil

Brown first 3 ingredients in the 1 tablespoon salad oil. Cook spinach according to package directions. Drain, reserving liquid; add water to make 1 cup. Stir spinach liquid and next 5 ingredients into meat mixture. Simmer 10 minutes. Combine spinach with remaining ingredients; spread in 13x9x2-inch baking dish. Top with meat sauce. Bake at 350° 30 minutes. Let stand 10 minutes before serving. Makes 8 to 10 servings.

Jiffy Chili-Hominy Bake

- 1 pound ground beef
- ½ cup chopped onion
- 1 1-pound can (2 cups) chili with beans
- 1 tablespoon chili powder
- 1 10½-ounce can condensed cream of chicken soup
- 1 1-pound 4-ounce can (2½ cups) yellow hominy, drained
- 2 tablespoons sliced ripe olives
- 2 ounces process American cheese, shredded (½ cup)

Cook ground beef and onion till meat is browned. Stir in remaining ingredients, except the cheese. Spoon into 2-quart casserole. Cover; bake in moderate oven (350°) for 25 minutes. Sprinkle cheese over top; continue baking, uncovered, 5 minutes. Makes about 6 servings.

Beef Cantonese with Ginger Rice

- ¼ cup soy sauce
- ¼ cup cooking sherry
- 2 tablespoons sugar
- ¼ teaspoon cinnamon
- 2 pounds beef chuck, cut in ½-inch cubes
- 1½ cups water
- 2 tablespoons cornstarch
- 2 tablespoons cold water
- 1 recipe Ginger Rice

Mix soy sauce, sherry, sugar, and cinnamon. Marinate beef in soy mixture 1 hour, stirring occasionally. Add 1½ cups water; simmer covered (*don't boil*) 1 hour or till tender. Blend cornstarch and 2 tablespoons cold water; add to meat mixture. Cook and stir till mixture thickens. Serve over GINGER RICE: Cook ½ cup chopped green onions 1 minute in 3 tablespoons hot salad oil. Add 2 tablespoons finely diced candied ginger and 4 cups hot cooked rice; toss lightly. Makes 6 to 8 servings.

236 • MEATS

Beef Stew with Sesame Biscuits

Cook 1 pound 1-inch cubes beef chuck in ¼ cup soy sauce 5 minutes, stirring frequently. Add 2 cups water. Cover; simmer 30 to 45 minutes or till almost tender. Add 4 carrots, cut in 1-inch pieces, 2 cups diced potatoes, 2 onions, quartered, 1 cup bias-cut celery slices, 1 teaspoon salt, and ¼ teaspoon garlic salt. Cover and simmer till meat and vegetables are tender, about 20 minutes. Mix 2 tablespoons *each* cornstarch and cold water; stir into stew; cook and stir till boiling. With a 1-inch cutter, remove centers from 7 or 8 packaged refrigerated biscuits. Pour *hot* stew into 2-quart casserole; place biscuits on top. Brush with melted butter; sprinkle with toasted sesame seed. Bake in hot oven (425°) 10 to 15 minutes or till done. Makes 6 servings.

Big-meal Combo

1 10½-ounce can condensed cream of chicken soup	2 1-pound cans (4 cups) small whole onions, drained
4 ounces sharp process American cheese, shredded (1 cup)	1 3-ounce can broiled sliced mushrooms, drained (½ cup)
¼ teaspoon salt	½ cup diced green pepper
2 1-pound cans (4 cups) tiny whole potatoes, drained	1 12-ounce can corned beef, chilled
	1 cup buttered soft bread crumbs or corn-flake crumbs

Combine soup, cheese, and salt; add vegetables. Pour into greased 8x8x2-inch baking dish. Cut corned beef in 8 slices; stand slices up in 2 rows in casserole. Top with crumbs. Bake in moderate oven (375°) 25 minutes or till hot. Makes 8 servings.

Beef Fondue

Salad oil
1½ pounds trimmed beef tenderloin, cut in ¾-inch cubes (3 cups)

Garlic Butter, Anchovy Butter, Tomato Steak Sauce, and Creamy Horseradish Sauce

Pour salad oil in beef fondue cooker or *deep* chafing dish* to depth of about 1½ inches. Place over direct heat on range and bring to 425° or just below smoking point. Then take to table and place over heating unit. Have beef cubes at room temperature in serving bowl. Set out small bowls of several of the butters and sauces. Each guest spears beef cube with fork, then holds it in hot oil until done as desired. He then dips it in a sauce on his plate.

Note: When salad oil cools so meat no longer cooks briskly, heat oil again on range. Treat hot oil with respect—be ever so careful in moving the pan.

* *Or* use an electric saucepan; oil can be heated at table, kept at proper temperature.

Garlic Butter

Whip ½ cup softened butter till fluffy. Stir in 1 clove garlic, minced. Makes ½ cup.

Anchovy Butter

Drain one 2-ounce can anchovies; place in mixer with ½ cup softened butter, 2 tablespoons olive oil, ½ teaspoon paprika, and ⅛ teaspoon pepper; beat smooth. Makes 1 cup.

Tomato Steak Sauce

Mix one 8-ounce can tomato sauce, ⅓ cup bottled steak sauce, 2 tablespoons brown sugar and 2 tablespoons salad oil. Bring to boil. Serve hot. Makes 1½ cups.

Creamy Horseradish Sauce

Combine 1 cup sour cream, 3 tablespoons drained prepared horseradish, ¼ teaspoon salt, dash paprika. Chill. Makes 1¼ cups.

Bavarian Wiener Supper

1 pound (8 to 10) frankfurters
1 10½-ounce can condensed cream of mushroom soup
½ cup mayonnaise
1 teaspoon caraway seed
1 1-pound can (2 cups) sauerkraut, drained
4 cups diced cooked potatoes
½ cup buttered soft bread crumbs
¼ teaspoon paprika

Halve 4 franks; reserve. Slice remaining franks ¼ inch thick. Mix soup and mayonnaise. Combine sliced franks with *half* of soup mixture, the caraway seed, and kraut; spread in an 11x7x1½-inch baking dish. Stir remaining soup mixture into potatoes; arrange around edge of dish. Combine buttered crumbs and paprika; sprinkle over potatoes. Arrange franks in design. Bake in moderate oven (350°) 30 minutes or till hot. Makes 5 or 6 servings.

Wiener Bean Pot

2 1-pound cans (4 cups) pork and beans in tomato sauce
1 envelope dry onion-soup mix
⅓ cup catsup
¼ cup water
2 tablespoons brown sugar
1 tablespoon prepared mustard
1 pound (8 to 10) frankfurters, sliced

Combine all ingredients in 2-quart casserole or bean pot. Bake uncovered in moderate oven (350°) 1 hour. Makes 6 to 8 servings.

Frank-and-Noodle Supper

- 1 1-pound 12-ounce can (3½ cups) tomatoes
- ½ cup water
- 1 envelope spaghetti-sauce mix
- 1 cup chopped celery
- 1 tablespoon instant minced onion
- 1½ teaspoons sugar
- 6 frankfurters
- 2 tablespoons butter or margarine
- 4 ounces (3½ cups) medium noodles
- 2 ounces sharp American cheese, shredded (½ cup)

For sauce, combine first 6 ingredients. Cut franks in thirds diagonally; brown in butter. Add noodles; pour sauce over, moistening all. Cover; cook over low heat, stirring occasionally, 25 minutes or till done. Sprinkle with cheese. Makes 4 servings.

Frank-Vegetable Medley

- ½ pound frankfurters (4 to 5), cut in 1-inch pieces
- ½ cup long-grain rice
- 1 8-ounce can (1 cup) tomato sauce
- 1 cup water
- 1 10-ounce package frozen mixed vegetables, slightly thawed
- ¼ cup chopped onion
- 1 teaspoon salt
- Dash bottled hot pepper sauce

Combine frankfurters with remaining ingredients in 2-quart casserole, breaking up frozen vegetables with fork. Bake, covered, in moderate oven (375°) for 1 hour or till heated through. Stir once or twice during baking time. Makes 6 servings.

Tenderloin-Noodle Treat

  6 ounces (about 3 cups) noodles
  6 slices pork tenderloin, ½ inch thick
  1 tablespoon shortening
  ½ teaspoon salt

  Dash pepper
  1 recipe Blue-cheese Sauce
  3 tablespoons chopped green pepper
  3 tablespoons chopped canned pimiento

Cook noodles in boiling salted water; rinse; drain. Brown tenderloin slices slowly on both sides in hot fat (takes about 15 minutes). Season with ½ teaspoon salt, dash pepper. Make BLUE-CHEESE SAUCE: Melt 3 tablespoons butter; blend in 3 tablespoons all-purpose flour, ¾ teaspoon salt, and dash pepper. Stir in 1 cup milk. Cook and stir till thick. Add 3 ounces blue cheese, crumbled (¾ cup); stir till cheese melts. Combine noodles, green pepper, pimiento, and sauce. Place in ungreased 10x6x1½-inch baking dish. Arrange meat on top. Bake at 350° 30 minutes or till done. Serves 6.

Veal Parmesan with Spaghetti

  6 thin veal cutlets (1½ pounds veal)
  2 tablespoons olive oil
  ½ cup chopped onion
  ¼ cup chopped green pepper
  ⅓ cup white wine
  1 1-pound can (2 cups) tomatoes
  2 8-ounce cans (2 cups) tomato sauce

  1 6-ounce can (⅔ cup) tomato paste
  1 clove garlic, minced
  1 tablespoon snipped parsley
  1 teaspoon oregano
  ½ pound long thin spaghetti, uncooked
  1 6-ounce package sliced Mozzarella cheese

Brown meat in oil. Remove meat; add onion and green pepper; cook till tender. Stir in next 7 ingredients. Add meat; cover; simmer ½ hour, stirring occasionally. Cook spaghetti according to package directions; drain. Remove half the sauce from meat; stir into spaghetti. Top cutlets with cheese; cover pan for 5 minutes. Arrange spaghetti and meat on platter; pass extra sauce and Parmesan.

Baked Corned-beef Burgers

- 1 12-ounce can corned beef, finely chopped
- ½ cup finely chopped green pepper
- ½ cup finely chopped onion
- Dash pepper
- ½ cup mayonnaise or salad dressing
- 1 beaten egg
- 1 tablespoon water
- ¾ cup fine dry bread crumbs
- ¼ cup fat
- 3 slices sharp process American cheese, halved daigonally
- 1 10¾-ounce can condensed cream of vegetable soup
- ⅓ cup milk
- 3 large English muffins, halved and toasted

Mix corned beef, green pepper, onion, pepper, and mayonnaise. Shape in 6 patties. Blend egg and water; dip patties into egg, then into crumbs. Brown lightly in hot fat. Arrange patties in 11x7x1½-inch baking pan. Place a cheese triangle on each patty. Combine soup and milk; heat; pour around patties. Bake in moderate oven (350°) 12 to 15 minutes or till heated through. Serve on hot muffin halves. Makes 6 servings.

Barbecued Pork and Bean Bake

Place two 1-pound cans baked beans in tomato sauce in a 13x9x2-inch baking dish. Prepare 5 or 6 lean rib pork chops. For each chop: dash with salt and pepper; spread lightly with prepared mustard; sprinkle with about 1½ tablespoons brown sugar; spread with about 1½ tablespoons catsup. Arrange chops over beans. With toothpick, attach 1 slice onion and ½ slice lemon to each chop. Bake in a slow oven (325°) about 1½ hours or till pork chops are fork tender. Garnish with parsley. Serve with crisp relishes and hot, crusty bread. Makes 5 or 6 servings.

Note: Barbecued rib fans are sure to enjoy this recipe with loin back ribs substituted for pork chops. Cut in serving-size pieces; prepare according to directions above.

Pork-chop Spanish Rice

　　5 pork chops, ½ inch thick
　1½ teaspoons salt
　　½ to 1 teaspoon chili powder
　　1 teaspoon monosodium
　　　glutamate
　　　Dash pepper
　　¾ cup long-grain rice*

　　½ cup chopped onion
　　¼ cup chopped green pepper
　　1 1-pound 12-ounce can
　　　(3½ cups) tomatoes
　　4 green pepper rings
　　　Shredded sharp process
　　　American cheese

Trim excess fat from chops; heat fat in heavy skillet. When you have about 2 tablespoons melted fat, remove trimmings. (Or, use salad oil instead of melting fat.) Brown chops slowly in hot fat; drain off excess. Combine seasonings and sprinkle over meat. Add rice, onion, and green pepper. Pour tomatoes over. Cover and cook over low heat about 30 to 35 minutes, stirring occasionally. Add green pepper rings and continue cooking, 5 minutes longer, or till rice and meat are tender. Before serving, sprinkle with shredded cheese. Makes 5 servings.

* *Or use packaged precooked rice, but add rice last 5 minutes of cooking.*

Southern Sausage and Egg Casserole

　　4 hard-cooked eggs
　　4 tablespoons butter or
　　　margarine, melted
　　¼ cup sifted all-purpose flour
　　½ teaspoon salt
　　　Dash pepper
　　2 cups milk

　　1 pound bulk pork sausage,
　　　cooked and drained
　　1 1-pound can (2 cups) golden
　　　whole kernel corn, drained
　　1 cup soft bread crumbs
　　　(1½ slices)

Slice 2 of the eggs into 1½ quart casserole. In saucepan, blend butter or margarine, flour, salt, and pepper. Add milk all at once. Cook, stirring constantly, till mixture is boiling and thickened. Stir in sausage and corn. Pour over sliced eggs. Slice remaining 2 eggs; arrange over top of sausage mixture. Sprinkle with bread crumbs. Bake in moderate oven (375°) for 20 to 25 minutes or till heated through. Makes 6 servings.

Pizza Supper Pie

1 stick packaged pastry mix	4 eggs
½ pound bulk pork sausage	½ cup milk
¾ cup chopped onion	4 ounces sharp American cheese, shredded (1 cup)
½ teaspoon oregano	
¼ teaspoon pepper	⅔ cup canned pizza sauce

Prepare one 9-inch pastry shell from pastry mix according to package directions, baking in very hot oven (450°) *only 7 minutes* or just till lightly browned. Remove from oven. Reduce temperature to 325°. Slowly brown sausage and onion, breaking up sausage with fork; drain. Add seasonings. Beat together eggs and milk; stir in sausage and cheese. Pour into pastry shell. Bake in slow oven (325°) 20 minutes or till knife inserted in center comes out clean. Spread top with pizza sauce. Serve immediately. Makes 6 servings.

Easy Mexican Skillet

 1 pound bulk pork sausage
 ¼ cup chopped onion
 ½ cup chopped green pepper
 1 cup uncooked elbow macaroni
 2 tablespoons sugar
 1 teaspoon salt
 1 teaspoon chili powder
 1 1-pound can (2 cups) tomatoes
 1 8-ounce can (1 cup) tomato sauce
 ½ cup dairy sour cream

Lightly brown meat; drain off excess fat. Add onion and green pepper; cook till tender. Stir in next 6 ingredients. Cover and simmer 20 minutes. Stir in sour cream; heat through. Pass grated Parmesan cheese. Serves 5.

Deviled Ham Elegante

 4 crisp rusks
 Prepared mustard
 1 4½-ounce can deviled ham
 4 hard-cooked eggs
 Dash Worcestershire sauce
 2 tablespoons finely chopped onion
 1 10½-ounce can condensed cream of mushroom soup
 ¼ cup milk

Spread tops of rusks with mustard, then with deviled ham. Heat in slow oven (325°) about 10 minutes. Chop 2 of the eggs and combine with remaining ingredients; heat till hot and spoon over rusks. Slice remaining eggs for garnish. Sprinkle with paprika. Makes 4 servings.

Ham Loaf in Cheese Crust

 1½ cups finely crushed rich round cheese crackers
 ¼ cup melted butter or margarine
 1 pound ground cooked or canned ham
 1 6-ounce can (⅔ cup) evaporated milk
 2 slightly beaten eggs
 ½ cup finely chopped onion
 ¼ cup finely chopped green pepper
 1 tablespoon prepared mustard
 1 tablespoon prepared horseradish
 ¼ teaspoon salt

For crust, mix cracker crumbs and butter; reserve 2 tablespoons. Press remaining crumbs over bottom and sides of a 9-inch pie plate. Bake in moderate oven (350°) 10 minutes. For ham filling, combine remaining ingredients; mix well.

Turn into baked crust. Sprinkle with reserved crumbs. Bake in 350° oven 45 to 50 minutes or till done. Let stand 5 minutes, then cut in wedges. Makes 6 servings.

Ham Medley

- 1 cup chopped celery
- ½ cup chopped green pepper
- ½ cup chopped onion
- 4 tablespoons butter or margarine, melted
- ¼ cup all-purpose flour
- ½ teaspoon salt
- Dash pepper
- 2½ cups milk
- 2 12-ounce cartons (3 cups) cream-style cottage cheese
- 4 cups ½-inch cubes cooked ham
- 1 8-ounce package noodles, cooked and drained
- 2 tablespoons butter or margarine
- ½ cup fine dry bread crumbs

Cook vegetables in the 4 tablespoons butter or margarine till tender; blend in flour, salt, and pepper. Stir in milk and cottage cheese; cook and stir till boiling. Stir in ham and noodles; transfer to 3-quart casserole. Combine remaining ingredients; sprinkle over top. Bake at 350° for 1 hour. Makes 10 to 12 servings.

Skillet Barbecue

- ½ cup chopped onion
- 2 tablespoons butter or margarine
- 1 cup catsup
- ⅓ cup water
- ¼ cup brown sugar
- 3 tablespoons vinegar
- 1 tablespoon prepared mustard
- 1 tablespoon Worcestershire sauce
- 1 12-ounce can luncheon meat, cut in julienne strips
- 6 hamburger buns, split and toasted

Cook onion in butter till tender, but not brown. Stir in catsup, water, brown sugar, vinegar, mustard, and Worcestershire sauce. Add luncheon meat. Simmer uncovered 15 minutes. Serve on toasted hamburger buns. Makes 6 servings.

Chevron Rice Bake

- 2 12-ounce cans luncheon meat
- 4 cups cooked rice
- 1 10-ounce package frozen peas, thawed **or** 1 1-pound can peas, drained
- 2 slightly beaten eggs
- 1 10½-ounce can condensed cream of chicken soup
- ½ cup milk
- ¼ cup snipped parsley
- ¼ cup chopped onion
- 1 teaspoon curry powder
- Dash pepper
- 1 1-pound 14-ounce can peach halves, drained
- Whole cloves

Slice contents of one can luncheon meat; reserve for top. Cut contents of other can in ½-inch cubes; combine with remaining ingredients except peaches and cloves. Spread in 13x9x2-inch baking dish. Stud peach halves with cloves; arrange, with

Meat and Macaroni Supper

- 1 medium onion, chopped (½ cup)
- 2 tablespoons butter or margarine, melted
- 1 10½-ounce can condensed cream of celery soup
- 1 8-ounce can (1 cup) tomatoes, cut up
- ¼ teaspoon thyme
- Dash pepper
- ½ 7-ounce package (1 cup) elbow macaroni, cooked and drained
- 1 12-ounce can luncheon meat, cut in 1x½-inch strips
- ¼ cup chopped green pepper
- 1 ounce process American cheese, shredded (¼ cup)

In medium skillet, cook onion in butter or margarine till tender but not brown. Stir in the soup, tomatoes, thyme, and pepper. Add the cooked macaroni, luncheon meat, and green pepper. Spoon into 1½-quart casserole. Top with shredded cheese. Bake, uncovered, in moderate oven (350°) for 35 to 40 minutes or till heated through. Makes 4 to 6 servings.

German "Pizza"

- 1½ tablespoons fat
- 3 medium potatoes, pared and thinly sliced
- Salt and pepper
- ½ cup chopped onion
- ½ cup chopped green pepper
- 2 cups julienne strips canned luncheon meat (1 12-ounce can) or ham
- 3 eggs
- 2 ounces sharp process American cheese, shredded (½ cup)

Melt fat in 10-inch skillet. Spread *half* the potato slices over bottom; sprinkle with salt and freshly ground pepper. Top with a layer of *half* the onion and *half* the green pepper, seasoning with salt and pepper. Arrange *half* the meat atop. Repeat layers of vegetables, *reserving* the remaining meat for garnish. Cover; cook over low heat till potatoes are tender, about 20 minutes. Break eggs into bowl; pour over potatoes, breaking yolks and spreading eggs evenly with a fork. Add meat, spoke-fashion. Cover and cook till eggs are set, about 10 minutes. Top with cheese; cover till cheese starts to melt, about 2 minutes. Center with parsley. Cut in wedges to serve. Makes 5 or 6 servings.

Baked Bean Pie

- 1 12-ounce can luncheon meat
- Maple-flavored or maple-blended syrup
- 1 1-pound 5-ounce can pork and beans in tomato sauce
- 2 tablespoons hot-dog relish
- 1 teaspoon instant minced onion
- 1 ounce sharp process American cheese, shredded (¼ cup)

Cut luncheon meat in 6 to 8 slices; brush each slice with syrup. Arrange meat slices around inner edge of 9-inch pie plate. In a saucepan, combine pork and beans, hot-dog relish, and onion; bring to boiling. Pour bean mixture into pie plate; sprinkle with shredded cheese. Bake in a moderate oven (350°) 20 minutes or till meat is lightly browned. Makes 3 to 4 servings.

Hot Salad and Cold Cuts

- ½ cup chopped onion
- 3 tablespoons bacon drippings or butter
- 4 ounces salami, cut in bite-size pieces
- 1 well-beaten egg
- 1 tablespoon sugar
- ¼ cup vinegar
- 2 tablespoons water
- 1 teaspoon salt
- ¼ teaspoon celery seed
- Dash pepper
- 4 cups hot cubed cooked potatoes (4 medium potatoes)

Cook onion in drippings till tender. Add salami; brown lightly. Combine next 7 ingredients; add to salami. Heat and stir till mixture thickens. Add potatoes; toss and heat through. Serve hot with COLD MEAT STACK-UPS: Spread one side of salami, liverwurst, and sharp-cheese-food rounds with Dijon-style prepared mustard. On Bologna slice, stack a slice each of large salami, liverwurst, and cheese, mustard side down. (Have each round smaller than the one below.) Anchor with toothpick topped with a stuffed green olive. Repeat, making 4 to 6 stacks.

Herbed Chicken Bake

- 2 cups dairy sour cream
- 1 teaspoon crushed dried tarragon*
- 1 teaspoon crushed dried thyme*
- 1 teaspoon salt
- 1 teaspoon paprika
- Dash garlic powder
- 4 large chicken breasts, halved
- 1 cup corn-flake crumbs
- 1 cup canned or cooked cleaned shrimp, split lengthwise
- ½ cup pitted ripe olives, quartered

Combine sour cream with herbs and seasonings. Dip chicken into sour-cream mixture, then roll in corn-flake crumbs. Place chicken pieces, skin side down, in well-greased 13x9x2-inch baking dish. Bake uncovered in moderate oven (350°) 40 minutes; turn chicken and bake 10 minutes longer. To the remaining sour-cream mixture, add shrimp and olives; spoon over chicken. Bake 10 minutes more. Trim with olives and a sprig of tarragon or parsley, if desired. Makes 8 servings.

  *Or use 3 to 4 teaspoons *each* snipped fresh tarragon and thyme.

Panamanian Chicken and Rice

Cut up a 2½- to 3-pound ready-to-cook broiler-fryer, season with salt. Mince 1 clove garlic; heat in ¼ cup salad oil. Brown chicken slowly in the oil; remove from skillet. Add 1 cup uncooked long-grain rice; brown slowly, stirring. Stir in one 12 ounce can (1½ cups) vegetable-juice cocktail, ¾ cup water, one 3-ounce can (⅔ cup) broiled sliced mushrooms (with liquid), 1 cup *each* chopped celery and onion, 1 teaspoon salt,

¼ teaspoon *each* marjoram and freshly ground pepper, and a pinch powdered saffron. Bring to boiling. Add browned chicken. Cover; simmer 35 minutes. Add 1 cup frozen peas, ½ cup pitted ripe olives, and 1 tomato, cut in wedges; season with salt and pepper. Cook covered 10 to 15 minutes. Makes 6 servings.

Chicken Cioppino

- 1 2½- to 3-pound ready-to-cook broiler-fryer chicken, cut up
- ¼ cup butter or margarine
- 1 recipe Italian Sauce
- 1 pound cleaned raw shrimp (about 1½ pounds in shell)

Season chicken with salt and pepper. Brown slowly in butter, turning once. Add Italian Sauce; cover and simmer till chicken is tender, about 35 minutes. Add shrimp, being sure to immerse in sauce. Cover and continue cooking just till shrimp are done, about 5 to 10 minutes. Serve in hot soup plates. Pass French bread. Makes 6 servings. ITALIAN SAUCE: Mix two 8-ounce cans (2 cups) tomato sauce, ½ cup cooking claret, ¾ cup chopped onion, 1 clove garlic, minced, 3 tablespoons snipped parsley, 1 teaspoon basil, crushed, 1 bay leaf, crushed, ½ teaspoon salt, and dash pepper.

Chicken-Chow Bake

- 2 cups diced cooked or canned chicken
- 1 10½-ounce can condensed cream of mushroom soup
- 1 8¾-ounce can (1 cup) pineapple tidbits
- 1 tablespoon soy sauce
- 1 cup celery slices
- 2 tablespoons chopped green onions
- 1 3-ounce can (2½ cups) chow-mein noodles

Combine all ingredients except noodles, mixing well. Gently fold in *1 cup of the noodles*. Turn into 8x8x2-inch baking dish. Sprinkle with remaining noodles. Bake in moderate oven (350°) 50 minutes or till hot. Makes 4 or 5 servings. Pass soy sauce.

Chinese Walnut Chicken

- 1 cup coarsely broken walnuts
- ¼ cup salad oil
- 2 chicken breasts (raw), boned and cut lengthwise in very thin strips
- ½ teaspoon salt
- 1 cup onion slices
- 1½ cups bias-cut celery slices
- 1¼ cups chicken broth
- 1 teaspoon sugar
- 1 tablespoon cornstarch
- ¼ cup soy sauce
- 2 tablespoons cooking sherry
- 1 5-ounce can (⅔ cup) bamboo shoots, drained
- 1 5-ounce can water chestnuts, drained and sliced
- Hot cooked rice

In skillet, toast walnuts in hot oil, stirring constantly. Remove nuts to paper towels to drain. Put chicken into skillet. Sprinkle with salt. Cook, stirring frequently, 5 to 10 minutes or till tender. Remove chicken. Add onion, celery, and *½ cup of the* chicken broth. Cook uncovered 5 minutes or till vegetables are slightly tender. Combine sugar, cornstarch, soy sauce, and cooking sherry; add remaining broth. Pour over vegetables. Cook and stir till sauce thickens. Add chicken, bamboo shoots, water chestnuts, and walnuts. Heat through. Serve with hot rice. Makes 4 to 6 servings.

Curry-top Chicken Pie

- ¾ cup sliced carrots
- 2 onions, cut in eighths
- ½ cup milk
- 2 tablespoons all-purpose flour
- 1 10¾-ounce can (1¼ cups) chicken gravy
- 1 cup drained canned or cooked peas
- 2 tablespoons chopped canned pimiento
- 2 cups diced cooked or canned chicken
- 1 recipe Curry Pastry

Cook carrots and onions in boiling salted water till tender; drain. Gradually stir milk into flour; add gravy. Cook and stir till thick. Add vegetables and chicken; heat to bubbling. Turn into an 8x8x2-inch pan. Top with Curry Pastry; crimp edge and cut slits. Bake in very hot oven (450°) 25 minutes or till browned. Makes 6 servings. CURRY PASTRY: Crumble 1 stick pastry mix into bowl; add 1½ teaspoons curry powder, then follow package directions. Roll to a 9-inch square, ⅛ inch thick.

Chicken-and-Stuffing Scallop

1 8-ounce package (3½ cups) herb-seasoned stuffing
3 cups cubed cooked or canned chicken
½ cup butter or margarine
½ cup all-purpose flour
¼ teaspoon salt
Dash pepper
4 cups chicken broth
6 slightly beaten eggs
1 recipe Pimiento Mushroom Sauce

Prepare stuffing according to package directions for dry stuffing. Spread in a 13x9x2-inch baking dish; top with a layer of chicken. In a large saucepan, melt butter; blend in flour and seasonings. Add cool broth; cook and stir till mixture thickens. Stir small amount hot mixture into eggs, return to hot mixture; pour over chicken. Bake in slow oven (325°) 40 to 45 minutes or till knife inserted halfway to center comes out clean. Let stand 5 minutes to set; cut in squares and serve with PIMIENTO MUSHROOM SAUCE. Mix 1 10½-ounce can condensed cream of mushroom soup, ¼ cup milk, 1 cup dairy sour cream, and ¼ cup chopped canned pimiento. Heat and stir till hot. Makes 12 servings.

Calico Chicken and Rice

Combine 2 cups dairy sour cream, ½ envelope or can (¼ cup) dry onion soup mix; set aside. Place two 2½- to 3-pound broiler-fryers, cut up, in Dutch oven. Add 2 cups water, 1 cup dry sherry, 1 teaspoon salt, dash pepper, ½ teaspoon basil. Cover; cook over low heat till tender, about 1 hour. Meanwhile, cook 2 cups long-grain rice, following package directions. Remove chicken from broth; cool. Cut in large pieces. Cook liquid in Dutch oven, uncovered, till reduced to 1½ cups. Blend in 1 10½-ounce can condensed cream of mushroom soup, ¼ cup chopped canned pimiento, ¼ cup snipped parsley. Stir in sour cream mixture, chicken, and rice. Cook and stir just till boiling. Makes 10 to 12 servings.

Creamy Chicken-Rice Casserole

Prepare 1 cup wild rice according to package directions. Cook ½ cup chopped onion in ½ cup butter or margarine till tender but not brown. Remove from heat; stir in ¼ cup all-purpose flour. Drain one 6-ounce can (1 cup) broiled sliced mushrooms, reserving liquid. Add enough chicken broth to liquid to measure 1½ cups; gradually stir into flour mixture. Add 1½ cups light cream. Cook and stir until mixture thickens. Add the wild rice, the mushrooms, 3 cups diced cooked chicken, ¼ cup chopped canned pimiento, 2 tablespoons snipped parsley, 1½ teaspoons salt, and ¼ teaspoon pepper. Place in 2-quart casserole. Sprinkle with ½ cup slivered blanched almonds. Bake in moderate oven (350°) 25 to 30 minutes or till hot. Makes 8 servings.

Ham and Chicken on Egg Puffs

- 2 tablespoons butter or margarine
- 3 tablespoons all-purpose flour
- ½ teaspoon salt
- 1 cup milk
- 4 well-beaten egg yolks
- 4 stiff-beaten egg whites
- Ham-Chicken Sauce

Melt butter; blend in flour and salt. Add milk. Cook, stirring constantly, till mixture thickens. Slowly stir hot mixture into egg yolks; fold in egg whites. Turn into greased 9x9x2-inch baking dish. Bake in moderate oven (350°) 30 minutes or till done. Cut in 6 to 8 servings. Serve *at once* with HAM-CHICKEN SAUCE: Cook ⅓ cup chopped onion in 2 tablespoons butter or margarine till tender; blend in 3 tablespoons flour. Add 1½ cups milk. Cook and stir till mixture thickens. Add 1 cup *each* diced cooked chicken and cooked or canned ham cut in julienne strips, ½ cup diced sharp process American cheese, 2 tablespoons chopped canned pimiento, and dash *each* nutmeg and pepper. Heat through, stirring often.

Turkey Cheese Puff

- 1 10-ounce package frozen broccoli
- 2 cups sliced cooked turkey
- 1 10¾-ounce can chicken gravy
- 2 egg whites
- ¼ teaspoon salt
- 2 egg yolks
- ¼ cup grated Parmesan cheese
- ¼ cup toasted slivered almonds
- Cheese Topper

Cook broccoli according to package directions; drain. Place in bottom of 10x6x1½-inch baking dish. Cover with turkey slices and top with gravy. Keep warm in 375° oven while preparing CHEESE TOPPER: Beat egg whites with salt to stiff peaks; set aside. Beat egg yolks till thick and lemon-colored, and fold into whites; then fold in cheese. Pour over hot turkey mixture. Top with almonds. Bake at 375° for 15 to 20 minutes or till golden. Makes 6 servings.

Quick Turkey Pie

- 2 cups packaged biscuit mix
- 1 tablespoon instant minced onion
- ⅔ cup milk
- ¼ cup chopped green pepper
- 2 ounces sharp process American cheese, shredded (½ cup)
- 4 tablespoons butter or margarine, melted
- ¼ cup all-purpose flour
- 1 teaspoon salt
- ½ teaspoon dry mustard
- Dash pepper
- 2 cups milk
- 1 teaspoon Worcestershire sauce
- ½ cup shredded carrot
- 2 cups diced cooked turkey

Combine biscuit mix and onion; stir in the ⅔ cup milk till mix is moistened. Pat into greased 9-inch pie plate. Sprinkle with green pepper and cheese. Bake in hot oven (400°) for 18 to 20 minutes or till golden. Meanwhile, blend butter or margarine, flour, salt, mustard, and pepper. Add the 2 cups milk and Worcestershire all at once. Cook and stir till mixture thickens and bubbles. Stir in carrot and turkey; heat through. Cut biscuit pie in wedges; top with turkey sauce. Makes 6 servings.

Turkey-Noodle Bake

- 1½ cups milk
- 1 10½-ounce can condensed cream of mushroom soup
- 3 beaten eggs
- 3 ounces (about 2¼ cups uncooked) fine noodles, cooked and drained
- 2 cups cubed cooked turkey
- 1 cup soft bread crumbs (1½ slices)
- 4 tablespoons butter or margarine, melted
- 4 ounces sharp process American cheese, shredded (1 cup)
- ¼ cup chopped green pepper
- 2 tablespoons chopped canned pimiento

Blend milk into soup. Stir in eggs; add remaining ingredients. Pour into 11x7x1½-inch baking dish. Bake in moderate oven (350°) for 30 to 40 minutes or till knife inserted in center comes out clean. Makes 6 to 8 servings.

Jiffy Turkey Paella

- 1 1-pound 12-ounce can (3½ cups) tomatoes
- 1 cup water
- ¼ cup cooking oil
- ¼ cup chopped onion
- ¼ cup chopped green pepper
- 1 teaspoon salt
- 1 teaspoon garlic salt
- Dash cayenne
- 1 cup long-grain rice
- 1 9-ounce package frozen artichoke hearts, thawed and quartered
- 2 cups diced cooked turkey
- ¼ cup sliced stuffed green olives

In large saucepan, combine tomatoes, water, oil, onion, green pepper, and seasonings. Stir in rice and artichoke hearts. Cover; bring to boiling. Reduce heat and simmer, covered, 25 minutes or till rice is tender, stirring occasionally. Stir in turkey and olives; heat to boiling. Makes 6 servings.

Chicken-Rice Divan

- 2 10-ounce packages frozen broccoli spears
- ½ cup shredded Parmesan cheese
- 6 large slices cooked chicken **or** 2 cups cubed chicken
- Salt and pepper
- 1 cup cooked rice
- 2 tablespoons butter or margarine
- 2 tablespoons all-purpose flour
- 1 cup milk
- 1 tablespoon lemon juice
- 1 cup dairy sour cream

Cook broccoli according to package directions; drain. Arrange in 11x7x1½-inch baking dish. Sprinkle with half the shredded Parmesan cheese; top with chicken. Season with salt and pepper; spoon on cooked rice. Prepare a medium white sauce: Melt butter in saucepan over low heat. Blend in flour; add milk all at once. Cook over medium heat, stirring constantly, till mixture thickens and bubbles; remove from heat. Stir in lemon juice; gently fold in sour cream and pour over chicken in casserole. Sprinkle with remaining Parmesan cheese. Bake in hot oven (400°) for 15 to 20 minutes or till lightly browned. Makes 6 servings.

Shrimp Buffet Casserole

- ½ cup chopped green pepper
- ½ cup chopped onion
- 2 tablespoons butter or margarine
- 3 cups cleaned cooked or canned shrimp
- 1 tablespoon lemon juice
- 2 cups cooked rice
- 1 10¾-ounce can condensed tomato soup
- ¾ cup light cream
- ¼ cup cooking sherry
- ¾ teaspoon salt
- ¼ teaspoon nutmeg

Cook green pepper and onion in butter till tender but not brown. Stir in remaining ingredients. Pour into 2-quart casserole. Bake in moderate oven (350°) 30 minutes or till hot. Trim with toasted almonds and parsley. Makes 6 to 8 servings.

Lazy Day Casserole

- 1¾ cups milk
- ½ cup cooking sherry
- 1 10½-ounce can condensed cream of chicken soup
- 1⅓ cups packaged precooked rice
- 1 4½-ounce can shrimp, drained, split lengthwise
- 1 5-ounce can lobster, drained and cut up
- 1 7½-ounce can minced clams, drained
- 1 3-ounce can broiled sliced mushrooms, drained (½ cup)
- 1 tablespoon parsley flakes
- ¼ teaspoon instant minced garlic
- Paprika
- ¼ cup toasted slivered almonds
- 2 tablespoons butter

Gradually stir milk and sherry into soup. Add next 7 ingredients. Turn into 2-quart casserole. Sprinkle with paprika and almonds; dot with butter. Bake in 350° oven 50 minutes. Makes 6 servings.

Shrimp* Thermidor

- ¼ cup chopped onion
- 2 tablespoons chopped green pepper
- 2 tablespoons butter or margarine
- 1 10¼-ounce can frozen condensed cream of potato soup
- ¾ cup light cream
- 2 ounces sharp process American cheese, shredded (½ cup)
- 2 teaspoons lemon juice
- 1½ cups cooked or canned shrimp, split lengthwise or 1 to 1½ cups canned tuna or crab meat, drained
- Puff-pastry shells

Cook onion and green pepper in butter till tender but not brown. Add soup and cream; heat slowly, stirring constantly, till blended. Bring just to boiling. Add cheese; stir to melt. Add lemon juice and shrimp.* Heat through. Serve in pastry shells. Makes 4 or 5 servings.

* Or crab or tuna.

Shrimp Chow Mein

Cook 1 cup *each* chopped onion, sliced celery, and chopped green pepper in ¼ cup hot salad oil 2 minutes; add 1 10½-ounce can condensed cream of mushroom soup. Blend 2 teaspoons cornstarch, ¾ cup cold water, and ¼ cup soy sauce; gradually stir into soup mixture. Cook and stir till mixture thickens. Cut 2 cups cleaned cooked or canned shrimp in half lengthwise; add along with one 3-ounce can broiled sliced mushrooms, drained (½ cup); one 5-ounce can (⅔ cup) water chestnuts, drained and thinly sliced; and one 1-pound can bean sprouts, drained. Heat thoroughly. Serve over 4 cups hot chow-mein noodles. Pass soy sauce. Makes 6 to 8 servings.

Luncheon Sea-food Bake

1 6½- or 7½-ounce can (1 cup) crab meat, drained
1 cup soft bread crumbs
1 cup mayonnaise or salad dressing
¾ cup milk
6 hard-cooked eggs, finely chopped
⅓ cup chopped onion
¼ cup sliced stuffed green olives
¾ teaspoon salt
Dash pepper
½ cup buttered soft bread crumbs

Break crab meat in chunks; mix with all ingredients except buttered crumbs. Pile in greased individual bakers or 1-quart casserole. Top with buttered crumbs. Bake in moderate oven (350°) 20 to 25 minutes or till hot. Trim with olive slices. Makes 6 servings.

Luncheon Shrimp Curry

- 2 pounds cleaned raw shrimp (2½ pounds in shell)
- 1½ cups **each** chopped onion and celery
- ½ cup butter or margarine
- 1 1-pound can (2 cups) applesauce
- 4 10½-ounce cans condensed cream of celery soup
- 1 6-ounce can (1⅓ cups) broiled sliced mushrooms (undrained)
- 2 tablespoons curry powder
- ¼ teaspoon salt

Halve shrimp lengthwise. Cook onion and celery in butter till almost tender. Stir in next 5 ingredients. Add shrimp. Simmer uncovered, stirring frequently, about 10 minutes. Serve over hot cooked rice. Offer curry condiments. Makes 10 to 12 servings.

Tuna-Noodle Casserole

- 6 ounces (3½ cups) medium noodles
- 1 6½- or 7-ounce can tuna
- ½ cup mayonnaise
- 1 cup sliced celery
- ⅓ cup chopped onion
- ¼ cup chopped green pepper
- ¼ cup chopped canned pimiento
- 1 teaspoon salt
- 1 10½-ounce can condensed cream of celery soup
- ½ cup milk
- 1 cup shredded sharp process American cheese
- ½ cup slivered blanched almonds, toasted

Cook noodles in boiling salted water till tender; drain. Combine noodles, drained tuna, mayonnaise, vegetables, and salt. Blend soup and milk; heat through. Add cheese; cook and stir till cheese melts. Add to noodle mixture. Turn into 1½-quart casserole. Top with almonds. Bake in hot oven (425°) about 20 minutes. Makes 6 servings.

Quick Tuna Bake

- 1 7½-ounce package macaroni-and-cheese dinner
- 3 tablespoons soft butter or margarine
- 1 8-ounce can (1 cup) tomatoes
- ½ cup milk
- 2 tablespoons instant minced onion
- 1 slightly beaten egg
- 1 6½- or 7-ounce can tuna, drained
- 2 tablespoons snipped parsley
- ¼ teaspoon salt
- Dash pepper
- 2 tablespoons corn flake crumbs

Cook macaroni according to package directions; drain. Add cheese (from packaged dinner) and butter. Toss to mix. Drain tomatoes, reserving liquid. Dice tomatoes; add with reserved liquid and remaining ingredients, except crumbs. Pour mixture into greased 1-quart casserole. Sprinkle with crumbs. Bake uncovered in moderate oven (350°) 35 minutes or till thoroughly heated. Makes 5 servings.

Tuna Croquettes with Pineapple

¼ cup chopped onion
2 tablespoons butter or margarine
2 tablespoons all-purpose flour
½ cup milk
1 6½- or 7-ounce can tuna, drained and flaked
2 cups cooked rice
1 slightly beaten egg

2 ounces sharp process American cheese, shredded (½ cup)
½ teaspoon salt
Dash pepper
1 cup packaged corn flake crumbs
⅓ cup fat

Cook onion in butter till tender; blend in flour. Add milk; cook and stir till mixture thickens and bubbles. Add next 6 ingredients. Chill several hours. Shape in 10 patties; roll in crumbs. Brown in hot fat 4 to 5 minutes on each side Makes 5 servings. Serve on BROILED PINEAPPLE SLICES: Combine 2 tablespoons *each* lemon juice and brown sugar, and 1 tablespoon melted butter; brush over 10 pineapple slices. Broil 3 to 4 minutes.

Tuna Jackstraw Casserole

- 1 4-ounce can (4 cups) shoestring potatoes
- 1 10½-ounce can condensed cream of mushroom soup
- 1 6½- or 7-ounce can tuna, drained
- 1 6-ounce can (⅔ cup) evaporated milk
- 1 3-ounce can broiled sliced mushrooms, drained (½ cup)
- ¼ cup chopped canned pimiento

Reserve 1 cup of shoestring potatoes for topper. Combine remaining potatoes with the other ingredients. Pour into 1½-quart casserole. Arrange reserved potatoes on top. Bake uncovered in moderate oven (375°) 20 to 25 minutes or until thoroughly heated. Trim with a sprig of parsley. Makes 4 to 6 servings.

Lemon Rice with Fillets

- ¼ cup chopped onion
- 2 tablespoons butter
- 2 cups cooked rice
- 2 tablespoons lemon juice
- 1 slightly beaten egg
- 2 pounds frozen fish fillets, partially thawed
- Melted butter

Cook onion in 2 tablespoons butter till slightly tender; stir into rice. Mix in lemon juice, egg, and dash salt. Place half the fillets in buttered 10x6x1½-inch baking dish; season with salt and pepper. Top with rice mixture, then remaining fillets. Brush with melted butter. Sprinkle with salt, pepper, and paprika. Bake at 375° about 35 minutes, brushing occasionally with melted butter. Makes 6 servings.

Company Creamed Tuna

- 2 tablespoons finely chopped onion
- 3 tablespoons butter or margarine
- 3 tablespoons all-purpose flour
- ¼ teaspoon salt
- Dash pepper
- 1¼ cups milk
- ½ cup dairy sour cream
- 1 6½- or 7-ounce can tuna, drained
- 3 tablespoons cooking sherry
- 2 tablespoons chopped parsley
- Toasted slivered almonds
- Puff-pastry shells

Cook onion in butter until tender but not brown. Blend in flour, salt, and pepper. Add milk; cook and stir until mixture thickens. Stir in sour cream. Add tuna, cooking sherry, and parsley. Heat through. Sprinkle with toasted almonds, if desired. Serve in pastry shells or spooned over toast points. Makes 4 servings.

Tuna-Rice Bake

- 1 6½- or 7-ounce can tuna
- 1 10½-ounce can condensed cream of celery soup
- ¾ cup packaged precooked rice
- 2 slightly beaten egg yolks
- ¼ cup milk
- 1 tablespoon lemon juice
- 2 tablespoons chopped canned pimiento
- 2 teaspoons instant minced onion
- 2 stiff-beaten egg whites

Break tuna in chunks; combine with *half* the soup and next 6 ingredients; fold in whites. Turn into greased 10x6x1½-inch baking dish. Bake at 350° 20 to 25 minutes or till set. Cut in 6 squares. Serve with PARSLEY SAUCE: Heat remaining soup with ½ cup milk and 1 tablespoon chopped parsley.

Creamy Tuna Ring

- ½ envelope (1½ teaspoons) unflavored gelatin
- 2 tablespoons cold water
- ¼ cup hot water
- 1 12-ounce carton (1½ cups) cream-style cottage cheese
- ¼ cup chopped green pepper
- 2 tablespoons finely chopped green onions
- ¼ teaspoon salt
- ½ envelope (1½ teaspoons) unflavored gelatin
- 2 tablespoons cold water
- 2 6½- or 7-ounce cans tuna, drained and flaked, **or** 1 1-pound can salmon, drained and flaked
- ½ cup chopped celery
- ¾ cup mayonnaise or salad dressing
- 2 tablespoons lemon juice

Soften 1½ teaspoons gelatin in 2 tablespoons cold water; dissolve in hot water. Beat cheese slightly; stir in dissolved gelatin, green pepper, onions, and salt. Chill till partially set.

Pour into a 5-cup ring mold. Chill till almost set. Meanwhile, soften 1½ teaspoons gelatin in cold water; dissolve *over* hot water. Mix remaining ingredients; stir in gelatin. Chill till partially set. Spoon over cheese layer. Chill till firm. Unmold. Makes 6 servings.

Leek Lorraine

1 9-inch unbaked pastry shell
1 1¾-ounce envelope dry cream of leek soup mix
1½ cups milk
½ cup light cream
3 slightly beaten eggs
6 ounces Swiss cheese, shredded (1½ cups)
1 teaspoon dry mustard
Dash pepper
1 4½-ounce can deviled ham
2 tablespoons fine dry bread crumbs

Bake pastry shell (have edges crimped high—filling is generous) in very hot oven (450°) for 7 minutes, or just till lightly browned. Remove from oven; reduce oven to 325°. In a medium saucepan combine soup mix and milk. Cook and stir till mixture boils; cool slightly. Stir in cream. Combine eggs, cheese, mustard, and pepper. Slowly stir in soup mixture. Mix together deviled ham and bread crumbs. Spread on bottom and sides of pie shell. Pour soup mixture over top. Bake in a slow oven (325°) about 45 to 50 minutes or till knife inserted in center comes out clean. Let stand about 10 minutes before cutting. Makes 6 servings.

French Bean Pot

2 pounds pork sausage links, halved
3 onions, sliced
3 tablespoons all-purpose flour
3 1-pound cans pork and beans in tomato sauce
1 8-ounce can (1 cup) tomato sauce
¾ cup cooking sherry
½ cup water
½ teaspoon salt
¾ teaspoon **each** crushed thyme and bay leaf
½ teaspoon crushed basil

Brown sausage in large skillet. Remove from pan; pour off fat, reserving ¼ cup. Cook onions and flour in reserved fat till flour is brown. Add sausage and remaining ingredients; heat to boiling Turn into 3-quart casserole or bean pot. Bake uncovered in slow oven (325°) 2 hours, stirring occasionally Makes 8 to 10 servings.

Sacramento Spanish Zucchini

- 1½ teaspoons salt
- 1 teaspoon monosodium glutamate
- ½ teaspoon chili powder
- Dash pepper
- 4 ½-inch pork chops
- ½ cup uncooked rice
- 1 1-pound 12-ounce can (3½ cups) tomatoes
- ½ cup **each** chopped green pepper, onion, and ripe olives
- 1 tablespoon sugar
- 2 cups thinly sliced zucchini squash
- ¼ cup shredded Parmesan cheese

Mix first 4 ingredients. Trim fat from chops and heat in skillet. Remove trimmings and brown chops, seasoning with *1 teaspoon of the* chili mixture. Drain off fat. Add rice, tomatoes, green pepper, onion, olives, and sugar. Border with zucchini; sprinkle all with chili mixture. Cover; cook, stirring occasionally, 1 hour or till pork is done. Top with cheese; cover to melt. Makes 4 servings.

Curried Eggs in Shrimp Sauce

- 8 hard-cooked eggs
- ⅓ cup mayonnaise or salad dressing
- ½ teaspoon salt
- ½ teaspoon curry powder
- ½ teaspoon paprika
- ¼ teaspoon dry mustard
- 1 recipe Shrimp Sauce
- 1 cup soft bread crumbs
- 2 tablespoons butter or margarine, melted

Cut eggs in half lengthwise; remove yolks and mash; mix with mayonnaise and seasonings. Refill egg whites; arrange eggs in 10x6x1½-inch baking dish. *Cover* eggs with Shrimp Sauce. Mix crumbs and melted butter; sprinkle around edge. Bake in moderate oven (350°) 15 to 20 minutes or till heated through. Trim with parsley. Makes 6 to 8 servings. SHRIMP SAUCE: Melt 2 tablespoons butter or margarine; blend in 2 tablespoons all-purpose flour. Stir in 1 10-ounce can frozen condensed cream of shrimp soup and 1 soup can milk; cook and stir till sauce thickens. Add 2 ounces sharp process American cheese, shredded (½ cup); stir till melted.

Hashed-brown Omelet

- 4 slices bacon
- 2 cups shredded cooked potatoes*
- ¼ cup chopped onion
- ¼ cup chopped green pepper
- 4 eggs
- ¼ cup milk
- ½ teaspoon salt
- Dash pepper
- 4 ounces sharp process American cheese, shredded (1 cup)

In 10- or 12-inch skillet, cook bacon till crisp. Leave drippings in skillet; remove bacon, and crumble. Mix potatoes, onion, and green pepper; pat into the skillet. Cook over low heat till underside is crisp and brown. Blend eggs, milk, salt, and pepper; pour over potatoes. Top with cheese and bacon. Cover; cook over low heat. When egg is done, loosen omelet. Fold in half. Makes 4 servings.

Or use packaged hash-brown potatoes, cooked.

Swiss Onion Bake

- 2 cups sliced onions
- 2 tablespoons butter or margarine
- 5 hard-cooked eggs, sliced
- 8 ounces process Swiss cheese, shredded (2 cups)
- 1 10½-ounce can condensed cream of chicken soup
- ¾ cup milk
- ¼ teaspoon pepper
- 8 ½-inch slices French bread, buttered

Cook onions in butter till tender but not brown. Spread in bottom of 10x6x1½-inch baking dish. Top with eggs, then with cheese. Mix soup, milk, and pepper; heat, stirring till smooth. Drizzle sauce over casserole (be sure some goes to bottom). Overlap bread slices on top. Bake in moderate oven (350°) 20 minutes or till hot. Broil to toast bread. Makes 5 servings.

Creamy Macaroni-Cheese Bake

- 2 cups uncooked elbow macaroni
- ⅓ cup mayonnaise or salad dressing
- ¼ cup chopped canned pimiento
- ¼ cup chopped green pepper
- ¼ cup finely chopped onion
- 1 10½-ounce can condensed cream of mushroom soup
- ½ cup milk
- 4 ounces sharp process American cheese, shredded (1 cup)

Cook macaroni according to package directions; drain. Combine with next 4 ingredients. Blend soup, milk, and ½ cup of the cheese. Stir into macaroni; place in 1-quart casserole. Top with remaining cheese. Bake, uncovered, at 400° for 20 to 25 minutes. Makes 4 to 6 servings.

Potluck Macaroni Bake

- 10 ounces (2½ cups) elbow macaroni
- ½ cup chopped onion
- ½ cup chopped green pepper
- ¼ cup butter or margarine
- 1 envelope dry tomato-soup mix
- 2 tablespoons all-purpose flour
- 3½ cups milk
- 6 ounces sharp process American cheese, shredded (1½ cups)
- 3 cups thin strips cooked ham **or** 1 12-ounce can luncheon meat, sliced
- Grated Parmesan cheese

Cook macaroni till tender in boiling salted water; drain. Cook onion and green pepper in butter till tender. Blend in soup mix and flour. Stir in milk. Cook and stir till mixture thickens. Stir in American cheese. Add macaroni and meat. Turn into 3-quart casserole. Sprinkle with Parmesan cheese. Bake uncovered in moderate oven (350°) 30 to 35 minutes. Makes 10 to 12 servings.

Oriental Rice Casserole

- ½ cup wild rice
- ½ cup uncooked long-grain rice
- 1 cup chopped onion
- 1 cup chopped celery
- 3 tablespoons butter or margarine
- ¼ cup soy sauce
- 1 3-ounce can broiled sliced mushrooms, drained (½ cup)
- 1 5-ounce can (⅔ cup) water chestnuts, drained and sliced
- ⅓ cup slivered almonds, toasted

Add washed wild rice to 2¼ cups boiling water, simmer covered 20 minutes; add white rice; bring to boiling; reduce heat, cover and cook 20 minutes longer.* Cook onion and celery in butter till tender. Mix all ingredients. Bake in 1½-quart casserole at 350° 20 minutes or till hot. Eight servings.

* *Or* prepare one 6-ounce package long-grain and wild-rice mix according to label directions. Reduce soy sauce in recipe above to 2 tablespoons.

Spanish Paella

- 1 3-pound ready-to-cook chicken, cut up
- 5 cups water
- 2 carrots, sliced lengthwise
- 2 onions, quartered
- 1 celery stalk with leaves
- 2½ to 3 teaspoons salt
- ¼ teaspoon freshly ground black pepper
- ⅔ cup long-grain rice
- 2 cloves garlic, crushed
- ¼ cup olive oil
- ¼ cup chopped canned pimiento
- ½ teaspoon oregano
- ¼ teaspoon Spanish saffron
- 1 cup frozen peas, broken apart
- ⅔ pound shelled raw shrimp (1 pound in shell)
- 1 10½-ounce can clams

Place chicken pieces in Dutch oven; add water and next 5 ingredients. Bring to boil, reduce heat, cover, and simmer 1 hour or till just tender. Remove chicken from stock; bone, cut up meat. Strain stock; save 4 cups. Fry rice and garlic in olive oil over medium heat, stirring constantly till rice is browned, about 10 minutes. Add reserved chicken stock, pimiento, oregano, and saffron. Cover, cook over low heat 15 minutes. Add chicken, peas, shrimp, and clams. Bring to boil, cover, then cook over very low heat 15 minutes. Makes 6 servings.

Quick Spanish Rice

½ cup chopped green pepper
½ cup chopped onion
1⅓ cups packaged precooked rice
¼ cup fat
1 beef bouillon cube
1¼ cups hot water
2 8-ounce cans (2 cups) tomato sauce
1 12-ounce can luncheon meat, cut in thin strips

Cook green pepper, onion, and rice in hot fat, stirring constantly, until lightly browned. Dissolve bouillon cube in hot water; add to rice along with the tomato sauce and meat; mix. Bring quickly to a boil; reduce heat and simmer uncovered 5 minutes or till rice is tender. Makes 5 servings.

Baked Mexican Enchiladas

Fry 12 canned or frozen tortillas in ⅓ cup hot salad oil, one at a time, just till softened. Heat one 15- or 10-ounce can enchilada sauce. Dip tortillas in enchilada sauce; spoon Cheese Sauce on each and sprinkle with *part of* 1 tomato, peeled and diced, and *part of* ½ cup chopped onion; roll up. Place, seam side down, in greased 11x7x1½-inch baking pan. Combine remaining Cheese Sauce and enchilada sauce; pour over casserole. Sprinkle with 2 ounces sharp process American cheese, shredded (½ cup). Bake in moderate oven (350°) 25 minutes. Makes 6 servings. CHEESE SAUCE: Melt ¼ cup butter; blend in ¼ cup all-purpose flour, ½ teaspoon salt, and ¼ teaspoon paprika. Add 2 cups milk; cook and stir until sauce thickens. Blend in 6 ounces shredded (1½ cups) cheese and 6 drops bottled hot pepper sauce.

SECTION 7

Outdoor Cooking

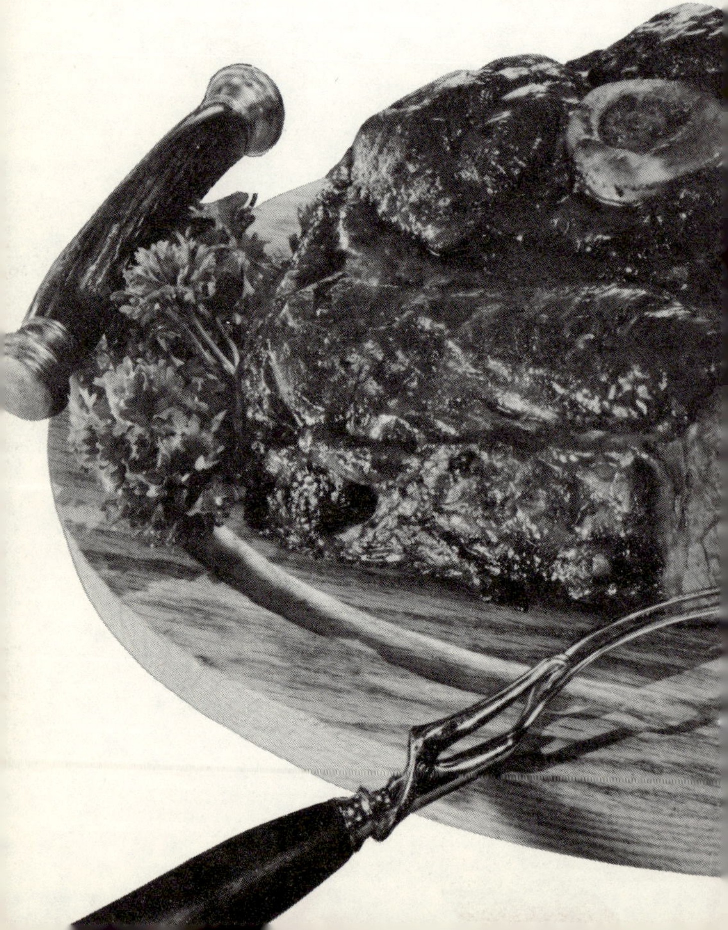

SECTION 7

Outdoor Cooking

Barbecued Chuck Roast

- 1 3-pound chuck roast, 1½ to 2 inches thick
- 1 teaspoon monosodium glutamate
- ⅓ cup wine vinegar
- ¼ cup catsup
- 2 tablespoons cooking oil
- 2 tablespoons soy sauce
- 1 tablespoon Worcestershire sauce
- 1 teaspoon prepared mustard
- 1 teaspoon salt
- ¼ teaspoon pepper
- ¼ teaspoon garlic powder

Sprinkle both sides of roast with monosodium glutamate. Place in a shallow baking dish. Thoroughly combine vinegar, catsup, cooking oil, soy sauce, Worcestershire sauce, mustard, salt, pepper, and garlic powder. Pour mixture over roast and marinate for 2 to 3 hours, turning once or twice. Place roast on grill or broiler pan and broil about 6 inches from heat. Turn roast and baste with marinade every 10 to 15 minutes. Broil a total of 35 to 45 minutes for a medium rare roast or till of desired doneness. Makes 6 to 8 servings.

Chef's Grilled Chuck Steak

- ½ cup chopped onion
- ½ cup lemon juice
- ¼ cup salad oil
- ½ teaspoon salt
- ½ teaspoon celery salt
- ½ teaspoon pepper
- ½ teaspoon thyme
- ½ teaspoon oregano
- ½ teaspoon rosemary
- 1 clove garlic, minced
- 2½ pounds chuck steak, ½-inch thick

Combine ingredients except steak. Marinate meat in mixture 3 hours in refrigerator, turning several times. Drain. Broil steak on grill over *hot* coals. Cook steak to doneness you like (about 30 minutes total time), turning once. Baste with marinade during broiling. Makes about 4 servings.

Swank Porterhouse Steak

- 1 2½- to 3-pound porterhouse or sirloin steak, about 2 inches thick
- ¾ cup finely chopped Bermuda onion
- 2 cloves garlic, minced
- Salt, pepper, and celery salt
- 3 tablespoons cooking claret
- 2 tablespoons soy sauce
- ¼ cup butter or margarine
- 1 3-ounce can broiled sliced mushrooms, drained (½ cup)

Slash fat edge of steak—don't cut into meat. Slitting from fat side, cut pocket in each side of lean, cutting *almost* to bone. Combine onion and garlic, seasoning with a dash of salt, pepper, and celery salt; use mixture as stuffing in steak. Mix cooking claret and soy sauce; brush on steak. Broil over *hot* coals a total of 25 minutes or till done to your liking, turning once—brush occasionally with soy mixture. Heat butter and mushrooms in a small pan, pour over steak. Slice across grain and serve sizzling! Makes 4 servings.

Beef and Bean Roll-ups

- 6 minute or cube beef steaks
- 6 tablespoons barbecue sauce
- 6 tablespoons pickle relish
- 1 1-pound can (2 cups) pork and beans in tomato sauce
- 3 tablespoons butter or margarine, melted

Pound steaks to flatten; sprinkle with salt and pepper. Spread *each* steak with 1 tablespoon barbecue sauce and top with 1 tablespoon pickle relish. Drain beans slightly; spoon onto steaks. Roll and fasten with toothpicks or skewers. Brush with melted butter or margarine and additional barbecue sauce. Broil for 10 minutes, turning once. Remove from grill; season with salt and pepper. Makes 6 servings.

Chateaubriand

Carefully trim fat from the surface of 2 to 2½ pounds Chateaubriand. Make a slanting cut, 2 inches deep, the full length of the Chateaubriand with a sharp, narrow-bladed knife held at a 45-degree angle. Make another cut, just as before, along opposite side of the Chateaubriand. Blend 4 ounces blue cheese and 1 tablespoon brandy. Spread cheese mixture in the openings formed by cuts. Skewer slashes closed with short skewers. Tie string around Chateaubriand at ends and in middle. Balance on spit; rotate over *hot* coals 1¼ to 1½ hours for medium rare. Serves 6 to 8.

Island Teriyaki

- ½ cup soy sauce
- ¼ cup brown sugar
- 2 tablespoons olive oil
- 1 tablespoon grated gingerroot **or** 1 teaspoon dry ginger
- ½ teaspoon monosodium glutamate
- ¼ teaspoon cracked pepper
- 2 cloves garlic, minced
- 1½ pounds top sirloin steak, cut in strips ¼-inch thick and about 1-inch wide
- Canned water chestnuts

Mix together first 7 ingredients. Add meat; stir to coat. Let stand 2 hours at room temperature. Lace meat accordion style on skewers; tip each end with water chestnut. Broil over *hot* coals 10 to 12 minutes; turn often and baste with marinade. Serves 4 or 5.

Teriyaki Burgers

- 1½ pounds ground beef
- 1½ cups soft bread crumbs (2 slices)
- ¼ cup chopped onion
- 2 slightly beaten eggs
- 2 tablespoons sugar
- 3 tablespoons soy sauce
- ¼ cup water
- 1 small clove garlic, crushed
- ¼ teaspoon monosodium glutamate
- Dash ginger

Combine ground beef with remaining ingredients; mix well. Shape in 6 patties or 3 larger "steaks." Broil 4 to 5 inches from heat for 10 minutes, turning once. Makes 6 burger or 3 "steak" servings.

Square Burgers

- 1 teaspoon instant minced onion
- ½ cup evaporated milk
- 1½ pounds ground chuck*
- 1 slightly beaten egg
- 1 teaspoon salt
- ¼ teaspoon monosodium glutamate
- Dash pepper
- 4 slices white bread, toasted and buttered
- 1 3½-ounce can French-fried onions **or** 1 4-ounce package frozen French-fried onion rings

Soak onion in evaporated milk 5 minutes; lightly mix with meat, egg, and seasonings. Place meat mixture on large sheet of waxed paper; lightly pat into a 9-inch square. Cut meat in 4 squares. With scissors, cut through waxed paper between burgers. Place, meat side down, on grill; peel off waxed paper. Broil over coals 4 to 5 inches from heat 5 minutes; turn and broil 3 to 4 minutes longer or till of desired doneness. Meanwhile, heat onion rings according to the label directions. Place each burger on a slice of toast; top with onion rings. Pass catsup and mustard. Makes 4 servings.

* If beef is lean, have 3 ounces of suet ground with this amount of meat.

Burgundy Beefburgers

- 2 pounds ground chuck*
- 1 cup soft bread crumbs
- 1 egg
- ¼ cup red cooking wine (not sweet)
- 2 tablespoons sliced green onions
- 1 teaspoon salt
- Dash pepper
- 2 tablespoons sliced green onions and tops
- ½ cup butter or margarine
- ¼ cup red cooking wine
- Butter or margarine
- 6 thick slices French bread, cut on the diagonal

In large bowl, toss first 7 ingredients with a fork till well mixed. Shape in 6 doughnut-shaped burgers, about 1 inch thick. For burgundy sauce, cook 2 tablespoons green onions in ½ cup butter till just tender; add ¼ cup wine. Brush burgers with the sauce. Broil over coals about 4 inches from heat for 9 minutes, brushing frequently with sauce. Turn burgers and broil 4 minutes longer or till of desired doneness, continuing to brush with sauce. Serve on buttered French bread slices. Heat remaining sauce to pass with burgers. Makes 6 servings.

* If beef is lean, have 4 ounces suet ground with this amount of meat.

Skewer Dogs

- 1 pound ground beef
- ¾ cup soft bread crumbs
- ¼ cup milk
- 2 tablespoons chopped onion
- 1 slightly beaten egg
- ½ teaspoon salt
- Dash pepper
- 6 frankfurters
- 1 cup catsup
- ¼ cup butter or margarine, melted
- ¼ cup molasses
- 2 tablespoons vinegar
- 6 slices bacon (optional)

Combine ground beef with next 6 ingredients; mix lightly. Divide meat mixture into 6 portions. Shape meat around franks, covering completely. (Roll kabobs between waxed paper to made uniform.) Chill. Insert skewers lengthwise through frankfurters. For Sauce: Combine catsup, butter, molasses, and vinegar; brush over kabobs. Wrap each kabob spiral-fashion with slice of bacon; secure with toothpicks. Broil 3 inches from heat about 15 minutes, turning as needed to cook bacon. Simmer sauce while kabobs are cooking; brush on kabobs just before removing from heat. Serve in toasted frankfurter buns; pass extra sauce. Makes 6 servings.

Sukiyaki Skewers

- ⅓ cup soy sauce
- ¼ cup sugar
- 1 teaspoon grated fresh gingerroot or ¼ teaspoon ground ginger
- 1 pound sirloin tip, cut in thin strips
- ½ pound fresh whole green beans
- 4 large carrots, cut into 3-inch sticks

For marinade combine soy sauce, sugar, and ginger. Add meat and let stand 1 to 2 hours. Meanwhile cook vegetables till barely tender. Wrap half the meat strips around bundles of 3 or 4 beans; repeat with remaining meat and carrot sticks. Thread kabobs on 2 parallel skewers, ladder-fashion. Brush with melted butter. Broil about 5 minutes, turning once.

Indoor-Outdoor Kabobs

- 1 envelope or can **dry** onion-soup mix
- ¼ cup sugar
- 1 cup catsup
- 1 cup water
- ½ cup vinegar
- ½ cup salad oil
- 2 tablespoons prepared mustard
- 2 slices lemon
- ½ teaspoon salt
- 1 pound round steak, cut in 1-inch cubes
- 4 medium potatoes, partially cooked and quartered
- Instant nonseasoned meat tenderizer
- 2 green peppers, cut in large pieces

For sauce, combine first 9 ingredients with several dashes bottled hot pepper sauce. Bring to boiling; reduce heat, simmer 20 minutes. Cool completely. Then add meat and potatoes; stir to coat. Marinate 2 to 3 hours. Remove meat; tenderize according to label directions. Thread on skewers with vegetables. Broil 5 inches from heat about 15 minutes; brush with sauce occasionally, turning once. Heat extra sauce to pass. Makes 4 servings.

Burger Mountains

- 1½ pounds ground chuck*
- 1 cup dairy sour cream
- ¼ cup Worcestershire sauce
- 1 tablespoon instant minced onion
- 1½ teaspoons salt
- 1 cup corn flakes
- Butter or margarine
- 2 hamburger buns, split
- 1 medium tomato, thinly sliced
- 1 medium unpared cucumber, thinly sliced
- ½ cup dairy sour cream
- 3 tablespoons milk
- 1 tablespoon crumbled blue cheese

Combine first 5 ingredients; blend thoroughly. Crush corn flakes slightly with hands; gently stir into meat mixture. Let stand ½ hour. To shape burgers, divide meat mixture in 4 portions and from each shape a 3½-inch patty and a 3-inch patty. (Patties will be about ¾ inch thick.) Broil in a wire broiler basket over *slow* coals, about 5 minutes per side. Meanwhile, butter buns and toast, cut side down, on grill. Place a large burger on each toasted bun half; then top each with a tomato slice and 3 cucumber slices. Add a smaller burger; spear with skewer to keep "mountain" in place. Drizzle with BLUE CHEESE SAUCE: In small saucepan, blend ½ cup sour cream, the milk, and blue cheese; heat through, stirring constantly. Serves 4.

* If beef is lean, have 3 ounces suet ground with this amount of meat.

Hilo Franks

- 1 cup apricot preserves
- ½ 8-ounce can (½ cup) tomato sauce
- ⅓ cup vinegar
- ¼ cup cooking sherry
- 2 tablespoons soy sauce
- 2 tablespoons honey
- 1 tablespoon salad oil
- 1 teaspoon salt
- 1 teaspoon grated fresh gingerroot **or** ¼ teaspoon ground ginger
- 2 pounds frankfurters

For the sauce, combine preserves, tomato sauce, vinegar, sherry, soy sauce, honey, salad oil, salt and grated gingerroot. Score the frankfurters on the bias. Broil franks over *hot* coals, turning and basting often with the sauce. Broil till hot through and glazed. Heat remaining sauce on edge of grill and pass with frankfurters. Makes 8 to 10 servings.

Florentine Franks

- 4 to 6 frankfurters
- 1 tomato, peeled, chopped, and drained
- 2 tablespoons shredded sharp process American cheese
- 2 tablespoons grated Parmesan cheese
- 1 small clove garlic, crushed
- ¼ teaspoon crushed oregano
- 4 to 6 slices bacon

Slit franks lengthwise, *cutting almost to ends and only ¾ the way through*. Combine tomato, cheeses, and seasonings; stuff in franks. Wrap each with a bacon strip, anchoring ends with toothpicks. Place franks, filling side down, on grill. Broil over *hot* coals turning often, about 10 to 15 minutes or till filling is hot and bacon crisp. Serve in frankfurter buns. Makes 4 to 6 servings.

Peanut-buttered Pork Loin

    2 boned pork loins (4 to 6   ½ cup orange juice
      pounds total)   ¼ cup creamy peanut butter

Tie pork loins together at 1½-inch intervals with the fat sides out. Balance roast on spit and secure with holding forks; insert meat thermometer. Season with salt and pepper. Arrange *medium hot* coals at rear of firebox, knock off ash. Put a foil drip pan in front of coals and under roast. Attach spit, turn on motor and lower hood. Roast until meat thermometer reads 185°. Allow about 3½ hours cooking time. Combine orange juice and peanut butter. When thermometer reads 185° brush the peanut butter sauce on roast and continue cooking and basting for 15 to 20 minutes. Makes about 15 servings.

Zesty Barbecue Pork Steak

    1 envelope dry tomato-soup mix   2 teaspoons Worcestershire
    ¼ cup dry onion-soup mix   sauce
    ½ cup Italian salad dressing   1 teaspoon prepared horseradish
    2 tablespoons vinegar   1 teaspoon prepared mustard
    2 cups water   6 pork steaks, ½ to ¾ inch
    2 tablespoons brown sugar   thick

In saucepan, combine soup mixes, salad dressing, and vinegar. Gradually stir in water. Add remaining ingredients except pork steaks. Bring mixture to boiling and let simmer 10 minutes. Slash edges of fat to keep steaks flat. Broil over *medium hot* coals for about 15 minutes. Turn and baste with sauce; broil 15 minutes longer. Baste on both sides before removing from grill. Makes 6 servings.

Luau Ribs

    1 13½-ounce can (1⅔ cups)   3 tablespoons soy sauce
      crushed pineapple   2 tablespoons Worcestershire
    ¼ cup molasses   sauce
    ¼ cup Dijon-style mustard   Dash pepper
    1 teaspoon monosodium   4 pounds spareribs or loin back
      glutamate   ribs
    3 tablespoons lemon juice

For glaze: Combine first 8 ingredients; set aside. Salt ribs; place bone side down on grill over slow coals. (Keep eye on heat—ribs tend to dry out and char with too much heat.) Grill about 20 minutes; turn meaty side down and grill till browned, about 10 minutes. Turn meaty side up and brush with the pineapple glaze; continue grilling without turning for 30 to 45 minutes, till meat is well done. (Loin back ribs will take longer.) Slide a piece of foil under thinner end of ribs if done before thicker end; continue cooking. Makes 4 to 6 servings.

Barbecued Ribs with Rodeo Sauce

1 cup catsup	1 tablespoon sugar
1 tablespoon Worcestershire sauce	1 teaspoon salt
	1 teaspoon celery seed
2 or 3 dashes bottled hot pepper sauce	4 pounds pork spareribs
	1 lemon, thinly sliced
1 cup water	1 large onion, thinly sliced
¼ cup vinegar	

For RODEO SAUCE: Combine first 8 ingredients; simmer 30 minutes. Salt ribs and place in rack over *slow* coals. Put barbecue lid on or hood down. Cook 1 hour. Brush ribs with Rodeo Sauce and peg on slices of lemon and onion with toothpicks. Continue to cook without turning ribs, 30 to 40 minutes or till done, brushing now and then with sauce. For smoke flavor, during last half hour, toss damp hickory chips or sawdust on coals. Snip ribs in servings with scissors. Makes 4 servings.

Abacus Ribs

- 4 pounds spareribs, cut in narrow strips
- 1 cup clear French dressing
- ½ cup finely chopped onion
- ½ cup chili sauce
- 2 tablespoons brown sugar
- 2 to 3 tablespoons lemon juice
- 2 tablespoons Worcestershire sauce
- Cooked or canned small whole onions

Rub ribs with salt and pepper; place in shallow baking dishes. Combine next 6 ingredients for marinade; pour over ribs, coating all. Let stand 2 hours at room temperature or overnight in refrigerator, spooning marinade over occasionally Drain, reserving marinade. Lace ribs on spit in accordion style, threading onions on as you weave in and out. Rotate over coals 45 minutes to 1 hour or until done, brushing frequently with marinade. Makes 4 servings.

Royal Ribs

- 2 tablespoons instant minced onion
- 1 tablespoon brown sugar
- 1 tablespoon whole mustard seed
- 1 teaspoon monosodium glutamate
- 2 teaspoons paprika
- 1 teaspoon crushed oregano
- 1 teaspoon chili powder
- 1 teaspoon cracked pepper
- ½ teaspoon salt
- ½ teaspoon ground cloves
- 1 bay leaf
- 1 clove garlic, minced
- 1 cup catsup
- ½ cup water
- ¼ cup olive oil or salad oil
- ¼ cup tarragon vinegar
- 2 tablespoons wine vinegar
- 2 tablespoons Worcestershire sauce
- 2 or 3 drops liquid smoke
- 4 pounds loin back ribs or spareribs

For sauce, combine all ingredients except ribs; stir well. Heat to boiling; simmer gently 20 to 25 minutes, stirring occasionally. Remove bay leaf. Sprinkle ribs with salt and place the slabs, bone side down, on grill of barbecue-smoker, away from the coals. Add dampened hickory to *slow* coals and close smoker hood. Hickory-barbecue about 3½ hours, basting with sauce the last half hour. Snip ribs in serving pieces. Makes 3 or 4 servings.

Sparkling Grilled Ham

- 1 1-inch slice fully cooked ham (about 1½ pounds)
- 1 cup sparkling Catawba grape juice (white)
- 1 cup orange juice
- ½ cup brown sugar
- 3 tablespoons salad oil
- 1 tablespoon wine vinegar
- 2 teaspoons dry mustard
- ¾ teaspoon ginger
- ¼ to ½ teaspoon cloves

Slash the fat edge of ham. Combine remaining ingredients; pour over ham in shallow baking dish. Refrigerate overnight or let stand at room temperature 2 hours, spooning marinade over several times. Broil ham slice over *slow* coals, about 15 minutes on each side, brushing frequently with marinade. Heat remaining marinade on edge of grill to pass. Makes 5 servings.

Lamb and Ham Kabobs

- ¼ cup salad oil
- ¼ cup dry red wine
- ¼ cup soy sauce
- ¼ cup tarragon vinegar
- 2 tablespoons chopped green pepper
- Dash pepper
- 1 clove garlic, crushed
- 1 pound lamb, cut in 1½-inch cubes
- ½ pound ham, cut in 1-inch cubes
- 1 medium onion, sliced and separated in rings

Combine first 7 ingredients; add lamb, ham, and onions. Stir to coat. Let stand 2 to 3 hours, turning meat occasionally. Alternate lamb and ham on skewers. Broil about 5 inches from heat 15 minutes or till done. Heat marinade to pass. Makes 4 servings.

Butterfly Leg of Lamb

- 1 5- to 6-pound leg of lamb
- 1 to 2 garlic cloves, minced
- 1 teaspoon salt
- 1 teaspoon **fines herbes**
- ½ teaspoon black pepper
- ½ teaspoon thyme
- ¼ cup grated onion
- ½ cup salad oil
- ½ cup lemon juice

Have meatman bone leg of lamb and slit lengthwise to spread it flat like a thick steak. (Note how it takes on the butterfly shape.) LEMON-MARINADE-BASTING SAUCE: In large glass dish or baking pan thoroughly blend remaining ingredients. Place butterfly leg in marinade. Leave at least one hour at room temperature, or overnight in the refrigerator, turning occasionally. Drain and save marinade. Insert 2 long skewers through meat at right angles making an X or place meat in a wire broiler basket. This will make for easy turning of the meat and keep meat from "curling" during cooking. Roast over *medium* coals 1½ to 2 hours turning every 15 minutes till medium or well done. Baste frequently with reserved marinade. Place meat on carving board and remove from basket or remove skewers. Cut across grain into thin slices. Makes 8 servings.

Patio Chicken Barbecue

- 1 8-ounce can (1 cup) tomato sauce
- ½ cup water
- ¼ cup molasses
- 2 tablespoons butter or margarine
- 2 tablespoons vinegar
- 2 tablespoons minced onion
- 1 tablespoon Worcestershire sauce
- 2 teaspoons dry mustard
- 1 teaspoon salt
- ¼ teaspoon pepper
- ¼ teaspoon chili powder
- 2 ready-to-cook broilers (2 to 2½ pounds each), cut in half lengthwise
- ½ cup salad oil
- Salt
- Pepper

In saucepan, combine tomato sauce, water, molasses, butter or margarine, vinegar, onion, Worcestershire sauce, dry mustard, 1 teaspoon salt, pepper and chili powder. Simmer mixture 15 to 20 minutes. Set aside. Brush halved broilers with salad oil and season with salt and pepper. Place bone side down on grill. Broil over *slow* coals 25 minutes; turn, broil 20 minutes. Brush with sauce. Continue broiling, turning occasionally and basting with sauce 10 to 15 minutes or till tender. Makes 4 servings.

Spinning Chicken

- 1 3- to 4-pound ready-to-cook broiler-fryer
- 1 teaspoon salt
- Dash pepper
- ½ cup chopped celery leaves
- ¼ cup snipped parsley
- ¼ cup chopped onion
- 2 tablespoons butter or margarine, melted
- ¼ cup catsup
- ¼ cup corn syrup
- 2 tablespoons lemon juice
- 2 tablespoons salad oil
- 2 tablespoons prepared mustard

Rinse chicken, pat dry with paper towels. Rub body cavity with salt and pepper. Combine celery, parsley, onion, and melted butter; place in body cavity. Fasten neck skin to back with nail or skewer. Tie with cord to hold nail. To mount chicken on spit, place holding fork on rod, tines toward point; insert rod through chicken (press tines firmly into the breast meat). To tie wings, use 24 inches of cord. Start cord at back; loop around each wing tip. Make slip knots so wings can't straighten. Tie in center, leaving equal ends. Now take an 18-inch piece of cord. Loop around tail, then around crossed legs. Tie very tightly to hold bird securely onto rod, leaving cord ends. Pull together cords attached to wings and legs; tie tightly. (If barbecuing more than one bird, fasten others on spit in same way, using holding fork for each; place birds close together.) Adjust holding forks and fasten screws tightly. Test balance. Place chicken on rotisserie, having *medium* coals at back and front of chicken and a drip pan under revolving bird. Roast chicken for about 2 hours without barbecue hood or about 1¾ hours with the barbecue hood down. Combine catsup, corn syrup, lemon juice, salad oil, and prepared mustard to make the tangy basting sauce. Use to baste the chicken occasionally during last 30 minutes of cooking. Makes 3 or 4 servings.

Sea-food Sword

- ¼ cup soy sauce
- ¼ cup salad oil
- ¼ cup lemon juice
- ¼ cup snipped parsley
- ½ teaspoon salt
- Dash pepper
- Fresh or frozen shrimp
- Fresh or frozen scallops
- Large stuffed green olives
- Lemon wedges

Combine first 6 ingredients for basting sauce. Peel and devein shrimp, leaving last section of shell and tail intact. Add shrimp and scallops to basting sauce; let stand 1 hour at room temperature, stirring now and then. On skewers, alternate shrimp (put shrimp on skewers in pairs, turning the second one upside down and reversing direction), scallops, olives, and lemon. Broil over *hot* coals, turning and brushing sea food frequently with sauce. Don't overcook.

Sonora Shrimp

- 1 cup bottled barbecue sauce
- 3 tablespoons lemon juice
- 1 tablespoon Worcestershire sauce
- 1 teaspoon dill weed
- 1 pound large shrimp, peeled and deveined

Combine first four ingredients for marinade and pour over shrimp; cover and let stand at least 6 hours or overnight in refrigerator, stirring occasionally. Cook shrimp on fine wire grill over *hot* coals about 6 to 8 minutes or till done, turning once and brushing often with marinade. Don't overcook! Heat remaining marinade on edge of grill and serve with the shrimp. Or, if you prefer, pass a lemon-butter sauce spiced with bottled hot pepper sauce and chili powder. Makes 3 or 4 servings.

Grilled Trout with Almonds

4 brook trout, cleaned	½ cup butter or margarine
¼ cup all-purpose flour	2 tablespoons slivered almonds
½ teaspoon salt	¼ cup lemon juice
Dash pepper	2 tablespoons snipped parsley

Remove heads from fish; wash and pat dry with paper towels. Combine flour, salt, and pepper; dip fish in seasoned flour. Place coated fish in an oiled wire broiler basket. Broil fish over *hot* coals 15 minutes or till fish flakes with a fork, turning once. Baste with ¼ cup melted butter. Melt remaining ¼ cup butter in a saucepan and add almonds. Brown almonds, stirring occasionally. Stir in lemon juice and parsley. Place grilled fish on warm platter and pour lemon sauce over. Makes 4 servings.

Barbecued Rock Lobster Tails

4 medium Rock lobster tails, frozen	1 teaspoon grated orange peel
¼ cup butter or margarine, melted	Generous dash **each** ground ginger, aromatic bitters, and chili powder
2 teaspoons lemon juice	

Thaw Rock lobster tails and cut off thin undershell membrane with kitchen scissors. Bend tail back to crack shell or insert long skewers lengthwise between shell and meat to prevent curling. Combine melted butter, lemon juice, orange peel, ginger, bitters, and chili powder; brush over lobster meat. Broil on grill over *hot* coals for about 5 minutes with meat side up.* Turn shell side up, brush with sauce and continue to broil 5 to 10 minutes longer or until meat has lost its transparency and is opaque. Serve immediately. Makes 4 servings.

* To broil lobster tails in range broiler: Prepare as above and place *shell side up* on broiler pan. Broil for about 5 minutes. Turn meat side up, brush with sauce and continue to broil 5 to 10 minutes longer.

Quick Onion Sauce

½ envelope (3 tablespoons) dry onion-soup mix	1 tablespoon prepared mustard
2 tablespoons sugar	¾ cup water
½ teaspoon salt	½ cup catsup
Dash freshly ground pepper	¼ cup vinegar
	1 tablespoon lemon juice

Combine all ingredients. Bring to boiling; reduce heat and simmer uncovered 10 minutes, stirring occasionally. Use as a basting sauce for hamburgers, and pass remaining sauce in a bowl. Or, use with grilled franks or with leftover pork or beef for barbecued sandwiches. Makes about 1½ cups.

Smoky Barbecue Sauce

- 1 8-ounce can (1 cup) tomato sauce
- 1 8-ounce bottle tomato-base meat sauce **or** 1 4½-ounce bottle steak sauce
- ½ cup water
- 1 teaspoon celery seed
- ¼ teaspoon liquid smoke

Combine all ingredients. Makes about 2¼ cups sauce or enough to baste 4 pounds of spareribs.

Rosy Marmalade Glaze

- ½ cup extra-hot catsup
- ⅓ cup orange marmalade
- 2 tablespoons finely chopped onion
- 2 tablespoons salad oil
- 1 tablespoon lemon juice
- 1 to 1½ teaspoons dry mustard

Combine all ingredients, blending well. Brush on ham, pork chops, or chicken the last 20 minutes of broiling time. (Use low heat to keep bright color of sauce.) Makes about 1 cup.

Herb-and-Honey Basting Sauce

- ¾ cup finely chopped onion
- 1 clove garlic, minced
- ¼ cup salad oil or olive oil
- 1 12-ounce can (1½ cups) pear nectar
- ½ cup white wine vinegar
- ¼ cup honey
- 2 tablespoons Worcestershire sauce
- 1 teaspoon prepared horseradish
- 1 teaspoon dry mustard
- 1 teaspoon salt
- ½ teaspoon thyme
- ¼ teaspoon rosemary
- ¼ teaspoon pepper

Cook onion and garlic in hot oil till tender but not brown. Add remaining ingredients; simmer uncovered 5 minutes. Use for marinating and basting chicken or other poultry for a barbecue. Pass extra sauce in a bowl. Makes 3¼ cups.

Sweet-Sour Sauce

- 1 cup sugar
- ½ cup white vinegar
- ½ cup water
- 1 tablespoon chopped green pepper
- 1 tablespoon chopped canned pimiento
- ½ teaspoon salt
- 2 teaspoons cornstarch
- 1 tablespoon cold water
- 1 teaspoon paprika

In a saucepan, combine first 6 ingredients and simmer 5 minutes. Combine cornstarch and 1 tablespoon cold water; add to hot mixture, and cook and stir till sauce thickens. Cool slightly. Add paprika.

Use to baste broiled shrimp and pass extra. Makes about 1½ cups sauce.

SECTION 8

Special Helps

DONE? THESE QUICK TESTS WILL TELL YOU

Automatic oven thermometers, or timers and portable meat thermometers, will mind time and temperature when you're roasting meat or poultry. Special thermometers will tell you when the candy has cooked long enough and when deep fat is just the right temperature for frying.

But there are other foods you can check best by look or touch. These simple tests are a part of cooking lore, the know-how of generations of good cooks. For some of the secrets that tell you when food is done, follow the pictures on the following pages.

Roast poultry

About 20 minutes before bird should be done, press thickest part of drumstick. If done, meat feels very soft, and you can move the drumstick up and down easily or twist it out of joint.

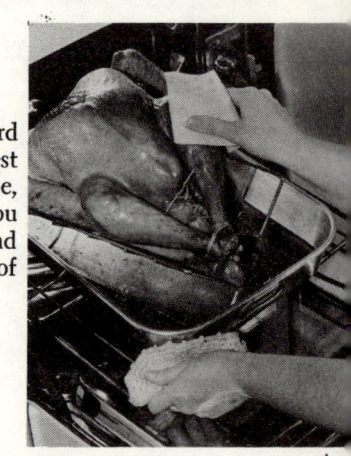

Bread and rolls

Touch dough lightly. If finger leaves slight dent, dough has risen till double and rolls are ready to go in the oven.

Cake

Insert toothpick or cake tester in center of cake. If it comes out clean, cake is done. Cake will also shrink slightly from sides of pan and will spring back when pressed lightly in center.

Griddle Cakes

When upper side of pancake is bubbly all over, under side is done. When a few bubbles have burst and the edge begins to appear dry, cake is ready to turn. To keep pancakes hot, place in a heavy pan over very low heat, cover but leave lid ajar. Or place rack in shallow pan and keep warm for a short time in very slow oven (250°).

Candy

If using a *thermometer*, clip to pan after syrup boils, being sure bulb is covered with boiling liquid, not just foam. Read with eyes level with fluid in indicator column; have syrup boiling.

Or, test candy with the *cold-water* method. Have ready small bowl of very cold water (but not ice water). To test candy, remove pan from heat. At once, while syrup is bubbling, drop a little syrup into the water. Hardness of ball formed indicates the temperature of the candy.

SPECIAL HELPS • 299

How to cook rice

Put 1 cup uncooked rice, 2 cups cold water, and ½ to 1 teaspoon salt in 2-quart saucepan; cover with tight-fitting lid. Bring to a vigorous boil; then turn heat as low as possible. Continue cooking 14 minutes. Do not stir or lift cover. Turn off heat; let rice steam, covered, for an additional 10 minutes. Makes 3 cups cooked rice. GLAMOROUS RICE RING, shown here, is a snap to make! Pack hot cooked rice—with some snipped parsley if you wish—into a ring mold (or custard cups). Turn out at once on hot platter. Put serving bowl in center. Fill with creamed ham or chicken.

How to cook spaghetti

A *large* pan is important to cook any pasta—spaghetti, macaroni, fine noodles, and lasagna. Use *lots of water*—3 quarts is minimum for cooking 8 ounces of pasta. Add 1 teaspoon salt for each quart water. Help prevent sticking by adding a teaspoon olive oil to the water, especially when cooking large pasta. Have water boiling vigorously. No need to break long spaghetti—hold a handful at one end, dip the other into the water. As spaghetti softens, curl it around in pan till immersed. Don't cover; stir at the start to prevent sticking. Keep water boiling. Cook till tender, but still firm. Don't overcook. Drain at once.

Neat way to frost a cake

Place four pieces of waxed paper over edge of cake plate. Place cake on plate. Paper will catch surplus frosting as you work.

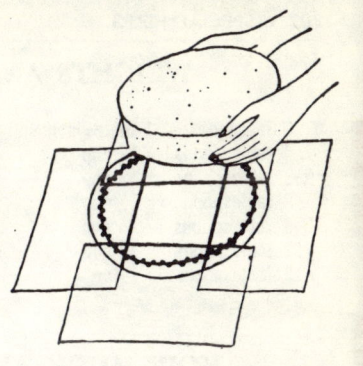

Frost between layers, then frost sides, and last of all, the top. If you wish, press finely chopped nuts against sides.

Decorate the top with a swirl of nuts. When you finish, carefully remove waxed paper—you have a spotless plate!

WEIGHTS AND MEASURES

3 teaspoons = 1 tablespoon
4 tablespoons = ¼ cup
5⅓ tablespoons = ⅓ cup
8 tablespoons = ½ cup
10⅔ tablespoons = ⅔ cup
12 tablespoons = ¾ cup
16 tablespoons = 1 cup

1 cup = 8 fluid ounces
1 cup = ½ pint
2 cups = 1 pint
4 cups = 1 quart
4 quarts = 1 gallon
8 quarts = 1 peck
4 pecks = 1 bushel

HOW MUCH AND HOW MANY

Butter, chocolate
2 tablespoons butter = 1 ounce
1 stick or ¼ pound butter = ½ cup
1 square chocolate = 1 ounce

Crumbs
20 salted crackers = 1 cup fine crumbs
12 graham crackers = 1 cup fine crumbs
22 vanilla wafers = 1 cup fine crumbs
8 to 9 slices zwieback = 1 cup fine crumbs
1 slice bread = ½ cup soft crumbs

Cereals
4 ounces macaroni (1-1¼ cups) = 2¼ cups cooked
4 ounces noodles (1½-2 cups) = 2¼ cups cooked
4 ounces spaghetti (1-1¼ cups) = 2½ cups cooked
1 cup uncooked rice (6½ to 7 ounces) = 3-3½ cups cooked
1 cup precooked rice = 2 cups cooked

Fruits, vegetables
Juice of 1 lemon = 3 to 4 tablespoons
Grated peel of 1 lemon = 1 teaspoon
Juice of 1 orange = 6 to 7 tablespoons
Grated peel of 1 orange = about 2 teaspoons
1 medium apple, chopped = 1 cup
1 medium onion, chopped = ½ cup
¼ pound celery (about 2 stalks), chopped = 1 cup

Cheese and eggs
1 pound process cheese, shredded = 4 cups
¼ pound blue cheese, crumbled = ¾ to 1 cup
12 to 14 egg yolks = 1 cup
8 to 10 egg whites = 1 cup

Nuts
1 pound walnuts in shell = 2 cups, shelled
¼ pound chopped walnuts = about 1 cup
1 pound almonds in shell = about 1 cup, shelled

EMERGENCY SUBSTITUTIONS

- 1 tablespoon cornstarch = 2 tablespoons flour
- 1 square (1 ounce) chocolate = 3 tablespoons cocoa plus 1 tablespoon butter
- 1 whole egg = 2 egg yolks
- 1 cup sour milk = 1 tablespoon lemon juice or vinegar plus sweet milk to make 1 cup
- 1 cup milk = ½ cup evaporated milk plus ½ cup water

CAN SIZES

- 8 ounce = 1 cup
- Picnic = 1¼ cups or 10½ to 12 ounces
- 12-ounce vacuum = 1½ cups
- No. 300 = 1¾ cups or 14 to 16 ounces
- No. 303 = 2 cups or 16 to 17 ounces
- No. 2 = 2½ cups or 20 ounces
- No. 2½ = 3½ cups or 29 ounces
- No. 3 cylinder = 5¾ cups or 46 fluid ounces
- No. 10 = 12 to 13 cups or 6½ pounds to 7 pounds, 5 ounces (equal to 7 No. 303 cans or 5 No. 2 cans)

Index

Abacus ribs, 286
Airy cheese rolls, 206
All-in-a-roll supper, 215
Almond peach torte, 158
Almonds
  grilled trout with, 292
  iced, 194
  maple ice cream, 190
  olive sauce, 62
Ambrosia, 114-15
Ambrosia chiffon pie, 150
Anchovy butter, 237
Angel cheesecake, 132
Apple-date squares, 171
Apple-melon toss with cheese, 109
Apple-stuffed pork tenderloin, 33
Apple top, 213
Apples
  carrot relish cups, 99
  cranberry tarts, 156
  peanut sandwiches, 219
  pear crumb pie, 146-47
  rutabaga and, 83
  stuffing, sausage and, 28
Applesauce puffs, 209
Apricot-glazed ham patties, 39
Apricots
  banana meringue pie, 144
  bran squares, 170
  frosted squares, 110-11
  golden roll-ups, 222
  spiced sweet potatoes and, 83
  tangerine mold, 176
Artichoke-pimiento bowl, 94
Artichoke velvet, 66
Asparagus delicious, 67
Asparagus toss with harlequin dressing, 94
Avocado-crab sandwiches, hot, 216
Avocado dressing, 107
Avocado fruit squares, 110
Avocado fruit toss, 109

Bacon
  Canadian, and bean bake, 36-37
  Yankee bake, 36
Bacon oriental, 35
Bacon spoon bread, 200-1
Baked Alaska, 128
  Melba, 129
Banana ambrosia ring, 212
Banana-apricot meringue pie, 144
Banana cream cake, 138
Banana oatmeal bread, 199
Barbecue
  chicken, 288-89
  frankfurters, 22
  pork chops, 32-33
    baked beans and, 241
  pork steak, 284
  sauce, 293
  skillet, 246
  Southern steak, 11
  spareribs, 285, 286
Barbecued chuck roast, 276
Barbecued lamb shanks, 42
Barbecued pot roast, 6-7
Barbecued rock lobster tails, 292-93
Bavarian cream, blueberry rice, 181
Bavarian-style savory stew, 9
Bavarian Wiener supper, 238
Beans
  baked
    barbecued pork and, 241
    Canadian bacon and, 36-37
    franks and, 24, 238
    French pot, 267
    hearty, 68
    pie, 248-49
    potluck, 67
  beef roll-ups, 277
  green
    Béarnaise, 67
    Mediterranean salad, 95
    savory, 68
    shoestring tossed salad, 106
    succotash, 86
    vegetable trio, 90
  salads, 95-96
    Mediterranean, 95
    Mexican, 95
    mustard, 96
    shoestring toss, 106
Beef, 4-23
  casseroles, *see* Casseroles—beef
  corned
    baked burgers, 241
    dinner, 14
    double-beef sandwiches, 220
    stag sandwiches, 217
  fresh-brisket feast, 7
  loaves, 17-19
    caraway, 21
    cranberry and, 19
    Italian style, 18
    mushroom, 17
    Parmesan, 19
    pizza, 22
    saucy, 230-31
  pot roast, 5-7
    Polynesian, 8-9
  roast, 4-5
    barbecued chuck, 276
    champion sandwiches, 220
    rolled rib, 4
    savory chuck, 4-5
  short ribs, saucy, 13
  stew
    burger skillet, 20
    oven, 8
    savory, Bavarian-style, 9
    with sesame biscuits, 236
  See also Beefsteak; Frankfurters; Hamburgers; Meat balls; Veal

INDEX • 305

Beef and bean roll-ups, 277
Beef Cantonese with ginger rice, 235
Beef fondue, 237
Beef Stroganoff, 12-13
Beefsteak, 9-16, 276-78
  bean roll-ups, 277
  California, 9
  Chateaubriand, 277
  chuck, grilled, 276
  flank, herb-stuffed, 10
  minute-steak scramble, 16
  porterhouse, swank, 276-77
  round steak
    chicken-fried, 14
    indoor-outdoor kabobs, 282
    roll-ups, 11
    sauerbraten, 15
  sirloin
    island teriyaki, 278
    oriental chi chow, 16
    quick Stroganoff, 12-13
    Southern Bar-B-Q, 11
    Stroganoff, 12
    sukiyaki skewers, 281
  Swiss, 13, 14
Beet relish, 69
Beet salads, 96
Beets with pineapple, 69
Biscuits, 210-11
  big, hamburger bake, 232
  Dixie corn-meal, 210-11
  hamburger supper pie, 20
  quick Parmesan, 211
  sesame, beef stew with, 236
Blintz pancakes, 222
Blue cheese, *see* Cheese—blue
Blueberries
  peach-a-berry cobbler, 160
  sauce, 222
Blueberry rice Bavarian, 181
Blueberry strata pie, 151
Borsch salad molds, 96
Bran apricot squares, 170
Bran muffins, cheddar, 210
Braunschweiger, 21
Bread, 198-204
  bacon spoon, 200-1
  cheese
    airy rolls, 206
    cheddar bran muffins, 210
    poppy-dot, 200
    quick Parmesan biscuits, 211
    sticks, 203
  corn, *see* Corn—bread
  Easter anise, 198
  loaves
    old-time herb, 204
    glazed raisin, 204
  nut
    glazed lemon, 201
    prune, 199
    walnut graham, 198
  oatmeal banana, 199
  onion
    French, 202
    supper, 200
Bridge meringue torte, 158-59
Broccoli casserole, 70-71
Broccoli italienne, 71
Broccoli Parmesan, 70
Brownies, 171
Brussels sprouts, blue cheesed, 71
Brussels sprouts polonaise, 71
Brussels sprouts soufflé, 71
Burgundy beefburgers, 279
Butter
  anchovy, 226
  garlic, 237
  whipped, 226
Butter-nut cake, 141
Butterfly leg of lamb, 288
Buttermilk waffles, 223
Butterscotch meringue bars, 168-69
Butterscotch swirls, 206-7
Butterscotch topping, 207
Butterscotch upside-down cake, 131

Cabbage
  Chinese, crabmeat with, 59
  See also Slaw
Caesar salad, 98
Cakes, 128-42
  banana cream, 138
  caramel ginger, 140
  cheesecake, 132-33
  chocolate, 130-31
  coffee, *see* Coffee cakes
  easy daffodil, 134-35
  frosty ribbon loaf, 139
  lemon tea, 165
  nut
    butter, 141
    peanut, quick, 136
  pineapple
    crunch, 137
    pudding and, 133
  prune spice, 139
  strawberry meringue, 134
  upside-down
    butterscotch, 131
    marmalade, 136
  vanilla wafer coconut, 137
  See also Baked Alaska; Fillings; Frostings; Pancakes
Calico chicken and rice, 254
California chicken, 9
California sweet-potato bake, 82
California vegetable bowl, 89
Campfire coleslaw, 96-97
Canadian bacon-bean bake, 36-37
Candied dill pickles, 101
Candied orange peel, 194
Candies, 192-94
  chocolate, *see* Fudge
Cantalope, 109
Caramel fudge, 193
Caramel ginger cake, 140
Caraway meat loaf, 21
Carioca cups, 185
Carrot relish cups, 99
Carrots, 72
  pickled, 99
  sunshine, 72
  zippy glazed, 72
Cashew drops, 168
Casseroles, 230-72
  beef, 230-37
    baked corned-beef burgers, 240
    big biscuit hamburger bake, 232
    burger in the round, 17
    Cantonese, with ginger rice, 235
    chili-hominy bake, 235
    for-the-crowd, 230
    fondue, 237
    German caraway meat balls, 232-33

306 • INDEX

Casseroles (cont'd)
  beef (cont'd)
    hamburger-biscuit supper pie, 20
    Italian hamburger bake, 231
    Italian sauce—spinach squares, 233
    ravioli, 234
    saucy loaves, 230-31
    stew with sesame biscuits, 236
    stuffed burger bundles, 18
  big-meal combo, 236
  broccoli, 70-71
  chicken, see Chicken—casseroles
  egg, 268-69; see also Eggs—casseroles
  ham, 244-45
    chicken and, on egg puffs, 255
    elegante, 244
    loaf in cheese crust, 244-45
    medley, 245
  luncheon meat, see Luncheon meat casseroles
  macaroni, 270
  pizza supper pie, 243
  pork, 241-43
    barbecued, and baked beans, 241
    easy Mexican skillet, 244
    French bean pot, 267
    sausage and egg, 242-43
    Spanish rice and, 242
    tenderloin-noodle treat, 241
  rice, see Rice—casseroles
  sea-food, see Sea-food—casseroles; Tuna—casseroles
  turkey, see Turkey casseroles
  veal Parmesan with spaghetti, 240-41
  vegetable, 267-68
  Wiener, See Frankfurters—casseroles
Cauliflower, cheese-frosted, 72-73
Cauliflower-cheese toss, 98
Cauliflower scallop, 73
Celery and luxe peas, 79
Celery-seed dressing, 124
Charlotte russe, 177
Chateaubriand, 277
Cheddar bran muffins, 210
Cheddar turkey casserole, 52
Cheese
  blue
    apple-melon toss with, 109
    bacon potatoes and, 82
    Brussels sprouts and, 71
    in Italian salad bowl, 106
    slaw, 97
    Waldorf salad, 108-9
  breads, see Bread—cheese
  cauliflower and
    frosted, 72-73
    toss, 98
  cottage, fluffy pineapple salad, 116
  cream, in peach Melba mold, 115
  fruit ring, 116-17
  macaroni: casseroles, see Macaroni—cheese casseroles
  macaroni salad, 118
  Mozzarella pizza loaf, 22
  Parmesan
    biscuits, 211
    broccoli, 70
    double potato bake, 81
    meat loaf, 19
    turkey puff, 255
    veal with spaghetti, 240-41
  sandwiches, see Sandwiches—cheese
  strawberry tarts, 156
  Swiss
    pear-Waldorf salad with, 109
    salami salad, 120
Cheese bread sticks, 203
Cheese buns deluxe, 215
Cheese crust, ham loaf in, 244-45
Cheese-frosted cauliflower, 72-73
Cheese marinated onions, 100-1
Cheese sauce, 272
Cheese-stuffed mushrooms, 76
Cheese-stuffed pork chops, 31
Cheese waffles, 224
Cheesecake, 132-33; see also Cakes—cheesecake
Cherry angel dessert, 184
Cherry crème parfaits, 183
Cherry mallow squares, 111
Cherry-rhubarb pie, 153
Chevron rice bake, 246-47
Chicken, 47-51, 288-90
  baked
    with dressing, 51
    sesame, 49
  barbecued, 288-89
  casseroles, 250-55
    Chinese walnut, 252
    chow bake, 251
    cioppino, 251
    curry-top pie, 252-53
    dinner elegante, 49
    ham and, 50-51
    ham and, on egg puffs, 255
    herbed, en casserole, 48
    herbed baked, 250
    scallop, stuffing and, 253
  casseroles with rice
    calico, 254
    creamy, 254
    divan, 258
    Panamanian, 250-51
  divan
    easy, 48-49
    rice and, 258
  salad, 118-19
  skillet cherry, 50
  spinning, 290
Chicken and dressing bake, 51
Chicken and ham, 50-51
Chicken and ham in tomatoes, 118-19
Chicken-and-stuffing scallop, 253
Chicken-chow bake, 251
Chicken cioppino, 251
Chicken dinner elegante, 49
Chicken-fried round steak, 14
Chicken livers and mushrooms, 76
Chicken Oahu, 47
Chicken rosemary, 47
Chili-hominy bake, 235
Chinese cabbage, crab meat with, 59
Chinese walnut chicken, 252
Chocolate, see Cakes; Cookies; Fudge; Puddings
Chocolate chiffon dessert, 176
Chocolate cloud soufflé, 174
Chocolate dream pie (low-calorie), 150-51
Chocolate malt bars, 172
Chocolate-mint dessert, 178-79

INDEX • 307

Chocolate-peanut bars, 169
Chocolate-raisin drops, 167
Chow mein
  shrimp, 260
  turkey, 52
  vegetable, 89
Clam puff, 57
Cobblers, 160-62
Cocoa-crust lime pie, 147
Coconut-oatmeal cookies, 167
Coconut vanilla wafer cake, 137
Coffee cakes, 212-14
Coffee-crunch dessert, 163
Coffee dot fudge, 192
Coffee-nut tortoni, 184
Cold cuts, *see* Luncheon meat casseroles
Compotes, fruit, 188-89
Confetti relish mold, 100
Cookies, 167-73
  butterscotch meringue bars, 168-69
  chocolate
    brownies, 171
    malt bars, 172
    peanut bars, 169
    pineapple squares, 170
    raisin drops, 167
  coconut-oatmeal, 167
  squares, 170-71
    apple-date, 171
    bran apricot, 170
    frosty strawberry, 173
    holiday fig, 172
    pineapple-chocolate, 170
Corn
  bread
    molasses, 203
    Dixie biscuits, 210-11
  fiesta, in tomato cups, 104
  on-the-cob, Western, 73
  oysters and scalloped, 73
  succotash, 86
Corn curry, 74
Corn waffles, 225
Corned-beef dinner, 14
Corned-beef stag sandwiches, 217
Crab
  Thermidor, 259
Crab Louis, 121
Crab meat with Chinese cabbage, 59
Crab sandwiches, *see* Sandwiches—crab
Cran-apple tarts, 156
Cranberries
  meat loaves, 19
  mince pie, 148
Cranberry-orange butter topping, 226
Cranberry-raisin sauce, 38
Cranberry-raspberry ring, 112
Cranberry sauce
  raisin and, 38
  roast duckling with, 54
Creole onions, 78
Croquettes
  tuna, with pineapple, 263
  turkey, 51
Crunches, dessert, 163-66
  coffee, 163
  deep dish grapefruit, 163
  Hawaiian fruit, 164-65
  lemon, 165-66
  pineapple cake, 137

Curried eggs in shrimp sauce, 268
Curried ham rolls, 38-39
Curries
  corn, 74
  sauce, 38-39
  shrimp, 261
Curry-top chicken pie, 252-53

Dad's Denvers, 218
Date dessert waffles, 225
Dates
  apple squares, 171
  choc-o-date dessert, 182
  pumpkin torte, 157
Desserts, 128-94
  date waffles, 225
  frozen, 189-90
    baked Alaskas, 128-29
    easy strawberry pie, 152-53
    lemon angel frost, 189
    lime refresher—low cal, 190
    maple-almond ice cream, 190
  molded, 175-79
  molded, chocolate
    chiffon, 176
    mint, 178-79
    mocha mousse, 175
  sauces, 191
  soufflé, 174
  squares, 178-80
  See also Cakes; Candies; Cobblers; Compotes; Cookies; Crunches; Pies; Puddings; Tarts
Deviled eggs, 59
Deviled ham elegante, 244
Deviled oysters on the half shell, 57
Deviled potato salad, 103
Dill pickles, candied, 101
Dill sauce
  lamb patties with, 45
  tomatoes with, 87
Dilly squash, 84
Dixie corn-meal biscuits, 210-11
Dressing
  chicken baked with, 51
  salad, *see* Salad dressing
  sausage-apple, 28
Dublin potato salad, 103
Dumplings, lamb stew with, 44

Easter anise bread, 198
Easter nest coffee cake, 212
Egg puffs, ham and chicken on, 255
Egg salad, 120
Eggplant, 75
Eggs
  casseroles, 268-69
    curried, in shrimp sauce, 268
    hashed-brown omelet, 269
    Southern sausage, 242-43
    Swiss onion bake, 269
  deviled, 59
Enchiladas, baked Mexican, 272

Fiesta corn in tomato cups, 104
Fiesta salmon bake, 59
Fig squares, 172-73
Figs, frosty stuffed, 193
Fillings
  meringue, 214
  pineapple, 137
  See also Toppers
Fish, *see* Sea-food

308 • INDEX

Florentine franks, 23, 283
Fondant, orange-butter, 193
Frankfurters, 22-25
  casseroles, 238-39
    Bavarian supper, 238
    bean bake, 24
    bean pot, 238
    noodle supper, 239
    noodle supper pie, 25
    vegetable medley, 239
  Hilo, 283
  island, 23
  pineapple speared, 23
  skewer dogs, 280
  tangy barbecue, 22
  wrap-ups, 24
Franks, Florentine, 23, 283
French bean pot, 267
French dressing, 123
French onion bread, 202
Frosted apricot squares, 110-11
Frosted cashew drops, 168
Frostings, cake, 142
  tutti-frutti, 140
Frosty mint cubes, 116
Frosty ribbon loaf, 139
Frosty strawberry squares, 173
Frosty stuffed figs, 193
Frozen orange-pecan molds, 112
Fruit-and-cheese ring, 116-17
Fruit cocktail cobbler, 160-61
Fruit compote, *see* Compotes
Fruit crumble, Hawaiian, 164-65
Fruit dressing, glossy, 124
Fruit freeze, oriental, 114
Fruit medley pie, 148
Fruit pies, *see* Pies—fruit
Fruit puffs, 209
Fruit salads, 109-17
  ambrosia, 114-15
  avocado, 109, 110
  bowls, 114
  chicken, 119
  frozen
    mint cubes, 116
    orange-pecan molds, 112
    oriental, 114
    strawberry-pineapple, 117
  melon, 113
    apple toss, with cheese, 109
    bowls—honey dressing, 113
    sparkling honeydew maid, 113
  molded, 111-12
    ginger-y citrus, 111
    orange-pecan, frozen, 112
    peach Melba, 115
  rings
    cheese and, 116-17
    cranberry-raspberry, 112
    red raspberry, 117
  squares, 110-11
Fruit-top pork chops, 32
Fruited chicken salad, 119
Fruited pot roast, 6
  Polynesian, 8
Fudge, 191-94

Garbanzo (Mexican) bean salad, 95
Garlic butter, 237
Garlic French dressing, 123
German caraway meat balls, 232-33
German "pizza," 248
Ginger caramel cake, 140

Ginger rice, beef Cantonese with, 235
Ginger sundae sauce, 191
Ginger-y citrus mold, 111
Gingersnap sauce, meat balls in, 21
Glazes
  carrot, 72
  ham, *see* Ham—glazed
  orange, for beets, 96
  raspberry, 132
  rosy marmalade, 293
Glazed lemon-nut bread, 201
Glazed raisin loaf, 204
Glazed squash with onions, 85
Glazed strawberry tartlets, 155
Glossy fruit dressing, 124
Graham bread, walnut, 198
Graham-cracker crust, 153
Graham crust, 133
Green beans, *see* Beans—green
Green pepper boats, garden, 79
Green peppers and tomatoes, 80
Ground beef, *see* Beef—loaves; Hamburgers; Meat balls
Ground lamb with lemon sauce, 45
Guacamole salad bowl, 107

Haddock-shrimp bake, 56
Ham, 37-40
  birds, veal and, 27
  casseroles, *see* Casseroles—ham
  chicken and, 50
    on egg puffs, 255
    in tomatoes, 118-19
  deviled, sandwiches, 218
  glazed
    balls, 38
    loaf squares, marmalade and, 39
    patties, apricot-glazed, 39
    pineapple-orange, 37
    sliced, with cranberry-raisin sauce, 38
  kabobs, lamb and, 287
  rolls, curried, 38-39
  Southern luncheon baked, 37
  sparkling grilled, 287
Ham and chicken on egg puffs, 255
Ham loaf in cheese crust, 244-45
Ham loaf—red mustard sauce, 40
Ham logs with raisin sauce, 40
Ham medley, 245
Ham salad, 118
Ham waffles, 224
Hamburger-biscuit supper pie, 20
Hamburgers and hamburger meat, 278-79
  all-in-a-roll supper, 215
  Burgundy, 279
  casseroles, 230-37
    big biscuit bake, 232
    biscuit supper pie, 20
    chili-hominy bake, 235
    for-the-crowd, 230
    German caraway meat balls, 232-33
    Italian bake, 231
    Italian sauce—spinach squares, 233
    ravioli, 234
    in the round, 17
    saucy loaves, 230-31
    stuffed bundles, 18
  Hong Kong, 217
  mountains, 282-83

INDEX • 309

Hamburgers (cont'd)
square, 279
stew, skillet, 20
teriyaki, 278
Harlequin dressing, asparagus toss with, 94
Hashed-brown omelet, 269
Hawaiian dazzler, 162
Hawaiian fruit crumble, 164-65
Herb-and-honey basting sauce, 294
Herbed chicken bake, 250
Herbed chicken en casserole, 48
Herbed fish, 61
Herbed leg of lamb, 41
Herb-stuffed flank steak, 10
Hilo franks, 283
Hominy-chili bake, 235
Honey-and-herb basting sauce, 294
Honey dressing for melon bowls, 113
Honeydew melon salads
apple toss with cheese, 109
melon balls—honey dressing, 113
sparkling maid, 113
Horseradish sauce, 237
Hot cross muffins, 207

Ice cream
maple-almond, 190
pumpkin squares, 179
Iced almonds, 194
Icings, see Frostings
Island franks, 23
Island sweet-sour pork, 30
Island teriyaki, 278
Italian dressing, 123
Italian hamburger bake, 231
Italian salad bowl, 106
Italian sauce, 251
Italian sauce—spinach squares, 233

Java tapioca parfait, 182
Jewel squares, 178, 180

Kugelhoff, 213

Lamb, 41-46
chops, 43
ground, with lemon sauce, 45
leg of, butterfly, 288
roast, 41
roll, savory, 42
shanks, barbecued, 42
skewered, 46
kabobs, ham and, 287
kabobs with plum sauce, 46
shish kabobs with onion marinade, 46
stew, 44-45
Lamb patties with dill sauce, 45
Lazy day casserole, 259
Leek Lorraine, 267
Lemon angel frost, 189
Lemon crisp, 166
Lemon rice with fillets, 264-65
Lemon sauce
ground lamb with, 45
marinade basting sauce, 288
potatoes in, 81
Lemon tea "cakes," 163
Lemon topping for pancakes and waffles, 226
Lemon turnips, 88
Lemonade pudding, 187

Lemondown fancy, 183
Lemons
frosting, 142
glazed nut bread, 201
pudding, see Puddings—lemon
Lima beans in vegetable trio, 90
Lime refresher—low cal, 190
Lobster
baked, Savannah, 58
lazy day casserole, 259
tails, barbecued rock, 292-93
Luau ribs, 284-85
Luncheon meat casseroles, 246-49
baked bean pie, 248-49
chevron rice bake, 246-47
German "pizza," 248
hot salad and, 249
macaroni supper, 247
skillet barbecue, 246
Luxe peas and celery, 79

Macaroni
cheese casseroles, 270
hot tuna salad, 108
meat supper, 247
Macaroni-and-cheese salad, 118
Maple-almond ice cream, 190
Maple syrup, 226
Maple waffles, 224
Marinades
cheese, for onions, 100-1
lemon basting sauce, 288
onion, 46
Marmalade glaze, 293
Marmalade ham-loaf squares, 39
Marmalade upside-down cake, 136
Marshmallow fudge topping, 191
Marshmallow-nut puffs, 192
Marshmallow-road fudge, 193
Marshmallow cherry squares, 111
Mashed potatoes step-by-step, 80
Meat balls
German caraway, 232-33
in gingersnap sauce, 21
gourmet, 21
ham, glazed, 38
Meat loaves
beef, see Beef—loaves
ham
in cheese crust, 244-45
marmalade squares, 39
with red mustard sauce, 40
Meat pies, see Pies—meat
Melba Alaska, 129
Melon bowls—honey dressing, 113
Melon salads, see Fruit salads—melon
Meringue
for baked Alaska, 128-29
butterscotch bars, 168-69
pies, see Pies—meringue
strawberry cake, 134
torten, see Tarts—meringue
Mexican bean salad, 95
Mincemeat-cranberry pie, 148
Mincemeat sundae squares, 191
Mint-chocolate dessert, 178-79
Minute-steak scramble, 16
Mocha mousse, 173
Molasses corn bread, 203
Mousse, mocha, 175
Mozzarella pizza loaf, 22

310 • INDEX

Muffins, 207-10
  cheddar bran, 210
  hot cross, 207
  orange-blossom, 208-9
  peanut-butter, 208
  puffs, 209
Mushroom pot roast, 7
Mushrooms, 76-77
  beef loaf, 17
  cheese-stuffed, 76
  pimiento sauce, 253
  zippy, 101
Mushrooms and chicken livers, 76
Mushrooms Mornay, 77
Mustard beans, 96

Noodles
  franks and, 25, 239
  tenderloin treat, 240
  turkey casserole, 257
  See also Macaroni; Spaghetti

Oatmeal banana bread, 199
Oatmeal-coconut cookies, 167
Olive-almond sauce, 62
Omelet, hashed-brown, 269
Onion marinade, shish kabobs with, 46
Onions, 78
  bread, *see* Bread—onion
  cheese marinated, 100-1
  Creole, 78
  glazed squash with, 85
  gourmet, 78
  leek Lorraine, 267
  sauce, quick, 293
  Swiss baked, 269
Orange-blossom muffins, 208-9
Orange-butter fondant, 193
Orange-glazed beets, 96
Orange sauce for pancakes and waffles, 226
Orange-thyme lamb chops, 43
Oranges
  candied peel, 194
  fruit salad
    frozen pecan molds, 112
    winter bowl, with walnut croutons, 114
  marmalade, *see* Marmalade
Oysters
  deviled, on the half shell, 57
  scalloped corn and, 74

Paella
  jiffy turkey, 257
  Spanish, 271
Panamanian chicken and rice, 250-51
Pancakes, 221-22
  toppers for, *see* Toppers for pancakes, waffles
Paprika Wiener schnitzel, 28
Pasta
  ravioli casserole, 234
  See also Macaroni; Spaghetti
Pastry, 143
  curry, 253
  flaky Danish crescent, 214
  shells, 155, 159
  See also Pies; Tarts
Pecan pumpkin pie, 149
Peach-a-berry cobbler, 160

Peach Melba mold, 115
Peach petal pie, 146
Peaches
  almond torte, 158
  cobbler, 160-61; *see also* Cobbler—peach
Peanut-and-apple sandwiches, 219
Peanut-butter fudge, 194
Peanut-butter muffins, 208
Peanut-butter waffles, 223
Peanut-buttered pork loin, 284
Peanut cake quick, 136
Pear-apple crumb pie, 146-47
Pear-Waldorf with Swiss cheese, 109
Peas, 78-79
  celery and luxe, 79
  quick Creole, 78
  vegetable trio, 90
Pecan-orange molds, frozen, 112
Peppers, green, *see* Green peppers
Perfection salad, 97
Pickled carrots, 99
Pickles, candied dill, 101
Pie crust, *see* Pastry
Pies, 143-53
  chocolate dream (low-calorie), 150-51
  fruit, 144-53
  meat
    curry-top chicken, 252-53
    frank-noodle, 25
    hamburger-biscuit, 20
    quick turkey, 256
  meringue, 143-44
    banana-apricot, 144
    cocoa-crust lime, 147
  pumpkin
    meringue, 144
    pecan, 149
Pilaf, sea-food, 55
Pimiento-artichoke bowl, 94
Pimiento mushroom sauce, 253
Pineapple
  cakes, *see* Cakes—pineapple
  company beets with, 69
  salads, 116-17
  tuna croquettes with, 263
Pineapple-chocolate squares, 170
Pineapple crunch cake, 137
Pineapple jewel squares, 180
Pineapple-orange glazed ham, 37
Pineapple sour cream pie, 145
Pineapple speared franks, 23
Pineapple topper, 135
"Pizza," German, 248
Pizza loaf, 22
Pizza supper pie, 243
Plum sauce, lamb kabobs with, 46
Polynesian beef, 8-9
Polynesian pork chops, 33
Poppy-dot cheese bread, 200
Pork, 29-34, 284-87
  chops, 31-33
    barbecue, 32-33
    barbecued, and baked beans, 241
    Cheese-stuffed, 31
    fruit-top, 32
    gourmet, 31
    Polynesian, 33
    Spanish rice and, 242
  loin, peanut-buttered, 284
  roast, 29

Pork (cont'd)
  sausage
    easy Mexican skillet, 244
    French bean pot, 267
    Southern egg casserole, 242-43
    strata, 35
  shoulder, 30
  spareribs, 34
    abacus, 286
    barbecued, with rodeo sauce, 285
    Cantonese, 286
    with caraway kraut, 34
    luau, 284-85
    royal, 286
  steak, barbecue, 284
  tenderloin
    apple-stuffed, 33
    noodle treat, 241
  See also Bacon; Ham
Pot de crème, 186
Pot roast, *see* Beef—pot roast
Potato salad, 102-3
Potatoes, 80-82
  baked, 81-82
  mashed, 80
    cottage, 81
  sweet, *see* Sweet potatoes
Potluck bean bake, 67
Potluck macaroni bake, 270
Prune nut bread, 199
Prune spice cake, 139
Pudding-and-pineapple cake, 133
Puddings, 180-87
  blueberry rice Bavarian, 181
  cherry, 183, 184
  chocolate
    carioca cups, 185
    choc-o-date dessert, 182
    frosting, 142
    nut, 188
    pot de crème, 186
  Java tapioca parfait, 181
  lemon
    lemonade, 187
    lemondown fancy, 183
    luscious frost, 185
  nut
    chocolate, 188
    coffee tortoni, 184
    walnut crunch, 164
  pumpkin chiffon, 180-81
  raspberry cream, 187
  Swiss molded, 175
Pumpkin golden hi-lighters, 205
Pumpkin date torte, 157
Pumpkin ice cream squares, 179
Pumpkin meringue pie, 144
Pumpkin pecan pie, 149

Raisin sauce, 40
  cranberry and, 38
Raisins
  chocolate drops, 167
  glazed loaf bread, 204
Raspberries
  in peach Melba mold, 115
  red, ring, 117
Raspberry-cranberry ring, 112
Raspberry cream pudding, 187
Raspberry glaze, 132
Raspberry ribbon pie, 152
Ravioli casserole, 234
Red mustard sauce, 40

Red raspberry ring, 117
Relish
  beet, 69
  molded salad, 99-100
    carrot cups, 99
    confetti, 100
  tomato, salad, 104-5
  vegetable medley, 89
Rhubarb-cherry pie, 153
Ribs
  short, saucy, 13
  spareribs, *see* Pork—spareribs
Rice
  blueberry Bavarian, 181
  casseroles, 271-72
    beef Cantonese with ginger, 235
    calico chicken and, 254
    chicken divan, 258
    chevron bake, 246-47
    creamy chicken, 254
    lemon, with fillets, 264-65
    oriental, 271
    Panamanian chicken and, 250-51
    quick Spanish, 272
    Spanish paella, 271
    tuna, 266
  in curried ham rolls, 39
  green, baked, 90
  Spanish, *see* Spanish rice
Rice-stuffed pork shoulder, 30
Roast
  beef, *see* Beef—roast
  lamb, *see* Lamb—roast
  pork, 29
  squab, 53
  veal, stuffed breast of, 28
Roast duckling with cranberry sauce, 54
Roast stuffed breast of veal, 28
Roast stuffed lamb, 41
Rock Cornish game hens, 55
Rodeo sauce, 285
Rolls, 204-7
  chef's salad in, 218-19
  supper all-in-a-, 215
Roman eggplant, 75
Rum royale cake, 130-31
Rutabaga and apple, 83

Sacramento Spanish zucchini, 268
Salad dressings, 123-24
  avocado, 107
  celery-seed, 124
  French, 123
  glossy fruit, 124
  harlequin, 94
  honey, 113
  Italian, 123
  nippy nectar, 124
  sour cream special, 123
  Thousand Island, 123
Salads, 94-122
  bean, *see* Beans—salads
  beet, 96
  Caesar, 98
  carrot, 99
  chicken, *see* Chicken—salads
  cold cuts and hot, 249
  egg, *see* Egg salad
  fruit, *see* Fruit salads
  guacamole, 107
  ham, 118-19
  hearty, 118-22

312 • INDEX

Salads (cont'd)
  macaroni
    cheese and, 118
    hot tuna and, 108
  molded, 96, 100, 111-12, 115-17, 120-21
  perfection, 97
  potato, see Potato salad
    in a roll, 218-19
  Sarah's, 105
  sea-food, see Seafood—salads; Tuna—salads
  spring soufflé, 100
  tomato, see Tomatoes—salads
  tossed, 106-9
  Waldorf, 108-9
  See also Slaw
Salami–hot cheese sandwiches, 219
Salami–Swiss cheese salad, 120
Salmon, fiesta baked, 59
Salmon or tuna ring, 62
Sandwiches, 215-20
  beef
    champion roast, 220
    corned-beef stag, 217
    double, 220
  chef's salad in a roll, 218-19
  cheese
    buns deluxe, 215
    salami and hot, 219
  crab, 216
  Dad's Denvers, 218
  peanut-and-apple, 219
Sarah's salad, 105
Sauces
  barbecue, 293
  blueberry, 222
  cheese, 272
  cranberry, see Cranberry sauce
  creamy horseradish, 237
  curry, 38
  dessert, see Desserts—sauces
  dill, see Dill sauce
  ginger
    gingersnap, 21
    sundae, 191
  herb-and-honey basting, 294
  Italian, 233, 251
  lemon, see Lemon sauce
  mincemeat sundae, 191
  olive-almond, 62
  onion, quick, 293
  pimiento mushroom, 253
  plum, lamb kabobs with, 46
  red mustard, 40
  raisin, see Raisin sauce
  rodeo, 285
  shrimp, 268
  sweet-sour, 294
  tartare, 58
  tomato steak, 237
  zippy, vegetable trio with, 90
Sauerbraten, round steak, 15
Sauerkraut Provençale, 84
Sausage-apple stuffing, 28
Sausage strata, 35
Sausages
  Braunschweiger, 21
  pork, see Pork—sausage
Scallops, broiled, 58
Sea-food, 55-62
  casseroles, 258-67
    baked lobster Savannah, 58
    crab meat with Chinese cabbage, 59
    fiesta salmon bake, 59
    lazy day, 259
    lemon rice with fillets, 264-65
    luncheon baked, 260-61
    luncheon shrimp curry, 261
    pilaf, 55
    shrimp buffet, 258
    shrimp chow mein, 260
    Spanish paella, 271
    Thermidor, 259
    tuna, see Tuna—casseroles
  herbed fish, 61
  salads, 120-22
    crab Louis, 121
    shrimp luncheon mold, 120-21
    see also Tuna—salads
Sesame-baked chicken, 49
Sesame biscuits, beef stew with, 236
Shish kabobs with onion marinade, 46
Shoestring toss, 106
Short ribs, saucy, 13
Shrimp
  curry, 261
  lazy day casserole, 259
  Sonora, 291
  Spanish paella, 271
Shrimp buffet casserole, 258
Shrimp-chicken cioppino, 251
Shrimp chow mein, 260
Shrimp-haddock bake, 56
Shrimp luncheon molds, 120-21
Shrimp on a skewer, 56
Shrimp sauce, curried eggs in, 268
Shrimp Thermidor, 259
Skewer dogs, 280
Slaw, 96-97
Sonora shrimp, 291
Soufflés
  Brussels sprouts, 71
  dessert, see Desserts—soufflé
  spring salad, 100
Sour cream pineapple pie, 145
Sour cream special, 123
Sour cream velvet frosting, 142
Sour-cream waffles, 225
Southern luncheon bake, 37
Southern sausage and egg casserole, 242-43
Southern steak Bar-B-Q, 11
Spaghetti
  pot roast with, 5
  veal Parmesan with, 240-41
Spanish paella, 271
Spanish rice
  pork-chop, 242
  quick, 272
Spareribs Cantonese, 34
Spareribs with caraway kraut, 34
Spinach delight, 84
Spinach in green rice bake, 90
Spinach squares, 233
Spinach toss, tangy, 106-7
Spoon bread, bacon, 200-1
Spring flower rolls, 204-5
Squab, 53
Squash, 84-85
  zucchini, see Zucchini
Steak
  beefsteak, see Beefsteak
  pork, barbecue, 284

INDEX • 313

Stew
  beef
    burger skillet, 20
    oven, 8
    savory, Bavarian-style, 9
  lamb, *see* Lamb—stew
Strawberries
  frosty squares, 173
Strawberry charlotte russe, 177
Strawberry-cheese tarts, 156
Strawberry meringue cake, 134
Strawberry-pineapple freeze, 117
Stuffing, *see* Dressing
Sukiyaki skewers, 281
Sunshine carrots, 72
Sweet potatoes, 82-83
Sweet-sour pork, island, 30
Sweet-sour sauce, 294
Swiss cheese, *see* Cheese—Swiss
Swiss onion bake, 269
Swiss pudding mold, 175
Swiss steak in foil, 13
Swiss veal foldovers, 25
Syrup, maple, 226

Tangerine-apricot mold, 176
Taos salad, 107
Tapioca, Java parfait, 182
Tart shells, 155, 159
Tartare sauce, 58
Tarts, 154-59
  almond-peach, 158
  citrus chiffon, 154
  cran-apple, 156
  meringue, 158-59
  pumpkin-date, 157
  strawberry, 155-56
Tenderloin-noodle treat, 240
Teriyaki burgers, 278
Teriyaki, island, 278
Thousand Island dressing, 123
Tomato relish salad, 104-5
Tomato steak sauce, 237
Tomatoes with dill sauce, 87
Tomatoes, 86-88
  green peppers and, 80
  oriental skillet, 88
  salads, 104-5
    chicken and ham, 118-19
    cups, fiesta corn in, 104
    relish, 104-5
  spicy whole, 86
Toppers
  apple, 213
  butterscotch, 207
  marshmallow fudge, 191
  pineapple, 135
  spicy, 209
  See also Fillings; Frostings; Glazes; Sauces
Toppers for pancakes, waffles, 226
Torten, *see* Tarts
Tortoni, coffee-nut, 184
Trout
  Farcie, 60
  grilled, with almonds, 292
Trout almondine, 60
Tuna
  casseroles, 262-67
    company creamed, 263
    creamy ring, 266-67
    croquettes with pineapple, 263
    jackstraw, 264

    noodle, 262
    quick baked, 262-63
    rice bake, 266
    Thermidor, 259
  salads, 107-8
    guacamole, 107
    hot macaroni, 108
    luncheon ring, 122
    Western, 108
  two-way oriental, 61
Tuna Florentine, 62
Tuna jackstraw casserole, 264
Tuna or salmon ring, 62
Tuna-rice bake, 266
Turkey casseroles, 52-53, 255-57
  cheese puff, 255
  cheddar, 52
  crêpes en casserole, 53
  jiffy paella, 257
  noodle bake, 257
  quick pie, 256
Turkey cheese puff, 255
Turkey chow mein, 52
Turkey croquettes, 51
Turkey-noodle bake, 257
Turnips, lemon, 88
Tutti-frutti frosting, 140

Upside-down cakes, *see* Cakes—upside-down

Vanilla wafer coconut cake, 137
Veal, 25-29
  birds, ham and, 27
  cutlets
    paprika Wiener schnitzel, 28
    Swiss foldovers, 23
  shoulder, braised rolled, 28
Veal chops, 28-29
Veal chops with olive sauce, 26
Veal Parmesan with spaghetti, 240-41
Veal Scaloppine, 27
Vegetable chow mein, 89
Vegetable medley relish, 89
Vegetable trio with zippy sauce, 90
Vegetables, 66-90
  casseroles, *see* Casseroles—vegetable
  frank medley, 239
  See also specific vegetables; salads

Waffles, 223-25
  corn, *see* Corn waffles
  toppers for, *see* Toppers for pancakes, waffles
Waldorf salad, 108-9
Walnut crunch pudding, 164
Walnut graham bread, 198
Whipped butter, 226
Wiener-bean bake, 24
Wiener bean pot, 238
Wiener schnitzel, 28
Wiener wrap-ups, 24
Wieners, *see* Frankfurters
William Tell coffeecake, 213
Winter orange bowl with walnut croutons, 114

Yankee bacon bake, 36

Zippy sauce, vegetable trio with, 90
Zucchini
  in California vegetable bowl, 89
  in Italian salad bowl, 106
  Sacramento Spanish, 268

THESE ARE AMERICA'S MOST-WANTED HOW-TO BOOKS FOR HOME AND FAMILY

The reason is simple. When you want to know the best way to do something you consult an authority on the subject. The foremost authority on subjects concerning the home and family is Better Homes and Gardens. It has been for over 40 years. That's why millions of Better Homes and Gardens Books are sold every year. That's why you should buy Better Homes and Gardens books when you want to know the best way of doing things. Great gifts for friends who feel the same. More than 50 titles in all.

Buy them wherever books are sold or send check or money order to Meredith Press, 1716 Locust, Des Moines, Iowa 50303.

New Cook Book $5.95
Handyman's Book $6.95
Our Baby (record book) $4.95
Stitchery and Crafts $5.95

Decorating Book $7.95
Story Book $2.95
Sewing Book $4.95